Shakespeare and Economic Theory

ARDEN SHAKESPEARE AND THEORY

Series Editor: Evelyn Gajowski

AVAILABLE TITLES

Shakespeare and Economic Theory David Hawkes
Shakespeare and Psychoanalytic Theory Carolyn Brown

FORTHCOMING TITLES

Shakespeare and Cultural Materialist Theory
Christopher Marlow
Shakespeare and Ecocritical Theory Gabriel Egan
Shakespeare and Ecofeminist Theory Rebecca Laroche
and Jennifer Munroe
Shakespeare and Feminist Theory Marianne Novy
Shakespeare and Film Theory Scott Hollifield
Shakespeare and New Historicist Theory Neema Parvini
Shakespeare and Posthumanist Theory Karen Raber
Shakespeare and Queer Theory Melissa Sanchez

Shakespeare and Economic Theory

David Hawkes

Bloomsbury Arden Shakespeare
An imprint of Bloomsbury Publishing Plc

B L O O M S B U R Y
LONDON • NEW DELHI • NEW YORK • SYDNEY

Bloomsbury Arden Shakespeare

An imprint of Bloomsbury Publishing Plc

Imprint previously known as Arden Shakespeare

50 Bedford Square	1385 Broadway
London	New York
WC1B 3DP	NY 10018
UK	USA

www.bloomsbury.com

BLOOMSBURY, THE ARDEN SHAKESPEARE and the Diana logo are trademarks of Bloomsbury Publishing Plc

First published 2015

© David Hawkes, 2015

British Library Cataloguing-in-Publication Data
A catalogue record for this book is available from the British Library.

ISBN: HB: 978-1-4725-7698-9
            PB: 978-1-4725-7697-2
            ePDF: 978-1-4725-7700-9
            ePub: 978-1-4725-7699-6

Library of Congress Cataloging-in-Publication Data
A catalog record for this book is available from the Library of Congress.

Series: Shakespeare and Theory, 1234567X, volume 1

Typeset by Fakenham Prepress Solutions, Fakenham, Norfolk NR21 8NN
Printed and bound in India

To Ali
büyük bir ciddiyetle yaşayacaksın bir sincap gibi
mesela – Nazim Hikmet

CONTENTS

Series Editor's Preface ix
Acknowledgements xii
Preface xiii

PART ONE   Economics in History and Criticism 1

1 'Will into appetite': Economics and
   Chrematistics 3
2 'The future comes apace': The Birth of
   Restricted Economy 17
3 The Last of the Schoolmen: The Marxist
   Tradition 33
4 'The hatch and brood of time': Beyond the
   Economy 51
5 Money as Metaphor: The New Economic
   Criticism 67

PART TWO   Economics in Shakespeare 89

6 'Going to the market-place': The Commons
   and the Commodity 91
7 'The soul of trade': Worth and Value 111
8 'Knaves of common hire': Wage Labour,
   Slavery and Reification 127

9 'Unkind abuse': The Legalization of Usury 143
10 'Lear's shadow': Identity, Property and
     Possession 161
     Conclusion: Magic and Alienation 179

Notes 185
Bibliography 203
Index 215

SERIES EDITOR'S PREFACE

'Asking questions about literary texts – that's literary criticism. Asking "Which questions shall we ask about literary texts?" – that's literary theory.' So goes my explanation of the current state of English studies, and Shakespeare studies, in my never-ending attempt to demystify, and simplify, theory for students in my classrooms. Another way to put it is that theory is a systematic account of the nature of literature, the act of writing, and the act of reading.

One of the primary responsibilities of any academic discipline – whether in the natural sciences, the social sciences, or the humanities – is to examine its methodologies and tools of analysis. Particularly at a time of great theoretical ferment, such as that which has characterized English studies, and Shakespeare studies, in recent years, it is incumbent upon scholars in a given discipline to provide such reflection and analysis. We all construct meanings in Shakespeare's texts and culture. Shouldering responsibility for our active role in constructing meanings in literary texts, moreover, constitutes a theoretical stance. To the extent that we examine our own critical premises and operations, that theoretical stance requires reflection on our part. It requires honesty, as well. It is thereby a fundamentally radical act. All critical analysis puts into practice a particular set of theoretical premises. Theory occurs from a particular standpoint. There is no critical practice that is somehow devoid of theory. There is no critical practice that is not implicated in theory. A common-sense, transparent encounter with any text is thereby impossible. Indeed, to the extent that theory requires us to question anew that with which we thought we were familiar, that which we thought we understood, theory constitutes a critique of common sense.

Since the advent of postmodernism, the discipline of English studies has undergone a seismic shift. And the discipline of Shakespeare studies has been at the epicentre of this shift. Indeed, it has been Shakespeare scholars who have played a major role in several of the theoretical and critical developments (e.g., new historicism, cultural materialism, presentism) that have shaped the discipline of English studies in recent years. Yet a comprehensive scholarly analysis of these crucial developments has yet to be done, and is long overdue. As the first series to foreground analysis of contemporary theoretical developments in the discipline of Shakespeare studies, *Arden Shakespeare and Theory* aims to fill a yawning gap.

To the delight of some and the chagrin of others, since 1980 or so, theory has dominated Shakespeare studies. *Arden Shakespeare and Theory* focuses on the state of the art at the outset of the twenty-first century. For the first time, it provides a comprehensive analysis of the theoretical developments that are emerging at the present moment, as well as those that are dominant or residual in Shakespeare studies.

Each volume in the series aims to offer the reader the following components: to provide a clear definition of a particular theory; to explain its key concepts; to trace its major developments, theorists, and critics; to perform a reading of a Shakespeare text; to elucidate a specific theory's intersection with or relationship to other theories; to situate it in the context of contemporary political, social, and economic developments; to analyze its significance in Shakespeare studies; and to suggest resources for further investigation. Authors of individual volumes thereby attempt to strike a balance, bringing their unique expertise, experience, and perspectives to bear upon particular theories while simultaneously fulfilling the common purpose of the series. Individual volumes in the series are devoted to elucidating particular theoretical perspectives, such as cultural materialism, ecocriticism, ecofeminism, economic theory, feminism, film theory, new historicism, posthumanism, psychoanalysis, and queer theory.

Arden Shakespeare and Theory aims to enable scholars, teachers, and students alike to define their own theoretical strategies and refine their own critical practices. And students have as much at stake in these theoretical and critical enterprises – in the reading and the writing practices that characterize our discipline – as do scholars and teachers. Janus-like, the series looks forward as well as backward, serving as an inspiration and a guide for new work in Shakespeare studies at the outset of the twenty-first century, on the one hand, and providing a retrospective analysis of the intellectual labour that has been accomplished in recent years, on the other.

To return to the beginning: what is at stake in our reading of literary texts? Once we come to understand the various ways in which theory resonates with not only Shakespeare's texts, and literary texts, but the so-called 'real' world – the world outside the world of the mind, the world outside the world of academia – then we come to understand that theory is capable of powerfully enriching not only our reading of Shakespeare's texts, and literary texts, but our lives.

Evelyn Gajowski
Series Editor
University of Nevada, Las Vegas

ACKNOWLEDGEMENTS

I owe a huge debt of gratitude to Lynn Gajowski for asking me to write this book, and for her superb editing of the manuscript. I'm also grateful to everyone at Bloomsbury for their support and assistance throughout, and especially to Emily Hockley for her prompt assistance in a tight spot. I'm thankful to the English Department at Arizona State University for providing me with a year's leave in which to complete the work. Departmental Chairs Maureen Goggin and Mark Lussier offered me every kind of help and encouragement along the way, Bruce Matsunaga, Phillip Karagis and Karen Silva were invaluable sources of practical aid, while colleagues like Cora Fox, Brad Irish, Joe Lockard, Eddie Mallott, Richard Newhauser and Brad Ryner provided invigorating conversation when it was most needed. I've been fortunate to work with doctoral students like Heather Ackerman, Jennifer Downer, Devori Kimbro and Michael Noschka, who have been helpful and inspiring beyond the call of duty. The friendship of Julia Friedman and L.G. Williams was profoundly encouraging and sustaining, and nothing at all would have been done without the loving kindness of Simten Gurac.

PREFACE

This book is divided into two parts. The first examines the tradition of economic Shakespeare criticism, paying particular attention to the schools of Marxist and new economic criticism. It also studies the concept of the 'economy' itself, as it develops from ancient Greece, through medieval and Renaissance England, and into our own postmodern era. There are two distinctions we must make before we can understand the term 'economy'. First, we need to differentiate between what the Greeks called 'economics' and what they called 'chrematistics'. For them, economics was the study of use-value; it analysed how the various possessions of a household might be most usefully employed. What the Greeks called 'chrematistics' was the study of exchange-value, of money and finance. Confusingly, the modern discipline of economics corresponds to what the Greeks called 'chrematistics'. The second distinction we must make is between the 'restricted' and the 'general' senses of 'economy'. Chrematistics implies a 'restricted' understanding of 'economy'. It excludes social and political considerations as 'exogenous' to its concerns. In contrast, ancient and medieval thought understood the term 'economy' in a 'general' sense. For Aristotle and Aquinas, economics included factors, such as ethics and aesthetics, that are now considered 'exogenous' to the economy. Shakespeare lived during the historical transition from economics to chrematistics, and thus also from a general to a restricted understanding of the economy. His interest to twenty-first century readers and audiences springs, in large part, from our location at an historical juncture when the economy once again seems to be in transition, this time from the 'restricted' to the 'general' sense of the term.

The book's second part concentrates on Shakespeare's works themselves. It examines the key words and ideas with which he depicted the epochal changes through which the English economy was passing, and it shows how he subtly adjusted their meanings to fit new circumstances and phenomena. Shakespeare depicts England's troubled transition from an economy based around use-value to a society organized around the pursuit of exchange-value. Although the concept of the economy was in the process of being restricted into its modern meaning, Shakespeare's work retains vestiges of the older, more general sense of the word, and he often conducts an ethical debate between these two senses of 'economy'. The vocabulary and concepts of modern 'economics' were first developed in early modern England and, as this book demonstrates, Shakespeare was an active and influential participant in that process.

PART ONE

Economics in History and Criticism

1

'Will into appetite': Economics and Chrematistics

I

What is 'the economy?' The significance of the term varies widely with time and place, and before we can explore 'economic' criticism of Shakespeare we need to know what the word meant to him. We should also clarify its significance for us, because its modern meaning is by no means as well-defined as we might think. Shakespeare lived through, observed, and chronicled the social and psychological effects of a remarkably rapid, and historically unprecedented, transition from one kind of economy to another. We need a preliminary understanding of that transition, and of the concepts and terminology in which Shakespeare discussed it, before we can begin to understand his treatment of economic matters.

The etymological root of 'economy' is the Greek *oikos*, meaning 'household', and in the ancient world 'economics' meant managing the resources of an aristocratic family. It was the theory and practice of providing for the household's needs by effectively using the materials at its disposal. Since a household included human beings, as well as material resources, economics also involved the relations between the people who made up the household. Ancient discussions of economics devote considerable attention to the relations between husband and wife, and between fathers and sons, as well as to the techniques of slave acquisition and management. The 'economy' in this sense includes the social roles ascribed to men and women, masters and slaves, adults and children, in addition to the material resources they produce and consume.

Yet if the economy involves these social relations, there is surely no human activity that could be excluded in principle from theoretical 'economics'. 'Economics' would have to include what we now call 'psychology', and 'sociology', and perhaps 'history', 'ethics' and 'aesthetics' as well. Modern economics is defined by its stern rejection of such 'exogenous' factors, and its disciplinary boundaries are strictly policed. To modern economic historians, it can therefore seem as though the concept of the 'economy' was absent from Greek thought altogether. As Moses Finley puts it:

> the ancients ... lacked the concept of an "economy," and, *a fortiori,* they lacked the conceptual elements which together constitute what we call "the economy." Of course they farmed, traded, manufactured, mined, taxed, coined, deposited and loaned money, made profits or failed in their enterprises. And they discussed these activities in their talk and their writing. What they did not do, however, was to combine these particular activities conceptually into a unit.[1]

From a modern perspective, the Greeks failed to identify sufficient common properties between their various productive and trading activities to forge them into a conceptual whole. The problem did not occur to the Greeks themselves, however, because they distinguished between 'economics' and the more specialized discipline of 'chrematistics'. The surviving Greek texts use 'economics' to refer to the realization and exploitation of use-value. They defined 'chrematistics' as the pursuit of exchange-value (money) as an end in itself. Paradoxically enough, what we call 'economics' today is what the Greeks called 'chrematistics'.

Modern economics, aspiring to the status of a specialist

science, strictly distinguishes between the 'economy' and social, cultural or political factors, which it calls 'exogenous', external to its concerns. It constructs the economy as a particular, delimited sphere of activity, and to this end it identifies 'economic' actions as those performed with the aim of maximizing the self-interest of the actor. This is a major departure from ancient economic assumptions, which, as we have seen, included human relations and society in the study of the *oikos*. Yet it corresponds closely to the chrematistic approach, which relies on the quantification of essential and natural qualities, and on their symbolic representation in abstract, objective form.

Chrematistics involves the translation of an object's intrinsic use-value into the symbolic terms of artificial exchange-value. In contrast to economics, which was an inherently useful and productive science, the Greeks regarded chrematistics as merely *banausic* knowledge. *Banausic* sciences were thought of as servile, because they were empirically associated with slaves and because, like slaves, they were regarded as means to ends beyond themselves. They therefore lacked the dignity of an end in itself or *telos*. In striking contrast to today's economists, the Greeks did not consider making money a worthwhile end in itself, but viewed it as a means to the higher end of providing the leisure in which to develop the soul. The cultivation of the soul was the purpose, the *telos*, of a human being. To take an exclusively chrematistic view of wealth was therefore to reveal a degraded, materialist and above all servile approach to the world.

Xenophon's Socratic dialogue *Oeconomicus* (360 BC) deals with personal character before turning to material goods. Indeed, its definitions of property and possessions are themselves dependent on subjective character. The tract argues that real wealth is use-value, so that a man truly owns only what he can use. One of the erroneous speakers, Critobulus, begins by defining the *oikos* in abstract terms. As he sees it, the *oikos* consists in possession, in attribution: the *oikos* is everything that 'belongs to' the landowner. Critobulus understands 'belong to' in the modern sense: 'of or pertaining to'. Socrates, however, argues that it is foolish to regard as wealth possessions which one cannot actually use. After all, a man may possess enemies. Enemies may belong to him, but they are not useful: they have no use-value for him. Socrates concludes that possessions that are not useful do not count as true wealth. Only things that a man both owns and can use are part of his *oikos*. Socrates defines the *oikos* as containing only 'what we may call a man's useful or advantageous possessions'. Economics is for him the study of use-value.

But usefulness is always *for* somebody. Use-value only exists, and it only becomes manifest, for particular human beings. By introducing usefulness into his definition of wealth, Socrates has therefore made that definition subjective. What is useful to one person might be useless to another. This raises the question of how usefulness can be realized: after all, many people may not even know how to use all of the goods in their possession. Socrates insists that use actually *is* wealth, so that those who do not use their goods properly do not really possess them as wealth: 'The same things, in fact, are wealth or not wealth, according as a man knows or does not know the use to make of them'. Critobulus eventually agrees, and draws the further inference that, to those who have no use for an object, its only use consists in exchange:

> To persons ignorant of their use flutes are wealth as saleable, but as possessions not for sale they are no wealth at all; and see, Socrates, how smoothly and consistently the argument proceeds, since it is admitted that things which benefit are wealth. The flutes in question unsold are not wealth, being good for nothing: to become wealth they must be sold.[2]

There are thus two kinds of wealth, the useful and the saleable, which contain two different kinds of value. Socrates defines use-value and exchange-value as matters of character. Use-value *is* exchange-value to those who cannot use their possessions, since all they can do with them is sell them. Furthermore, exchange-value can also be use-value, provided its possessor has the character to make use of it. Socrates emphasizes that use-value is the only true wealth:

CRITOBULUS

You seem to say, Socrates, that money itself in the pockets of a man who does not know how to use it is not wealth?

SOCRATES

And I understand you to concur in the truth of our proposition so far: wealth is that, and that only, whereby a man may be benefited ... Let money then, Critobulus, if a man does not know how to use it aright – let money, I say, be banished to the remote corners of the earth rather than be reckoned as wealth.

(ibid.)

The argument then circles back to the beginning. Even enemies can, as it turns out, be reckoned as wealth, providing one knows how to use them properly. The quality of enmity, like usefulness, demands a subjective element – all enemies are enemies of somebody. It is impossible for anyone to be a purely objective enemy. And as Shakespeare would explain at length, it is perfectly possible to 'use' one's enemies to one's own 'advantage'. Indeed anything that belongs to a man can either be part of his *oikos* or not, depending on his ability to realize its use-value.

The *Economics* attributed to Aristotle takes the same approach as Xenophon's dialogue. Its primary concern is human relations: Michel Foucault describes it as 'a master's manual ... [which] purports to be an art of governing, and not so much things as people'.[3] Like Xenophon's Socrates, Aristotle considers the *oikos* as the sphere commanded by a private individual landowner, which includes land, buildings, livestock and people. He identifies the two basic elements of the *oikos* in order of importance: 'The component parts of a household are (1) human beings, and (2) goods and chattels'. The householder's prime requisite is a wife, and acquiring her entails mastery of a whole array of cultural conventions and social niceties: 'We should have ... as part of economics, to make proper rules for the association of husband and wife; and this involves providing what sort of a woman she ought to be'.[4] Even when he turns to material goods, the first category Aristotle discusses is human: 'Of possessions, that which is the best and the worthiest subject of economics comes first and is most essential – I mean man. It is necessary therefore first to provide oneself with good slaves' (1344a22–5). In ancient Greece, then, economics was concerned mostly with matters that modern economists would consider external to their field.

II

The feeling would have been mutual. The Greeks thought of the pursuit of financial profit as a non-economic matter. For them, economics was concerned with use-value; the accumulation of exchange-value was the business of chrematistics. They believed that the acquisition of money (chrematistics) was not, rightfully or naturally, an end in itself, but rather a means to the higher end of realizing use-value (economics). This teleological subordination is also an ethical hierarchy, so that anyone who prioritizes acquiring money above using it properly is making a moral as well as a logical error. Such a person would reveal their servile mentality by falsely objectifying what is properly subjective. According to this teleological ethic, actions and ideas were evaluated according to how effectively they served their final cause, purpose, or *telos*. It was the purpose of exchange-value to realize utility: the purpose of money was to buy useful things. To regard chrematistics as an end in itself is therefore to make an egregious logical and ethical error. As Karl Polanyi points out, this ethic accords well with what historians and anthropologists tell us about 'traditional' societies:

> The outstanding discovery of recent historical and anthropological research is that man's economy, as a rule, is submerged in his social relationships. He does not act so as to safeguard his individual interest in the possession of material goods; he acts so as to safeguard his social standing, his social claims, his social assets. He values material goods only in so far as they serve this end.[5]

Before the sixteenth century, all human societies perceived chrematistics as a means to the higher end of economic utility. Aristotle also applied this teleological reasoning to aesthetics. He differentiated between an inferior, 'chrematistic' art, which is created for the purpose of making money, and a superior, 'autotelic' art which, as the term suggests, is an end in itself.[6] For Aristotle, autoteleology was a *sine qua non* of true art, and he established a tradition of artists priding themselves on their contempt for commercial considerations which continued at least until Modernism. Karl Marx evidently derived his aesthetics as well as his economics from Aristotle, and wholeheartedly endorsed the virtues of autotelic art: 'In no sense does the writer regard his works as a *means*. They are *ends in themselves*'.[7]

Such opinions must have been difficult to sustain for an enthusiastic Shakespearean like Marx, because Shakespeare is a notable exception to the traditional aesthetic disregard for commerce. He wrote for money throughout his life. In fact, he seems to have stopped writing as soon as he had accumulated the means to live comfortably without working. The Elizabethan public theatre in which he worked was among the earliest entertainment industries, and it was regularly castigated by its opponents for its commercial aesthetics. Indeed, this criticism was echoed by many professional playwrights, such as Ben Jonson and Thomas Dekker. They had to appeal to the public in order to live, however, and Shakespeare was no different. Several of his plays show unmistakable signs of having been manipulated to maximize their market appeal. The addition of an extra witch scene in *Macbeth*, and the re-appearance of the popular Falstaff in *The Merry Wives of Windsor* seem to have been motivated by commercial considerations. In fact, we can presume this true of Shakespeare's work as a whole. It simply would not exist in its present form had its author not been driven by 'chrematistic' motives.

And yet the tradition of Western aesthetics, within which Shakespeare always worked, and whose major assumptions he evidently endorsed, unequivocally denigrates such base motives as contrary to art's essential nature. Thinkers from Aristotle to Marx and beyond insisted that art should disregard the profit motive and be an end in itself. It seems, then, that Shakespeare's work embodies a contradiction. It adheres to a classical aesthetic morality, and yet its core *raison d'être* violates classical aesthetics in the most blatant fashion. I would suggest that this contradiction is the source of Shakespeare's fascination for the people of early modern England. It moulds the content of his work as well as its form: many of his plays depict malcontents, individualist schemers for profit and advancement, who prefigure the ruthlessly acquisitive *homo economicus* described by Thomas Hobbes. Shakespeare portrays such figures with enough sympathy that we are forced to take their complaints and aspirations seriously. But the forces of degree and hierarchy finally quell the ambitions of Cade, Iago, Edmund and their ilk, and it seems that Shakespeare still regarded the energies that were being liberated by the development of a market economy as threatening and destructive. He understood them, however, and he also understood their influence on his own aesthetic practice. He surveyed the emerging world of commodities and exchange-value with the same kind of fascinated foreboding that its maturity evokes in twenty-first-century observers.

III

Part of the reason for the ethical distinction between use-value and exchange-value concerns their respective limitations. Use-value is limited by nature. Since it cannot be separated from physical possession of the object, it cannot be expanded beyond natural, physical limits. But exchange-value is artificial and non-material. It only exists in the human mind. Money is not part of nature. It is only a conventional sign. In theory there is no reason why it should not reproduce infinitely, after the manner of linguistic representation. As today's economists insist, the economy can and must 'grow' without regard for natural limitations. This distinction between economics and chrematistic was noted by Jacques Derrida:

> For Aristotle, it is a matter of an ideal and desirable limit, a limit between the limit and the unlimited, between the true and finite good (the economic) and the illusory and indefinite good (the chrematistic).[8]

For Xenophon and Aristotle, to be truly wealthy was to use money properly. People with the wrong kind of character can never enjoy wealth, though they may well possess money. Aristotle describes such people as natural slaves. Natural slavery is subservience to one's own desires, and a person suffering from such internal slavery will never know how to use his possessions correctly. Aristotle draws here on the Platonic theory of the soul. In the *Republic* Plato constructs an ethical hierarchy within the soul, with reason at the top and appetite at the bottom. People who serve their appetites are following their most servile impulses for, just as the function of the slave is to serve the higher ends of his master, so the function of the appetite is to serve reason. Those who prioritize appetite above reason thus reveal themselves as natural slaves. Plato uses the pursuit of money as the paradigm of enslavement to our lowest desires, which are:

denoted by the general term appetitive, from the extraordinary strength and vehemence of the desires of eating and drinking and the other sensual appetites which are the main elements of it; also money-loving, because such desires are generally satisfied by the help of money ... If we were to say that the loves and pleasures of this third part were concerned with gain, we should then be able to fall back on a single notion; and might truly and intelligibly describe this part of the soul as loving gain or money.[9]

This and similar passages lie behind St Paul's declaration that the love of money is the root of all evil. They exert the profoundest influence on Western habits of thought in every era. They depend upon the distinction between chrematistics, a necessary but inferior species of knowledge, and economics. Devotion to chrematistics is characteristic of natural and empirical slaves; only a natural master can understand or devote himself to economic pursuits. More than anything else, 'economics' in the ancient world meant self-mastery, the dominance of reason over appetite within the individual soul. As Foucault puts it: 'the government of an *oikos* presuppose[s] that one has acquired the ability to govern oneself' (160). This is the 'economic' attitude to wealth that Shakespeare inherited. It is epitomized by Iden in *2 Henry VI*:

> This small inheritance my father left me
> Contenteth me, and worth a monarchy.
> I seek not to wax great by others' waning
> Or gather wealth I care not with what envy;
> Sufficeth that I have maintains my state,
> And sends the poor well pleased from my gate.[10]

This conservative, communal, charitable attitude to wealth is the dialectical opposite of chrematistics. A chrematistic approach ignores use-value, it does not ask what wealth is *for*. Rather it takes an exclusively quantitative approach, identifying wealth with exchange-value, thus rendering it potentially unlimited and thus – given the inherently avaricious nature of fallen man – guaranteeing that people will devote themselves to its pursuit, with disastrous moral and practical consequences. Shakespeare foresees the long-term effects of chrematistics in various works, and he often compares them unfavourably with the traditional economy whose passing he mourns. For instance, Ulysses in *Troilus and Cressida* speaks from a perspective that we would regard as 'conservative'. His purpose is to defend 'degree', or hierarchy. In the process however, he engages in a powerful and perspicacious critique of the false equality promoted by chrematistics. 'Degree being vizarded', he observes, 'Th'unworthiest shows as fairly in the mask' (1.3.83–4). If hierarchy is hidden, true 'worth' will be occluded behind the egalitarian façade of quantitative equivalence. If society is abandoned to the market, all traditional customs, institutions and relations will dissolve in a chaos of atomistic competition:

> Take but degree away, untune that string,
> And hark what discord follows. Each thing meets
> In mere oppugnancy. The bounded waters
> Should lift their bosoms higher than the shores
> And make a sop of all this solid globe;
> Strength should be lord of imbecility,
> And the rude son should strike his father dead;
> Force should be right; or rather, right and wrong,
> Between whose endless jar justice resides,
> Should lose their names, and so should justice too.
> Then everything includes itself in power,
> Power into will, will into appetite;
> And appetite, an universal wolf,
> So doubly seconded with will and power,
> Must make perforce an universal prey
> And last eat up himself.

(1.3.109–24)

What Shakespeare and his contemporaries noticed about the transition from an economic to a chrematistic society was the unprecedented, and profoundly counter-intuitive, commodification of three things that, according to traditional ontological assumptions, could never be commodified: land, labour and money. These terms are rather misleading. They disguise the true nature of the transition from feudalism to capitalism. 'Land' means not only the literal soil, but the entire environment: that which surrounds us. The commodification of 'land' meant the commodification of our external surroundings – of the objective world itself. Equally, 'labour' does not only mean the energies exerted during work hours; it refers to human life *per se*, to subjective activity considered as a whole.[11] The commodification of 'land' and 'labour' entailed a total transformation in humanity's understanding of its self. In the words of Joyce Oldham Appleby:

> The critical step in establishing a market momentum is the alienation of land and labor. When these fundamental components of social existence come under the influence of the price mechanism, social direction itself passes to economic determinants … Regular market dealings in land and labor required that the perception of the uniqueness of persons and things be replaced by the peculiar cognitive processes of market calculations.[12]

The term 'money' is also misleading in this context. The human experience is inevitably semiotic, and financial representation is only one of many signifying systems by which the human mind mediates between itself and its objective environment. Language is another, and so is art. As money's nature began to change, parallel changes took place in other media. The Elizabethan public theatre, for example, was widely recognized as an aesthetic analogue to the economic marketplace. Financial and linguistic developments were experienced, and expressed, as analogous, or homologous. Fernand Braudel describes the growth of a popular mistrust of money during the Renaissance: 'This uneasiness was the beginning of an awareness of a new language. For money is a language (we too must be forgiven for using a metaphor); it calls for and makes possible dialogues and conversations; it exists as a function of these conversations'.[13] The commodification of money implies the commodification of mediation *per se*. The commodification of land, labour and money therefore means the commodification of human existence in its entirety: our subjectivity, our objectivity, and the mediation between the two. As Karl Polanyi explains:

> labor and land are no other than the human beings themselves of which every society consists and the natural surroundings in which it exists. To include them in the market mechanism means to subordinate the substance of society itself to the laws of the market ... But labor, land, and money are obviously *not* commodities; they postulate that anything that is bought or sold must have been produced for sale is emphatically untrue in regard to them. In other words, according to the empirical definition of a commodity they are not commodities. Labor is only another name for human activity which goes with life itself ... Land is only another name for nature ... Actual money, finally, is merely a token of purchasing power which, as a rule, is not produced at all, but comes into being through the mechanism of banking or state finance. None of them is produced for sale. The commodity description of labor, land, and money is entirely fictitious.[14]

Despite being fictitious in theory, however, the commodification of labour, land and money is empirically true in practice. Land, labour and money really *are* bought and sold in the modern economy. For Polanyi, therefore, that economy depends upon universal acceptance of a demonstrably false state of affairs. Although they have not been produced for sale, human life, the environment and the media of exchange can all be commodified. They can be treated as sources of exchange-value, in insouciant disregard of nature, reason and custom alike. But commodification always comes with a price.

To summarize: today's definition of 'economics' is diametrically opposed to the traditional understanding of the term. Economics in the ancient sense was the science of utility. Its aim was to realize use-value, which it regarded as subjective. Today's economics is what the ancients called 'chrematistics'. It is the science of exchange, and its aim is the acquisition of exchange-value, or money, which is objective. Economics in the ancient sense was openly dependent on character; today's economics claims to be scrupulously impersonal. The shift from the ancient to the modern notion of economics entails a revision in our entire view of the world, away from an essentially qualitative outlook, which sees things in terms of their essences, and towards a quantitative approach, which evaluates things by their relations to other things. The modernist cultural shift from essential to relational identity is inseparable from the rise of the modern sense of 'economics'. Perhaps Shakespeare appeals to us today because of the unparalleled insight with which he chronicles that transition.

2

'The future comes apace': The Birth of Restricted Economy

I

We have seen that the modern notion of the 'economy' as a clearly-defined sphere of behaviour with its own laws and conventions was foreign to ancient thought. It remained foreign in medieval Europe, where 'scholastic' philosophers like Thomas Aquinas developed Aristotle's ideas into concepts like the 'moral economy' and the 'just price'. The scholastics stressed that market transactions should be judged in ethical terms. The 'just price' theory rejected the determination of value by the market, holding that the true value of an object was inherent in the uses to which it could be put, and that nothing should be sold or bought at a price egregiously at odds with the prevailing norm. Martin Luther expressed the core of the doctrine succinctly: 'It should not be thus, "I may sell my wares as dear as I can or will," but thus, "I may sell my wares as dear as I ought to or as is right and fair'.[1] Such notions specifically insisted on deploying exogenous considerations such as ethics in economic reasoning.

By the end of the Middle Ages, as David McNally observes: 'the market dictated the internal organization of the English farm: prices, profits, wages, and rents were increasingly determined by market conditions'.[2] Nevertheless, throughout the sixteenth century most commentators still followed the ancient tradition, using the term 'economy' to mean the administration of a single household. Richard Huloet's revised Latin-English Dictionary of 1572 translated 'Economie' as 'Household ordering, or gouernaunce'.[3] A section of Giles Fletcher's *Of the Russe Common Wealth* (1591) was headed 'oeconomie or private behavior' and was devoted to the 'Emperor's' management of his own household. Sixteenth-century writers on economics usually acknowledged their debt to Aristotle. In 1583 Anthony Marten's translation of Peter Martyr Vermigli's *Commonplace Book* emphasizes human relations as an economy's essential components: 'Oeconomie (or household government) as appeareth by Aristotle's Politics hath three societies: namely of a husband and wife, of a parent and children, of a Lord and Servants'.[4]

The distinction between 'economics' and 'chrematistics' remained intact throughout the sixteenth century. A commentary on Aristotle's *Politics,* published in English in 1598, carefully distinguishes between 'economy' and the acquisition of possessions: 'That therefore Oeconomie and the acquisitive faculty, are not all one, it may hence appear, because it belongeth to the one to furnish with goods, and the other to use them: for to what art pertaineth it to use goods in a family, but unto the art of Oeconomie?'[5] The commentator identifies economics with the realization of use-value; the acquisition of money is for him non-economic. He also follows Aristotle in noting that the chrematistic acquisition of exchange-value is a subordinate means to the higher end of managing economic utility: 'the skill of acquiring and getting is servant to the skill of housekeeping, called Oeconomie' (ibid.).

This sense of 'economy' was still prevalent in the first two decades of the seventeenth century. In 1609 William Perkins subtitled his *Christian Oeconomie* 'A short survey of the right manner of erecting and ordering a familie', and in 1614 Richard Braithwaite equated his 'Oeconomy' with his 'private family'.[6] By the 1620s, however, the 'economy' was outgrowing its ancient significance, and the word was increasingly used in a more general, frequently figurative sense. In 1621 Matthew Kellison referred to 'the Oeconomie of Morall life',[7] and in 1632 Samuel Torshell described the Israelites as 'under the Oeconomy of Moses'.[8] The following year Henry Hawkins referred to the 'economie of the Heavens'[9] and James Hart wrote on 'the oeconomie of the body'.[10] In such usages, the term expands beyond household affairs, and comes by analogy to designate any self-contained system of exchange.

This originally metaphorical extension of the term 'economy' enabled the invention of the 'economy' in the modern sense of the term. In the 1620s, merchant-theorists like Gerard de Malynes, Thomas Misselden and Thomas Mun – the famous 'three M's' – began the process of isolating 'economic' activity in order to study it and improve its efficiency. As Appleby notes, it was in this debate that '[f]or the first time economic factors were clearly differentiated from their social and political entanglements' (41). In 1621 Mun effectively declared the economy's independence from political control when, having described the means by which England could acquire *specie* by trade, he felt able to proclaim that 'this must come to pass by a necessity beyond all resistance'.[11] Mun's shockingly new claim was that, as the authentic expressions of basic human nature, 'economic' laws and tendencies possessed an autonomous power that placed them beyond the control of any subjective agency. As McNally puts it: 'By focusing on the necessary laws which governed the interaction of prices, the balance of trade and specie flows, Mun treated economic phenomena as susceptible of analysis which was both scientific and objective, that is, as comprehensible without reference to the "subjective" decisions of individual economic agents' (31).

Diana Wood also notes that '[i]t was not until the early Renaissance period that people started to reflect on specifically economic topics',[12] but her phrasing here suggests that economic topics were there all along, waiting to be discovered by the first sharp-eyed scientist to appear. In reality, as

Wood's own work amply demonstrates, the economy was not discovered but invented. Certain perennial modes of human behaviour were identified as sharing a common characteristic, which marked them off from all other types of behaviour and defined them as 'economic' in nature. The first modern students of the economy abandoned Plato's internal ethical hierarchy as impossibly idealistic, arguing that appetite could never be wholly controlled by reason. They imagined the economy as the aggregate of those human actions that were performed with the aim of satisfying 'appetite' or, in other words, maximizing the individual self-interest of the actor.

In contrast to the medieval 'moral economy', these early modern students of 'political economy' thought of their field as an area in which moral strictures against avarice and self-seeking could legitimately be suspended. Instead of seeking the significance of economic transactions by asking what they are *for*, in pursuit of Aristotle's final cause or *telos*, modern students of the economy followed the new scientific principles laid down by Francis Bacon, and confined themselves to analysing people's actual behaviour. The birth of 'political economy' meant reconceiving behaviour that had previously been regarded as avaricious, ambitious and self-interested as merely natural, and thus morally neutral. Until the seventeenth century, economic commentators always exhorted their readers to fair-mindedness and equitable dealing. They routinely excoriated selfishness.[13] They were first and foremost moralists for, as Anthony Parel notes, medieval 'economics was essentially a moral science, and not an autonomous behavioural science'.[14] It was necessary to dispose of this moralistic legacy before 'the economy' could be analysed as if it were a natural phenomenon. Once this had been achieved, the way was clear for the emergence of theoretical 'political economy'. This discourse first took shape in late sixteenth- and early seventeenth-century England. As Oswald Spengler pointed out:

That which we call national economy today is built up on

premises that are openly and specifically English. Credit-money, in the special form imparted to it by the relations of world-trade and export-industry in a peasantless England, serves as the foundation whereupon to define words like capital, value, price, property.[15]

By 'national economy', Spengler means the economics of the *polis,* political economy, or what we call 'economics' today. The terminology and concepts of modern economics took shape in sixteenth- and early seventeenth-century England. Power was shifting from the landed wealth of the aristocracy to the moneyed wealth of the bourgeoisie. 'Let all my land be sold' (2.2.150) declares the noble Timon of Athens on finding himself in debt. But his Steward informs him that it is insufficient to cover the interest, and: 'The future comes apace' (2.2.153). This was a timely warning. Although the earliest tracts to discuss economic matters in modern terms began to appear in the 1620s, their authors were working with a vocabulary and conceptual repertoire that had been developed decades earlier. Neal Wood remarks that 'The intellectual foundations of political economy ... were laid in early Tudor times'.[16] Shakespeare was thus a witness at the birth of the economy. He was also an active participant in the initial formation and early development of 'political economy'. No writer has been as influential as Shakespeare on the English language, and countless of his economic neologisms and idiosyncratic phrases are still used daily by millions of people who have no idea of their source. His work both describes and participates in the construction of economics as we know it today.

II

As historians like Max Weber have shown, the Calvinist concept of 'total depravity' played a vital role in preparing the intellectual ground for modern economics.[17] Following St Augustine, Calvin claimed that the Fall had rendered humanity entirely alien from God. In the *Institutes of the Christian Religion,* he declared that 'all parts of the soul were possessed by sin after Adam deserted the fountain of righteousness', so that the soul's 'entire nature is opposed to supernatural grace' and 'all that proceeds from [man] is to be imputed to sin'.[18] Although other passages in the *Institutes* seem to qualify the severity of this doctrine, Calvin's arguments for total depravity were ratified by the Synod of Dort in 1617, and their influence on popular psychology during Shakespeare's lifetime is incalculable. For many sixteenth- and early seventeenth-century Calvinists, human action was sinful by definition. There was no point in trying to change the innate selfishness of human beings, and the pursuit of self-interest must be accepted as an ineradicable element of fallen human nature.

This reasoning informed Thomas Hobbes's *Leviathan,* which claimed that, in their natural condition, human beings would ineluctably seek to maximize their personal advantage without restraint. In the absence of legal force, Hobbes believed, human society is a *bellum omnia contra omnes.* Hobbes conceived of this 'war of all against all' as the condition of primitive humanity, destined to be historically superseded by civilization. As many subsequent commentators have observed, however, this state of universal individualism is almost entirely absent from the 'primitive' hunter-gatherer societies Hobbes had in mind, which actually tend to be rather communistic. It is however strikingly reminiscent of the conditions pertaining in *laissez faire* capitalist economies, such as the one inhabited by Hobbes himself. In the view of C. B. Macpherson, Hobbes's philosophical empiricism led him to assume that the competitive, individualist, market-oriented society whose development he was observing revealed permanent truths about human nature. What Hobbes took for man in the state of nature was, according to Macpherson, 'civilized man with only the restraint of law removed', and the 'war of all against all' simply reflected the conditions of seventeenth-century England, which 'approximated closely to a possessive market society'.[19]

According to Macpherson, Hobbes was generalizing from empirically observed phenomena which were historically very recent, and geographically very limited. It was specifically Shakespeare's England that witnessed the birth of Hobbesian man, and of a civilization that Polanyi calls 'economic in a different and distinctive sense, for it chose to base itself on a motive only rarely acknowledged as valid in the history of human societies ... namely, gain' (30). Like Polanyi, Fernand Braudel identifies an epochal shift in human consciousness as taking place over what he calls the 'long sixteenth century' from 1450 to 1640. Commenting on Braudel's concept, Immanuel Wallerstein observes:

> This was the period in which was created a European world-economy whose structure was unlike any that the world had known before. The singular feature of this world-economy was the discontinuity between economic and political institutions.[20]

As the work of Braudel, Wallerstein and Polanyi shows, the modern conception of the economy involved the reversal of traditional values, because of a basic alteration in the relative positions of economy and social relations. Put simply, modernity involves the conquest and colonization of society by the economy. In the words of Polanyi: 'Instead of economy being embedded in social relations, social relations are embedded in the economic system' (57). Furthermore, the economic system was originally conceived as consisting solely of self-seeking behaviour. As a result, comments Appleby, the emergence of capitalism in sixteenth-century England involved a 'break with conventional opinions about human nature' because 'capitalism is the first economics system that depends upon greed' (2011, 20, 23).

The secular implications of Calvinist theology grew clear over the early seventeenth century, and by 1653 Joseph Lee could call it an 'undeniable maxime, That every one by the light of nature and reason will do that which makes for his greatest advantage'.[21] Within a century of Shakespeare's death, Bernard de Mandeville's 'The Grumbling Hive' (1705) had developed the concept of total depravity into a fully-fledged rationalization of economic selfishness. Mandeville's allegory describes a hive of bees, all of whom are relentlessly pursuing their own interest. The paradoxical result is the peace and prosperity of the hive as a whole: 'Thus every Part was full of Vice, / Yet the whole Mass a Paradise'.[22] If, as Calvin suggested, human nature was innately depraved, to hold it to any absolute moral standard would be absurdly self-righteous. It would be preferable, as Mandeville's parable suggested, to channel sinfulness in directions which would advance the material condition of society as a whole:

> Luxury
> Employ'd a Million of the Poor,
> And odious Pride a Million more:
> Envy it self, and Vanity,
> Were Ministers of Industry;
> Their daring Folly, Fickleness,
> In Diet, Furniture and Dress,
> That strange ridic'lous Vice, was made
> The very Wheel that turn'd the Trade.

> (180–8)

Mandeville's poem was the climax of a tendency, in place since the late sixteenth century, whereby, in Appleby's words: 'the acceptance of the personal drive for private gain as a legitimate and ineradicable human quality became integrated into new theories about the economy' (1978, 95). The discourse of political economy constructed a *cordon sanitaire,* dividing the rest of culture and society from the sordid selfishness of 'economic' behaviour. The economy was the realm of unrestricted human nature, in which Hobbes's *bellum omnia contra omnes* could be conducted within relatively safe confines, without risking the stability of society as a whole. This meant isolating 'economic' thoughts and actions from the social totality, within which they had previously been deeply embedded. It meant a transition from 'economics' to 'chrematistics'.

To think in chrematistic terms is to impose an alien, artificial exchange-value upon a natural, physical use-value. This was a difficult enough habit of mind to acquire with regard to material possessions. When applied to human beings, to the environment by which human beings live, and to the media of representation through which human beings experience their environment, this process of commodification seemed absurd as well as unjust. But whatever their subjective attitude to such changes, the people of Shakespeare's England were objectively living through precisely such a transformation. For large-scale exchange to take place, an artificial equivalence, a symbolic common denominator, must be imposed upon the individual objects of exchange. When people sell their time, which is indistinguishable from their lives, in exchange for wages, this process of 'reification' is imposed upon human beings, with a corresponding impact on the psyche itself. Furthermore, a chrematistic economy must also make a commodity of money. The medium of exchange must become an object of exchange, and this meant first relaxing, then abolishing, the ancient prohibition on usury. Like 'man' and 'nature', 'money' must be reconceived as something that can be bought and sold on the market. Shakespeare slightly predated political economy by a strictly chronological standard: he died in 1616, while Thomas Mun's *A Discourse of Trade* was not published until 1621. As we shall see, however, he understood the ideological undercurrents that would soon bear fruit in the birth of the restricted economy, and he represents them in uniquely perspicacious style at every stage of his career.

III

The last decades of the twentieth century saw the dawn of historical and cultural era known as 'postmodernism'. The 'postmodern' era is distinguished from previous epochs by the fundamental significance it attributes to the economy. In the words of Timothy Mitchell:

> During the second half of the twentieth century, economics established its claim to be the true political science. The idea of "the economy" provided a mode of seeing and a way of organizing the world that could diagnose a country's fundamental condition, frame the terms of its public debate, picture its collective growth or decline, and propose remedies for its improvement, all in terms of what seemed a legible series of measurements, goals, and comparisons.[23]

With the deliberate organization of society around the market, the economy grows ever more influential over politics, culture and personality. In fact, since twenty-first-century economics involves consumption as much as production, and therefore necessarily takes account of the psychologies and social circumstances of consumers, many commentators now argue that the term 'economy' has expanded so far as to have become entirely figurative. We are moving, it is said, from a restricted to a general sense of 'economy'. Although Asger Sorenson has claimed that '[t]he notion of a general economy can be traced back, at least, to Rousseau's article on "economy" for the French Encyclopedia of 1755',[24] the implications of this development were not explored until the postmodern era. One of the earliest theorists of the 'general economy' was Georges Bataille, who declared that

> the extension of economic growth itself requires the overturning of economic principles – the overturning of the ethic that grounds them. Changing from the perspectives of *restrictive* economy to *general* economy actually accomplishes a Copernican transformation: a reversal of thinking: and of ethics.[25]

According to Bataille, this newly generalized, figurative understanding of the 'economy' returns the concept to its ancient form, in which psychology was more important than finance: 'The exposition of a *general economy* implies intervention in public affairs, certainly, but first of all and more profoundly, what it aims at is consciousness' (41). In addition to invading the psyche, economics has also colonized the sphere of semiotics. The electronic money of the twenty-first century is a system of efficacious representation. Having moved through incarnations as precious metals and bank-notes, money is now acknowledged as a sign, albeit a sign with practical power. This has inspired theorists like Jean Baudrillard, Marc Shell and Jean-Joseph Goux to argue that money is susceptible to semiotic analysis, just like any other sign. This insight has produced the genre of literary criticism known as 'New Economic Criticism', as practised by such critics as Mary Poovey, Regina Gagnier and Walter Benn Michaels. Some professional economists, such as Deirdre McCloskey, have also begun to study the verbal devices and rhetorical manoeuvres by which, they argue, the field of 'economics' is constructed.

In his famous essay 'From a Restricted to a General Economy', Jacques Derrida cites Bataille's account of how, by expanding the 'economy' beyond the sense in which it is 'restricted to commercial values ... [t]he *general economy* ... makes apparent that excesses of energy are produced, and that by definition, these excesses cannot be utilized.

The excessive energy can only be lost without the slightest aim, consequently without any meaning'.[26] For Derrida, the transition from restricted to general economy entails the loss of referentiality, as signs become autonomous of 'any meaning'. We saw above how Aristotle understands use-value as limited by the natural, physical constraints of objects, while he presents exchange-value as potentially limitless because it consists of pure representation. In Derrida and Bataille, the 'restricted' economy corresponds to the Greek 'economics', while the 'general' economy allows value to reproduce indefinitely, thus recalling the Greek concept of 'chrematistics'.

In 'From a Restricted to a General Economy', Derrida claims that phenomenology – the study of how things appear to the human mind – 'corresponds to a restricted economy ... limited to the meaning and the established value of objects, and to their *circulation*' (271). In the restricted sense of 'economy', representation is referential: money designates commodities, and signs designate referents. In the general, figurative sense of 'economy', however, value or meaning is no longer produced from the simple relation of sign to referent. This economic development is paralleled by the structuralist linguistics of Ferdinand de Saussure, in which meaning no longer emerges from the interaction between the verbal sign and an extra-linguistic referent. Rather, meaning is produced by the combination of signifier and signified, which are both elements within the sign. Semiotic significance thus becomes non-referential at approximately the same historical moment, and in roughly the same philosophical manner, as financial value.

The kind of economies Bataille describes – Native American *potlatch* ceremonies, Aztec human sacrifices – are based upon pure expenditure, not on the creation of value. Like post-Saussurean linguistics, they threaten the production of referential meaning itself. As Derrida puts it, they gesture towards a non-financial 'economy', which would be related 'not to the *telos* of meaning, but to the *indefinite* destruction of value' (271). Applied to linguistics, Derrida believes that this 'general economy' can revolutionize the making of meaning:

> It multiplies words, precipitates them one against the other, engulfs them too, in an endless and baseless substitution whose only rule is the sovereign affirmation of the play outside meaning.
>
> (274)

Meaning escapes the referential paradigm, which Derrida associates with the 'restricted' sense of economy, and is instead endlessly deferred along a chain of signifiers with no ultimate referent. Derrida describes the 'general economy' as a 'potlach of signs' (ibid.). In another canonical essay, 'White Mythology' (1974), he outlines the kinship between money and metaphor, and the relation between value and meaning. Despite the apparent radicalism of his claims, however, it is not hard to see in Derrida's 'general economy' the semiotic counterpart of the non-referential financial representations – the swaps, options and futures, the 'derivatives' that refer not to any external referent but only to other forms of money – that dominate the 'casino capitalism' of the postmodern era.

In the wake of Bataille and Derrida, it has become common for postmodernist philosophers and literary critics to use the term 'economy' in a purely metaphorical sense, referring to 'symbolic economies', 'libidinal economies', 'the political economy of the sign' and 'the economy of desire'. In reaction against this tendency, critics such as Douglas Bruster have argued for retaining a strict division between the literal and the figurative uses of the term 'economy'. Bruster constructs a polarity between two kinds of 'economic' criticism. First, we have what he calls 'the *Wall St. Journal* sense of "economy," which is 'a system involving money, credit, debt, profit, and loss'. Bruster conceives of this restricted sense of 'economy' as 'literal'. On the other hand, we have 'the metaphoric sense of "economy," which can encompass non-financial themes and behaviour'.[27] In my own response to Bruster's article I argue that this distinction between literal and metaphoric 'economies' does not hold water:

> "money, credit, debt, profit, and loss"... do not refer to objective things; they are figurative terms for relations between people ... It would never have occurred to the people of Renaissance England to separate the "economy" from the rest of life, and such a separation is manifestly untenable in the postmodern environment, when the "market" saturates every aspect of experience.[28]

In spite of Bruster's cogent case, it seems to me that the postmodern condition has returned us to the condition of pre-modern England, insofar as 'economic' matters are once again conceptually inseparable from moral, cultural or aesthetic considerations. Like Shakespeare, we are confronted by a 'general' economy. Shakespeare's work indicates that concepts and concerns that were until recently considered part of the restricted economy affected the entire range of sixteenth- and seventeenth-century life. He observed and reflected on the earliest emergence of 'economics' from the surrounding discursive fields, and because of this his viewpoint appears increasingly apposite in our era, when the 'economy' is once more expanding to fill the entire experiential landscape.

But if we are to accept that Shakespeare's depiction of economic affairs is appropriate to twenty-first-century society, we must depart from literary critical orthodoxy. Until quite recently, most critics who took economic issues seriously were Marxists, and Marxism assumes that history is a progressive narrative, evolving and developing, so that each era constitutes a practical and theoretical advance on the last. From the Marxist perspective, a sixteenth-century critique could never be applied to twenty-first-century economics, simply because human knowledge has objectively advanced over the last five centuries. Today's pro-capitalist, neo-classical economists would heartily concur. But this conception of history as evolution has recently been challenged by postmodernist thinkers, most famously Jean-François Lyotard, who announced the end of the 'grand narratives' that purport to explain history as a whole by the imposition of a progressive *telos*. The implications of abandoning such teleologies have been aptly summarized by Silvia Federici:

> capitalism was not the product of an evolutionary development bringing forth economic forces that were maturing in the womb of the old order ... Capitalism was the counter-revolution that destroyed the possibilities that had emerged from the anti-feudal struggle – possibilities which, if realized, might have spared us the immense destruction of lives and the natural environment that has marked the advance of capitalist relations worldwide. This much must be stressed, for the belief that capitalism "evolved" from feudalism and represents a higher form of social life has not yet been dispelled.[29]

In a tragic irony, their teleological view of history persuaded many Marxists that capitalism must represent a progressive advance on feudalism, simply because it grew to predominance at a later date. This view was sustainable as long as capitalism could be seen as a temporary stage on the road to socialism. But the recent collapse of practical alternatives to capitalism has made it easier to recognize its emergence as a tragic error, a historical wrong-turn that seems increasingly likely to prove humanity's terminal mistake. To reconceive capitalism in this way is to abandon Marx's notion of inevitable historical development. As the next chapter will show, however, this does not entail abandoning Marx's description of capitalism's psychological, ethical or aesthetic effects. Shakespeare anticipated and influenced that description, for he recognized in early capitalism the same essential characteristics that inspired Marx's critique.

3

The Last of the Schoolmen:
The Marxist Tradition

I

Karl Marx loved William Shakespeare. Marx's daughter
Eleanor recalled that 'Shakespeare ... was the Bible of our
house, seldom out of our hands or mouths ... By the time I
was six I knew scene upon scene of Shakespeare by heart'.[1]
Her brother-in-law Paul Lafargue confirmed that '[Marx's]
respect for Shakespeare was boundless: he made a detailed
study of his works and knew even the least important of his
characters'.[2] Marx's correspondence indicates that he often
filtered his most intimate, personal experiences through the
medium of Shakespearean characters. In 1856 he wrote to
Engels that 'Little Jenny called Pieper "Benedick the married
man," but little Laura said: Benedick was a wit, he is but "a
clown" and "a cheap clown" too. The children are constantly
reading their Shakespeare'.[3] In the same year he declared to his
wife: 'And I do love you, more than the Moor of Venice ever
loved ...'.[4] As S. S. Prawer comments:

> The Shakespeare-cult rife in the Marx household was noted
> by many observers – it brought about regular meetings of
> a Shakespeare-reading society called "The Dogberry Club"
> in Marx's house, which Marx is known to have attended
> and enjoyed, as well as contacts with Frunivall and the
> English Shakespeare Society.

(395)

Throughout his career, Marx packed his writings with Shakespearean allusions, from his earliest articles quoting Shylock in defence of peasants' rights to his invocations of Mistress Quickly in *Capital*. Prawer argues persuasively that by constantly peppering his work with literary references – also including a varied host of other literary giants, with Aeschylus and Goethe among his favourites – Marx was deliberately fulfilling a theoretical imperative. In his early journalism for the *Rheinische Zeitung*, this takes the form of a 'spirited game, played by journalists who could be sure that their readers would catch Shakespearean allusions without difficulty and would refer them to their original context' (38). In his later work, however, this habit is consciously put to work in the philosophical pursuit of the Hegelian totality: '[Marx] needs to quote from, and allude to, literary works to suggest the complex relationships and interconnections which he sees between the different activities of men' (72).

According to Prawer, the result is that 'even when [Marx] is engrossed in economic studies he makes constant mental cross-reference to literature' (72). He returns repeatedly to key characters like Shylock, who 'is never far from Marx's thoughts when he considers the behaviour of nineteenth-century entrepreneurs and the principles of nineteenth-century economists' (130). Reaching for a figure to convey the economic metaphor of 'confidence', Marx turns instinctively to Shakespeare: 'The person who exhibits such confidence equates – like Shylock! – a "good" man with a man who can pay'.[5] He was naturally attracted to the character of Thersites, the cynical plebeian voice in *Troilus and Cressida*, and in general Marx admired Shakespeare's ability to capture elements of the *Zeitgeist* within his individual characters, who inhabit the fertile borderlands between allegory and realism. In a letter of criticism to Ferdinand Lasalle concerning his play *Franz von Sickengen*, Marx urged the author 'to *Shakespearize* more, while now I see *Schillerizing*, the transformation of individuals into mere mouthpieces for the spirit of the time as your greatest fault'.[6] Apparently it was the combination of credible individual personalities with expressions of his age's most fundamental underlying socio-economic tendencies that attracted Marx to Shakespeare. In the same letter to Lasalle, Marx's collaborator Friedrich Engels advances Shakespeare as the archetypal poet of the modern era:

> The characteristics which sufficed in antiquity are no longer adequate in our age, and in this, it seems to me, you could have paid more attention to the significance of Shakespeare in the history of the development of the drama.[7]

It may surprise us to find Marx and Engels interested in a sixteenth-century author because of his modernity. But these nineteenth-century thinkers were well aware that the essential outline of modern psychology had first become visible three centuries earlier, and they revered Shakespeare as one of the first to have glimpsed it. The interest Marx and Engels took in Shakespeare was more than recreational. Shakespeare's treatments of economic themes, his strategic deployment of economic metaphors, even his fluctuating and sensitive economic vocabulary, exerted a profound and openly acknowledged influence on their own theories.

II

Shakespeare frequently invokes the conventional axioms of Aristotelian-Scholastic economics, and many of his dramas depict the crisis to which those axioms were being subjected during his lifetime, as a money-based, market economy began to dissolve traditional ideas and social arrangements. This no doubt goes some way to explaining Marx's enthusiasm for him. While Shakespeare's critique of capitalism may have inspired Marx, however, the alternative values espoused by the playwright were less amenable to revolutionary inter-pretation. Shakespeare usually attacked capitalism from a conservative perspective, deploring its disruption of stable institutions and traditional class relations. The Marxist theory that capitalism breeds its own gravedigger in the form of the revolutionary proletariat is utterly foreign to his world-view.

Nor did the playwright's own class position dispose him to sympathy with the lower orders. John Shakespeare, William's father, was a substantial landowner and local official who was also twice convicted of usury. Shakespeare himself prospered as a playwright and a part-owner of Blackfriars' and the Globe Theatre, and he invested his profits in property in both Stratford and London. David Armitage notes that Shakespeare 'bought the large house called New Place in 1597, inherited a share in two other houses in Stratford in 1601, invested in land around Stratford in 1602 and 1603, and bought a half-share of the Corporation's tithe-holdings in 1605'.[8] He was personally involved in acrimonious struggles over enclosure, and he was fined for hoarding corn in time of dearth. In class terms, Shakespeare was an upwardly-mobile bourgeois with a strong ideological loyalty to feudalism.

As a result, Marxist Shakespeareans find themselves in an oxymoronic position, as Richard Levin pointed out when he suggested that 'some of [Shakespeare's] plays denigrate the kind of individualism and acquisitiveness that came to be associated with capitalism, but this denigration is based on an endorsement of feudal values'.[9] As Levin goes on to remind us, however, this ought to be counted as a point of agreement between Shakespeare and Marx, for '[t]here is a similar tendency to idealize feudalism in Marxist thought ...' (ibid.). The article in which Levin expressed these views brought a barrage of furious replies from Leftist scholars, which were eventually published as a volume entitled *Shakespeare Left and Right* (1991). This volcanic reaction revealed the severity of their dilemma. Marxist Shakespeareans are inevitably troubled by the sheer distance, ideologically and historically, between their world-view and the 'Elizabethan world-picture' reflected in the texts they study. As the famous Hungarian Marxist Georg Lukács readily admitted, Shakespeare himself was fascinated by individual psychology, and paid little attention to the underlying economic factors that Marxists considered vital. In Lukács' words, the Bard neglected to consider 'the abstract':

> What does this mean? It means that the tragic content of *Julius Caesar* is the strange character of four men, Caesar, Brutus, Cassius and Antonius, whose interaction spells tragedy for Brutus. It means that the play contains nothing of the abstract struggles from that age, a struggle between the declining Roman aristocratic republic and the new Caesarism. It means that in *Coriolanus* it is not the confrontation of aristocrats and plebians, but the baseness of Sicinius, Brutus and Aufidius, and Volumnia's great nobility that leads to Coriolanus' death. It means, that in the historical struggles portrayed in Shakespeare's dramas of English history, it is not English feudalism that collapses … in the end, Henry VII marks not the triumph of the new over the old, but the success of the noble hero against the monumental villain [Richard the Third].[10]

Here Lukács constructs a typical but surely false polarity between individual character and 'abstract' historical processes. He criticizes Shakespeare's failure to portray the 'abstract' social and economic causes which, in his opinion, lie behind their surface manifestations in individual personalities: 'when the tribunes scold the people for fawning on Caesar, they talk only about the people's ingratitude to Pompey, and not about the struggle against tyranny' (137). But if supposedly impersonal forces inevitably manifest themselves in individuals, they can surely be studied through individual thoughts and behaviour. Furthermore, the Roman historical context that Shakespeare describes was indeed notable for a shift in public discourse from the political to the personal. In fact this was precisely the grievance of the real-life anti-Caesarian conspirators, who feared the power of Caesar's personality cult. Lukács sometimes seems to wish Shakespeare had shared his own belief in the Marxist doctrine that economic factors are the true determining elements in society, and that by comparison individual characters are mere epiphenomena. As Sharon O'Dair observes:

> Shakespeare's plays pose difficulty for critics who, in addressing inequality and subordination in them, look primarily to Marx and Marxian class analysis for interpretive help or theoretical grounding, thereby ignoring or discounting the established and competing model of stratification in the early modern period, that is, one revealed in a hierarchy of status, in which an economy of prestige takes place over an economy of money.[11]

Victor Kiernan concurs, noting that, for Marxists, Shakespeare's 'plays seem to raise an immediate difficulty ... We are shown no tragic clash between the feudal aristocracy and the class destined to supplant it'.[12] Despite such differences however, it remains true that Marx and Shakespeare shared a broadly similar theoretical outlook. Like the Bard, Marx judged capitalism from an Aristotelian perspective. Thus the great English historian R. H. Tawney perceptively called Marx 'the last of the schoolmen'.[13] It was only natural for Marx to appreciate Shakespeare's dramatic, passionate enactments of Aristotelian reasoning in its death throes. Indeed, Marx considered Shakespeare a serious authority on economic matters, and often cited him to that effect, quoting Timon of Athens' excoriating anti-financial diatribe on several occasions. This famous speech gets to the heart of the Aristotelian case against exchange-value. It provided the medium through which Marx applied Aristotle to modern economics. Having exiled himself from Athens in disgust at the economic selfishness of its inhabitants, Timon sits cursing outside the city walls. He digs in the earth for roots to eat:

What is here?
Gold? Yellow, glittering, precious gold?
No, gods, I am no idle votarist.
Roots, you clear heavens! Thus much of this will
make
Black, white; foul, fair; wrong, right;
Base, noble; old, young; coward, valiant.
Ha, you gods! Why this? What this, you gods? Why,
this
Will lug your priests and servants from your sides,
Pluck stout men's pillows from below their heads.
This yellow slave
Will knit and break religions, bless the accurs'd,
Make the hoar leprosy ador'd, place thieves,
And give them title, knee and approbation
With senators on the bench. This is it
That makes the wappen'd widow wed again;
She whom the spital-house and ulcerous sores
Would cast the gorge at, this embalms and spices
To th'April day again. Come, damn'd earth,
Thou common whore of mankind, that puts odds
Among the rout of nations, I will make thee
Do thy right nature.

(4.3.25–45)

Here Shakespeare combines the Hellenic conception of exchange-value as artifice with the Hebraic injunction against fetishizing 'the works of men's hands',[14] to produce a witheringly accurate diagnosis of money's effects. When he read this speech, Marx was living through the final dissolution of feudal, *ancien regime* Europe, the seeds of which he discerned in sixteenth-century England, and the root of which he located in the rise to power of money. He evidently found his impressions confirmed by Timon's agonized alienation, in which Shakespeare encapsulates the origins of the ideology whose maturity Marx was observing three centuries later. In the *Economic and Philosophic Manuscripts of 1844* Marx claims that 'Shakespeare excellently depicts the real nature of money' in Timon's speech, by stressing two of its properties:

1   It is the visible divinity – the transformation of all human and natural properties into their contraries, the universal confounding and overturning of things: it makes brothers of impossibilities.

2   It is the common whore, the common pimp of people and of nations. The overturning and confounding of all human and natural qualities, the fraternization of impossibilities – the divine power of money – lies in its character as man's estranged, alienating and self-disposing species-nature. Money is the alienated ability of mankind. That which I am unable to do as a man, and of which therefore all my individual essential powers are incapable, I am able to do by means of money. Money thus turns each of these powers into something which in itself it is not – turns it, that is, into its contrary.[15]

These two key insights conveyed by Shakespeare to Marx have been confirmed by history. First, money transforms essence into appearance. Second, money transforms human beings into things. Both of these insights can be found in Aristotle, so Shakespeare was working within a long tradition. But Shakespeare gives Timon a particularly impassioned exposition of money's implications, and this vehemence no doubt stems from the historical location of both Timon and Shakespeare at the birth of a market-oriented society. On the basis of Shakespeare's rendition of Aristotle, Marx would construct his theories of 'commodification' as the imposition of symbolic exchange-value upon authentic use-value, and of wage labor as the systematic reification of humanity. Although Marx certainly drafted them into the service of his theory, it is important to remember that these ideas precede him by millennia. They have also enjoyed a lengthy post-Marxist career as the primary inspirations behind postmodernists like Gilles Deleuze, Guy Debord and Jean Baudrillard, and they continue to inspire *avant garde* thinkers like Slavoj Žižek, Michael Hardt and David Graeber to this day.

Despite their disproportionate influence and extensive afterlife, however, Marx's actual comments on Shakespeare are few and far between. He is scarcely more expansive on general questions of literature or aesthetics. Such asides as do survive are neither lengthy nor rigorous enough to provide a solid theoretical foundation for literary critical practice, and so Marxist critics have been forced to extrapolate their methodology from Marx's economic and philosophical observations. On this basis, they practise what they take to be a Marxist method in their own work. In its earliest, crudest form, this amounted to 'economic determinism': the belief that economic factors determine all other phenomena. This approach has become known by the derogatory name 'vulgar Marxism', and it was the dominant strain in Marxist thought during the late nineteenth and early twentieth centuries.

Today though, in a notable historical irony, economic determinist arguments are made mostly by strident advocates of capitalism. Echoing capitalism's earliest defenders like Hobbes and Mandeville, twentieth-century pro-capitalists like Friedrich Hayek and Ayn Rand argued that the pursuit of self-interest, manifested in the market economy, is the authentic expression of human nature. They believe that human beings have evolved into selfish individualists by inexorable, quasi-Darwinist progress, and that economic self-interest is the real motive lurking behind all human activity, however altruistic it may appear. Any attempt to mitigate the effects of the market on the rest of society can thus easily be denigrated as a violation of nature. Market behaviour is the pure, unmediated expression of humanity, and *homo economicus* is man in his natural condition.

III

We should remember here that this morality is the diametrical opposite of ancient and medieval ethics. According to Socrates, Aristotle and Aquinas, humans realize their nature by fulfilling their purpose, their *telos*. This cannot mean indulging appetite, for we share appetite with the animals and so it cannot be the definitive human characteristic. It cannot mean the pursuit of money, for after the necessities have been provided, money is merely an adjunct to the satisfaction of appetite. The definitive human characteristic is reason. Reason is what sets us apart from the beasts. The exercise of reason, the intellectual cultivation of the soul, is thus the end or purpose of human life, and the fulfilment of human nature. The purpose of economics is to make such a life possible. But the capitalist morality of modernity reversed this ethical system, suggesting that the fulfilment of appetite, by means of money, was true human nature and thus the proper purpose of human society.

The clear implication of such thinking was that human beings are entirely material creatures, driven by entirely physical needs. On both the political 'Left' and the 'Right', economic determinism has invariably been accompanied by materialist theories of subjectivity, which reflect the reifying effects of commodification. Throughout the 1960s and 1970s, Marxists like Louis Althusser and post-Marxists like his pupil Michel Foucault advanced influential materialist accounts of human identity. Today, such theories are frequently used to advocate a market mentality, and disciplines like 'Leadership Studies' take inspiration from ideas about the self that were first developed by allegedly progressive thinkers in the humanities. A recent article in the *Journal of Business Ethics* entitled 'The Ethics of Managerial Subjectivity' was devoted to 'managing subjectivity as an ethical enterprise in relation to organizational structures and norms, and 'examin[ing] the manager as a moral subject in relation to subjectivity at work'.[16] Thus the philosophical discourse of 'structures' and 'subjectivity' seeps into managerial practice. The authors explicitly base their research on the theories of Michel Foucault, whose materialist account of subjectivity informs the work of many other management and leadership theorists who may or may not know his texts at first-hand.

This new, pro-capitalist form of materialist determinism has successfully insinuated itself into the twenty-first-century popular mind. Today, materialism and capitalism are considered entirely compatible. For most of the twentieth century, however, the argument that economic self-interest determines people's thoughts and behaviour was closely identified with Marxism. The difference is that for Marxists the determining factor was the collective interests of social classes, while the pro-capitalists look to the self-interest of individuals as the driving force behind social developments. But both sides agree that the economy is, in some sense, more real than the rest of society, and that it is the cause of other social phenomena. Strangest of all from a twenty-first century perspective, pro- and anti-capitalists both ascribed these functions to the economy on the grounds that it was *material*. The twentieth century equated the material with the real, and both with the economic.

In accordance with these assumptions, late nineteenth and early twentieth-century Marxists claimed that philosophy, religion, art and literature – 'ideology', to use Marx's term – constituted a 'superstructure', which was built upon and determined by the substantial 'base' of 'material', economic factors. This tended to produce critics who believed that Shakespeare's characters must be interpreted in the light of their economic position, usually as reflected in their social class. Bertolt Brecht expressed the classical Marxist interpretation of the plays as presenting the transition from feudalism to bourgeois society:

From the feudal point of view the new love (Romeo, Antony), the new thinking (Hamlet), the new demand for freedom (Brutus), the ambition (Macbeth), the new self-regard (Richard III), are deadly. From the bourgeois point of view the feudal-type restrictions are deadly.[17]

Like Marx and Engels, Brecht praised Shakespeare because, living as he did at the dawn of the capitalist era, he was able to observe capitalism's effects on subjectivity with the penetration afforded by novelty. According to Ernst Bloch, Shakespeare even anticipated Brecht's most famous dramatic device, the 'alienation effect', in which the actor or script calls attention to the artifice in which they are engaged:

> The *locus classicus* for this kind of estrangement is still Hamlet, in the play within the play ... [which] is entitled "The Mousetrap," and it actually becomes one even while presenting itself as an account of faraway events. This verges upon Brecht's instrument of estrangement.[18]

The idea that economics, expressed in social class, was the primary influence on literary form remained typical of Marxist criticism for most of the twentieth century. In 1977 Paul Delany provided a concise summary of this approach:

> The analysis will take as its point of departure Marx's view of the English Renaissance as a transitional stage between the dominance of the feudal aristocracy and that of the commercial bourgeoisie, which consolidated its power over England's destiny in 1688. My concern will be with the effects of this transition on social and personal relations: that is, with shifts in consciousness that pertain to the cultural "superstructure" rather than to the direct results of changes in the mode of production.[19]

Social and personal relations are thus conceived as epiphenomena that are caused by economic factors. The latter are imagined as somehow deeper or more fundamental than the former. Delany goes on to describe what this will mean when applied to the text: 'I shall assume ... that the opposition between the party of Lear and the party of Regan, Goneril, and Edmund is not merely a conflict between good and evil persons; it conveys also a social meaning that derives from the contemporary historical situation as Shakespeare understood it' (24). This putative contrast between social and psychological factors was characteristic of twentieth-century Marxism. In *Shakespeare: A Marxist Interpretation,* A. A. Smirnov urged Marxist critics to 'make the transition from the psychological to the social antithesis',[20] to trace what the Bard presented as personal issues to their socio-economic causes. Today, however, this looks like a false dichotomy. The 'conflict between good and evil persons' is surely inseparable from the 'contemporary historical situation'; it is not necessary to choose between moral psychology and socio-economic analysis. L. C. Knights made this point long ago, taking issue with John Palmer who

> at the end of an excellent chapter on *Coriolanus,* says, 'The politics are ... in the last analysis incidental. Shakespeare is intent on persons, not on public affairs'. But this is an over-sharp distinction. In Shakespeare's political plays – not least in *Coriolanus* – politics are shown as an affair of persons ... In Shakespeare, when great public events are involved, there is an opening of inner, as well as of social, perspectives.[21]

In contrast to Knights, Delany distinguishes personality from politics, because for him the 'historical situation' means specifically the economic situation. He considers economics and personal morality to be different areas of experience, the first of which determines the second. In this he is typical of Marxist materialism. In its most extreme forms, which were usually to be found in Communist states, vulgar Marxist criticism brazenly subordinated aesthetics to political and economic expedience. The dour conclusion reached in 1929 by the Theatre Discussion Group in Soviet Ukraine would soon echo throughout the Communist world: 'The foundational role of the theatre should not lie in entertainment, nor in aesthetic delight, but in its social significance'.[22]

This didacticism was enforced by the government-sanctioned publication in Moscow in 1935 of P. A. Martov's *The Soviet Theatre*. Martov informed his readers that the Repertory Company of the People's Commissariat of Education 'does not permit the performance of plays which are socially insignificant or harmful, and it assists the theaters in the correct interpretation of a play'.[23] The Chinese Communists offered similar assistance. The puritanical pragmatism of their aesthetics was epitomized by Mao Zedong's Talks at the Yenan Forum on Literature, which insisted that all literary criticism must be 'correct' and 'political', and that literature must be evaluated on the basis of its 'objective effects'.[24] In practice this tended to produce formulaic, class-based claims like Yang Zhouhan's 1958 assertion that Shakespeare 'not only opposed feudalism but also transcended the limits of bourgeois ideas, and therefore was also against the bourgeoisie'.[25]

This portrayal of Shakespeare as a genius straining to break free of the limitations imposed by his bourgeois perspective became canonical behind the Iron Curtain. Having been praised by Marx and Engels, the Bard was ripe for appropriation by the forces of international Socialism. Thus on the four-hundredth anniversary of Shakespeare's birth the official Soviet newspaper *Pravda* declared:

> The whole extent of Soviet art ... is closely bound up with the heritage of Shakespeare. In our eyes, this titan of the Renaissance was never an honoured classic; he has always been our contemporary, a participant in that great struggle for the fair future of mankind to which the Soviet people are also committed.[26]

This subordination of aesthetics to politics was a regrettable result of the base/superstructure model. Crude as it may appear, however, that model also produced many critical insights. In *A Marxist Study of Shakespeare's Comedies* (1979), Elliot Krieger used it effectively, to explain the movement, found in all Shakespeare's comedies, from a 'primary world' of realism, conflict and evil to a 'secondary world' of fantasy, reconciliation and the triumph of good. Krieger argues convincingly that the apparent harmony and concord of the 'second world' actually reflect specifically aristocratic class values, which Shakespeare shows victorious over the insurgent, bourgeois morality represented by the 'first world'. He invokes the Marxist theory of false consciousness to explain that 'Because it creates the illusion that class interests are universal interests, the second world functions as an ideological system ...'[27] According to this reading, the reconciliations of Shakespeare's comic resolutions are not timeless assertions of universal values, but calculated and faintly shabby rationalizations, designed to make the hierarchical society advocated by aristocrats appear natural and thus permanent. The final acts of the comedies generally involve a restatement of the 'great chain of being', the vital element in what E. M. W. Tillyard called 'the Elizabethan world-picture', where everything in creation occupies its own, divinely-appointed place within the overall harmony. Krieger notes the convenience of this world-view as a justification of class hierarchy: '[b]y attributing the arrangement of the social structure to an immaterial force outside of human action and control, the belief in harmony articulates the fantasy that nature – or heaven – itself sanctions and determines the extant class structure' (10).

For Marxists such as Krieger, then, the supposedly universal values expressed in Shakespeare's comedies are in fact part of the ideological superstructure. They reproduce and perpetuate aristocratic assumptions by presenting them as eternal verities. In spite of their overtly conservative message, however, Krieger also finds an oppositional dialectic at work within the plays. In a movement that recalls the Hegelian *aufhebung*, whereby the synthesis both transcends and reproduces the poles of the precedent opposition, the 'second world' is altered and undermined in the process of negating the 'first world':

> The dramatic form of the comedies, which I will call dialectical, negates the second-world ideology. While the ideology within the play states that static hierarchies and ordered structures constitute and determine a social ideal, the form of the play demonstrates that material conditions can be transformed, replaced, or negated by human action. In this regard the dialectical dramatic form negates the static ideology that the protagonists express through the dramatic contents.
>
> (7)

Economic determinism defined both pro- and anti-capitalism throughout the twentieth century. Both sides of this opposition also endorsed a materialist determinism: they believed that the sphere of ideas was determined by the supposedly 'material' sphere of the economy. These two forms of determinism – economic and materialist – seemed comfortably compatible during the industrial era, when it was easy to identify the economy with the production of material goods. It is less clearly relevant to the post-industrial, exchange-based economies of the present day, however, and after the Second World War several Western Communists began to rethink their mental picture of the economy as the motor driving the rest of society. As early as 1938 Georg Lukács observed:

> Under capitalism ... the different strands of the economy achieve a quite unprecedented autonomy, as we can see from the examples of trade and money – an autonomy so extensive that financial crises can arise directly from the circulation of money.[28]

This departs from the conventional Communist materialism that conceived of material production as the determining force in the economy. From there it was a relatively small step to the conclusion that the ideological superstructure might, under certain conditions, achieve a similar autonomy from the economic base. A few years earlier, the Italian Communist leader Antonio Gramsci had already developed his theory of 'cultural hegemony', by which the ruling class made its domination appear natural through its manipulation of culture. Literature and aesthetics were therefore valid spheres of class struggle, which need not be limited to the economic arena. In the wake of Gramsci, other thinkers like Louis Althusser conceded the 'relative autonomy of the superstructures',[29] admitting that ideas can sometimes change or develop separately from the material base. But committed as he was by his membership of the French Communist Party to imagining the proletariat as the vanguard of the revolution, Althusser was transfixed by a vision of class warfare, and unable to break entirely with economic determinism. The intellectual tension produced by this dilemma is perceptible in the strained formulation by which he asserted 'determination in the last instance by the (economic) mode of production' (ibid.).

However, the empirical condition of post-war Europe made economic determinism hard to sustain, even 'in the last instance'. The identity, politics and ideology of many people in the Western world were clearly influenced by their race, gender and sexual orientation, in addition to their social class. The 'vulgar Marxist' response to such developments is accurately encapsulated in Richard Levin's admittedly hostile summary:

> for Marxists (at least the orthodox ones) everything depends on class. According to their theory, class oppression is the real cause of race and gender oppression, which will end when – and only when – the capitalist class system is replaced by a classless socialist society.

(48)

As we have seen, Levin advanced this contention in a deliberately provocative article, but the resulting controversy suggests that he touched a sensitive nerve. It is indeed true that their loyalty to radical politics imprisons many otherwise sophisticated thinkers in a dogmatic economic determinism, and that this often commits them to a doctrinaire faith in a 'materialism of the last instance'. [30] Levin cites such evidence as Toril Moi's claim that opposition to 'patriarchy and sexism ... necessarily also entails opposition to capitalism' and Gayle Greene's assertion that 'sexism and the values of patriarchy are inherent in capitalism' since 'their root is economic'.[31] Since the determining role of the economy was as widely accepted on the political right as on the left, moreover, such materialist theories easily survived the collapse of the Communist political project.

4

'The hatch and brood of time': Beyond the Economy

I

The dogmatic materialism espoused by many literary critics often springs from a residual loyalty to Marxist politics. But would a movement away from economic determinism, or even away from materialism, necessarily involve a departure from Marxism? Although Lenin's ultra-materialist reading of Marx in *Materialism and Empirico-Criticism* ensured that reductive materialist determinism remained the orthodoxy of institutional communism, there has always been a dissident tradition that emphasizes Marxism's dialectical, Hegelian heritage. It is true that Marx often suggests that economic factors determine ideas. In 1859 he observed:

> a distinction should always be made between the material transformation of the economic conditions of production, which can be determined with the precision of natural science, and the legal, political, religious, aesthetic or philosophical – in short, ideological forms in which men become conscious of this conflict and fight it out.[1]

However, Marx's dialectical method is logically incompatible with materialist determinism. Marx took his theory of dialectics from Hegel, who emphasized the doctrine known as the 'interpenetration of opposites'. This ancient idea, as adapted by Hegel, inspired Marx with its insight that each pole of a logical contradiction determines the other. It would be impossible to conceive of the concept 'good', for example, without thereby bringing the opposite concept of 'evil' into existence. The concepts 'good' and 'evil' are only significant in relation to each other, they need each other to exist, and in this sense 'good' is actually constitutive of 'evil', its apparent opposite. Marx applies this dialectical logic to every situation. It allowed him to perceive, for instance, that the opposition between capital and labour is ultimately an illusion, because the former is the externalized, objectified form of the latter. Capital and labour form a mutually definitive binary opposition.

Because it insists on the mutual determination of apparent opposites, dialectical thought is incompatible with materialist determinism, which posits a one-way determination of ideas by matter. It is also incompatible with the idea that the economy is the ultimate cause of ideas. Given the fundamental importance of dialectics to his mature theory, therefore, it is hard to avoid concluding that Marx's economic determinism was a youthful rhetorical flourish, best disregarded in the interpretation of his mature work. This conclusion finds support in remarks made by Marx's closest friend and colleague, Friedrich Engels:

> there is only one point lacking, which, however, Marx and I always failed to stress enough in our writings and in regard to which we are all equally guilty. That is to say, we all laid, and were bound to lay, the main emphasis, in the first place, on the derivation of political, judicial and other ideological notions, and of actions arising from those notions, from basic economic facts. But in so doing we neglected the formal side – the ways and means by which these notions, etc., come about – for the sake of the content.[2]

What distinguishes Marx's method from political economy is not economic determinism but dialectics. In Hegel's *Phenomenology of Mind* (1807), which exerted a seminal influence on Marx's generation of German students, dialectics is used to demonstrate the inter-connectedness of all experience, from the formation of personal identity to the course of world history. The task of the dialectician is to locate individual phenomena within the over-arching 'totality', and it is only in this context that phenomena can be grasped in their full significance. However, the totality has been rendered imperceptible to immediate experience by the universal alienation imposed by capitalist modernity, and the consequent fragmentation of life into discrete 'fields' or 'spheres' of activity and interest – what the idealist Hegelian T. S. Eliot called the 'dissociation of sensibility'. Doug Brown summarizes this basic contention of Hegelianism:

> Polanyi and Lukács shared a belief that market society had, in its brief history, destroyed essential organic bonds that had held together the substance of pre-capitalist societies … with the disembedding of economy from society and its self-regulation by market motives and forces, not only was there a separation of the economic spheres from the state (or polity) but the economic sphere tends to dominate the state.[3]

A Hegelian might well acknowledge the primacy of economic motives at the current historical juncture, but he or she would see it as a contingent result of alienation, not as a universal part of the human condition. Such a critic would therefore not insist that, say, Hamlet's procrastination is directly caused by the growing obsolescence of the aristocracy in a bourgeois world – although a 'vulgar' Marxist might well make such a claim. Georg Lukács' philosophy vacillated along with his political relations with the Hungarian and Soviet Communist Parties, but he summed up the Hegelian Marxist position aptly: 'it is not the primacy of economic modes in historical explanation that constitutes the decisive difference between Marxism and bourgeois thought, but the point of view of totality'.[4]

This lesson was soon assimilated into literary criticism. In 1964 Arnold Kettle committed Marxist heresy when he declined to limit his interpretation to the restricted economy, insisting that Shakespeare's work must also be understood through the 'social, artistic, political, religious, scientific' changes that were taking place as he wrote.[5] By the 1950s the retreat from economic determinism was joined even by many materialist Marxists, who used Gramsci's concept of 'hegemony' to involve culture in the class struggle. This could only be reconciled with materialism by interpreting culture itself as part of the material realm, and even claiming, in Althusser's formulation, that 'Ideas have disappeared as such'.[6] Today this argument is also made with ever-increasing confidence by cognitive neuroscientists and evolutionary psychologists, who literally identify ideas with the material processes of the brain. In the Anglophone world, the proposition that ideas are actually material has been highly influential on literary criticism, where it has produced the movement known as 'Cultural Materialism'. This genre's name alludes to Gramsci's recognition of the class struggle's cultural dimension. Its founding father was the Welsh Marxist Raymond Williams, whose *Culture and Society* inspired such contemporary Shakespearean critics as Alan Sinfield, Jonathan Dollimore and John Drakakis.

In his influential *Marxism and Literary Criticism* (1976), Terry Eagleton distinguished Marxism from the 'sociology of literature', which 'concerns itself chiefly with what might be called the means of literary production, distribution and exchange in a particular society – how books are published, the social composition of their authors and audiences, levels of literacy, the social determinants of "taste"'.[7] Eagleton finds Marxism's competitive advantage in its ability to locate both the texts it examines and the method by which it examines them within the historical totality: 'The originality of Marxist criticism ... lies not in its historical approach to literature, but in its revolutionary understanding of history itself' (ibid.). Eagleton made a similar point in *Criticism and Ideology* (1978):

Historical materialism stands or falls by the claim that it is not only not an ideology, but that it contains a scientific theory of the genesis, structure and decline of ideologies. It situates itself, in short, outside the terrain of competing "long perspectives," to theorise the conditions of their very possibility.[8]

Eagleton's work extrapolated from Pierre Macherey's *Towards a Theory of Literary Production* (1966), which argued that literary texts can reveal ideological contradictions by imposing pre-existent, formal structures upon the inchoate blur of human experience. According to Macherey, the critic's task is to discover, by means of these ideological contradictions in the text, the material, historical contradictions that have produced them. Once again we find the typical Marxist assumption of superior explanatory power: the Marxist critic not only identifies features of the text, but explains them by reference to extra-textual history, which is conceived as material and especially as economic.

II

This extra level of perceived explanatory power led many critics to espouse a rhetorical and methodological commitment to 'materialism' up to and beyond the end of the twentieth century. As Ivo Kamps noted in 1995: 'Over the last decade and a half, we have witnessed the rapid ascendancy of materialist Shakespearean criticism in Great Britain and the United States'.[9] By this date, however, literary critics rarely used the word 'materialism' in its strict philosophical sense: they did not usually suggest that ideas are entirely determined by, or that they can be reduced to, the material circumstances under which they occur. In fact, 'materialism' was frequently employed as a synonym for 'historicism', as in Jonathan Dollimore and Alan Sinfield's Introduction to their landmark anthology *Political Shakespeare* (1985). The authors define the term 'cultural materialism':

> 'Materialism' is opposed to 'idealism:' it insists that culture does not (cannot) transcend the material forces and relations of production. Culture is not simply a reflection of the economic and political system, but nor can it be independent of it. Cultural materialism therefore studies the implication of literary texts in history.[10]

Dollimore and Sinfield's careful phrasing, which denies the *determination* of culture by economics but asserts that culture is inevitably *influenced* by economics, reflects an astute effort to assimilate Althusser's 'relative autonomy of the superstructures' into literary theory. But it is difficult to see why 'materialism' so defined is opposed to 'idealism'. Idealist criticism does not necessarily claim transcendence; it is perfectly capable of locating the texts it studies in their historical contexts – it simply regards that context as consisting of ideas. Yet literary critics persisted in using 'materialism' and 'historicism' interchangeably. In his Introduction to *Shakespeare Left and Right* (1991), Ivo Kamps summarized the political division among Shakespeareans:

> Put simply, the prevailing sentiment on the Right is that Shakespeare transcends his historical moment – he is not for an age but for all time – because his genius allowed him to capture what is most true, universal, and enduring about human nature. A recent wave of counter-criticism, however, has focused close attention on the various ways in which the playwright's texts participate in, are subversive of, or

reflect on Renaissance institutional practice and ideologies
designed to oppress and control the people.

(1)

For critics like Kamps, universal statements about human
nature are necessarily politically conservative. This is not only
because they ignore the historical determinations of character
and ideas, but more specifically because they fail to recognize
particular class interests, which rest ultimately on economic
factors. This understanding of 'ideology' can be traced to
Marx's *The German Ideology* (1845–6):

> Each new class which puts itself in the place of one ruling
> before it is compelled ... to represent its interest as the
> common interest of all the members of society ... It has to
> give ideas the form of universality, and represent them as
> the only rational, universally valid ones.[11]

However, the Marxist emphasis on class grew less pronounced
by the late twentieth century, as economic determinism
gradually loosened its hold on radical critics. Unlike
Althusser, Kamps does not even invoke the economy as
a 'last instance'; for him, the definitive characteristic of a
Leftist critic is a concern with oppression of any description.
In their Introduction to *Marxist Shakespeares* (2001), Jean
Howard and Scott Cutler Shershaw conceded that '"class"
relations cannot be considered to possess a priority in the
colloquial sense, a greater immediacy or practical relevance
to any and all human situations' (7). Some Marxist critics
had already distinguished between historicism (the belief
that attitudes, ideas and behaviours are determined by the
historical situation in which they arise) and materialism (the
belief that such phenomena are determined by the material
situation in which they arise.). For example, when L. C.
Knights declared that 'Shakespeare's political characters bring
their world with them',[12] he was reminding his readers that

the figures represented in the history plays are products of
their time, but he did not suggest that their class position
or economic circumstances was the key to understanding
them, as a vulgar Marxist might have done. It is true that the
examples that Knights provides of the kind of historical details
he considers significant are economic in scope:

> Readers of Shakespeare will hardly need to be reminded of
> the part played in the total action of *Henry IV, Part II*, by
> the evocation of life on a Gloucestershire manor, where the
> well-chain must be mended and the headland sown with
> red wheat, and where Mouldy's old mother will have no
> one to do 'her husbandry and her drudgery' if he goes off
> to the wars.

(35)

Knights' point, however, is not to reduce character to an
expression of economic interests but to maintain an awareness
of the social totality. He finds the source of Shakespeare's
'political wisdom' in his

> awareness of the fact ... that society, far from being an
> aggregation of individuals, is a network of inter-personal
> relationships – the person himself depending for his very
> sense of self on those myriad vibrations of liking, disliking,
> validation and challenge that extend almost indefinitely in
> all directions.

(51)

Later generations of Marxists echoed this praise of
Shakespeare's ability to show how social forces and personal
foibles blend together in their influence on human behaviour.
In the words of Victor Kiernan: 'Shakespeare's protagonists
are fully developed as individuals, but not cut off from the
social whole' (33). Such a protagonist's 'passions are not his
own solely, but well up from the social condition, or, more

distinctly, out of the conditions men collectively forge for themselves at a given time' (ibid.). This is historicism, certainly, but it is not materialism, still less economic determinism. In fact, it recalls the dialectical, totalizing approach of Hegel, and Shakespeare's susceptibility to Hegelian reading doubtless goes some way towards explaining his appeal to Marxist critics.

We should not underestimate Marxism's achievement in introducing historicism to Shakespeare studies. For centuries it had indeed been assumed that Shakespeare's appeal lay in his transcendence of history, his access to universal truths about general human nature. This attitude was inscribed in Shakespeare criticism from the very beginning, when the Bard's rival and contemporary Ben Jonson announced him to be 'not of an age but for all time'. It was famously canonized by the eighteenth-century sage Dr Samuel Johnson, who felt that:

> Shakespeare is ... the poet of nature; the poet that holds up to his readers a faithful mirror of manners and of life. His characters ... are the genuine progeny of common humanity ... His persons act and speak by the influence of those general passions and principles by which all minds are agitated, and the whole system of life is continued in motion.[13]

Jonson and Johnson value Shakespeare for his insight into 'common humanity', the essential core of human nature which, they believe, remains irreducibly constant regardless of time or place. Harold Bloom makes similar claims for Shakespeare, but as the title of his *Shakespeare: The Invention of the Human* (1999) indicates, he sees the Bard as producing the modern concept of human nature under specific historical circumstances, rather than as miraculously discovering eternal verities. Virtually all critics now accept that the characters, plots and messages conveyed by literary texts are historically contingent. Marxism is therefore not distinguished by its historicism, nor by its materialism, nor even by its economic determinism, all of which are shared by other critical schools. If Hegelian Marxism is distinguished by its emphasis on the totality, what distinguishes materialist Marxist criticism is its emphasis on class, and especially on class conflict, as the root cause of historical change.

Because Marx claimed that the key to history was held by the proletariat, Marxist critics often display an interest in Shakespeare's lower-class characters and their passages of plebeian discourse. For many of Marx's more romantic followers, the proletariat's logical position as the antithesis of capital issued in a vague sympathy for all oppressed and marginal characters, regardless of whether their oppression is economic in nature. Many radicals have evaluated Shakespeare by this standard. To nineteenth-century liberals like William Hazlitt, he seemed deplorably lacking in sympathy for the underdog. Hazlitt deduced the playwright's opinion from *Coriolanus*:

> The people are poor; therefore they ought to be starved. They are slaves; therefore they ought to be beaten. They work hard; therefore they ought to be treated like beasts of burden. They are ignorant; therefore they ought not to be allowed to feel that they want food, or clothing, or rest, that they are enslaved, oppressed, and miserable.[14]

Twentieth-century critics tended to interpret Shakespeare's sympathies differently. L. C. Knights applauded what he took to be Shakespeare's empathetic portrayal of poverty in the figure of Poor Tom: 'In *King Lear* ... we are invited to make vividly present to our imagination what it feels like to be homeless, starving and half-naked' (37). Knights pointed out that Shakespeare captured class conflict in the language used by the various social ranks, noting 'a strain of colloquial and idiomatic speech which, even in the early plays, contrasts with, and to some extent undermines the formal rhetoric' (36).

Shakespeare's interest in plebeian life is a product of his personal involvement in capitalism. The public theatres of his time were commercial enterprises. In fact, as Daniel Vitkus notes, 'the earliest joint-stock companies in England were the London theatre companies'.[15] They made money by the innovative method of charging admission. More than any previous art-form in English history, Shakespeare's plays were created as commodities. They were written for the purpose of profiting by market exchange. H. Rick Smith has shown how Shakespeare selected and adapted his story-lines on the basis of their previously-established market appeal: 'Shakespeare's history plays are rooted in the prior cultural consumption of entertainment and narrative commodities'.[16] Because they needed to appeal to the 'groundlings' (as those who stood in the theatre's cheapest sections were known) most of Shakespeare's plays contain one or two scenes of lowbrow, knockabout comedy featuring plebeian characters. One of the reasons for Shakespeare's attraction to Marxists is the attention he devotes to such ordinary folk as the 'rude mechanicals' of *A Midsummer Night's Dream*, the Porter in *Macbeth*, or the pedlar Autolycus in *The Winter's Tale*. In twentieth-century Britain, this sympathy for the underclass coalesced with the intellectual project known as 'history from below', which attempted to unearth the experience of marginalized or 'subaltern' groups in every kind of document.

However, there are obvious problems in applying a Marxist class analysis to Shakespeare's work. Marx's studies were carried out in the mid-nineteenth century, when the abstract forces of capital and labour were clearly, visibly incarnated in the opposed social classes of bourgeoisie and proletariat. In the twenty-first century, however, virtually every member of Western society fits Marx's definitions of both a proletarian (one who sells his labour-power for wages) and a bourgeois (one who lives by capital investments). The logical contradiction between capital and labour-power has not been diminished – the former is still the alienated, symbolic manifestation of the latter – but it has been internalized. In the third millennium, the contradiction between capital and labour-power is manifested not in class struggle, but in the psychological processes of single individuals. That does not mean that the capital/labour-power dialectic is irrelevant to literary analysis. On the contrary, it means that this contradiction will be visible at the psychological, ethical and aesthetic levels as well as the economic.

III

Like Aristotle, Marx was a 'teleological' thinker. He believed that economic history was progressing, naturally and inevitably, towards the end, or *telos*, of communism. The first generation of Marxist critics gamely made a case for reading Shakespeare in a similarly teleological fashion. For instance, Alick West defended *King Lear* against charges that it presents a nihilistic, meaningless world by arguing that Kent, the noble servant who rebels against his master's injustice, is the standard-bearer of a better, future society, rather than a conservative adherent to feudal notions of loyalty. A.L. Morton claimed that Shakespeare's history plays revealed ineluctable historical processes, depicting the inevitable emergence of absolute monarchy out of the feudal system. Morton quotes the Earl of Warwick in *2 Henry IV* to show that Shakespeare anticipated the dialectical approach to history, in which 'weak beginnings lie intreasured. / Such things become the hatch and brood of time' (3.2.85–6).[17]

We have seen how their shared materialism caused a striking concurrence between communists and capitalists. Engels, Lenin, Hayek and Rand are unanimous in their fundamental conviction that human behaviour is ultimately determined by economic motives. Marx struggled to reconcile this opinion with the history of aesthetics, which he takes to be characterized by degeneration from the ancient ideal:

It is well known that certain periods of highest development of art stand in no direct connection with the general development of society, nor with the material basis and the skeleton structure of its organization. Witness the example of the Greeks as compared with modern art or even Shakespeare ... Is the view of nature and of social relations which shaped Greek imagination and thus Greek [mythology] possible in the age of automatic machinery and railways and locomotives and electric telegraphs? Where does Vulcan come in as against Roberts & Co., Jupiter as against the lightening rod, and Hermes as against the Credit Mobilier?[18]

According to the assumptions of economic determinism, the material advances of modern society should inevitably have brought about corresponding progress in aesthetics. Yet even by modern standards of evaluation, the art of economically primitive ancient Greece seems superior to the products of our own epoch. This furnishes Marx with a contradiction that he never managed to resolve: 'the difficulty does not lie in understanding that the Greek art and epos are bound up with certain forms of social development. It rather lies in understanding why they still afford us aesthetic enjoyment and in certain respects prevail as the standard and model beyond attainment' (ibid.).

But this is only a 'difficulty' for an economic determinist. If one does not believe that economic developments determine aesthetics, so that the two develop in tandem, there is nothing strange about the modern world's appreciation of ancient art. Although Marx was committed to the Victorian faith that economic history is progress, he was forced to admit that aesthetic history did not follow the same pattern of inexorable advance. Later generations of Marxist critics would attempt to reconcile this contradiction using the concept of the 'totality'. For Lukács, the ability to perceive the 'social whole' within a work of art meant, first of all, identifying the work's references to the cultural and economic circumstances which made its production possible. It meant interpreting the classics of the past in the light of their place in history:

> For aesthetics, our classical heritage is that great art that presents the totality of man, the whole man in the totality of his social world ... These theoretical and practical perspectives determine the criteria on the basis of which Marxist aesthetics recaptures the classics. The Greeks, Dante, Shakespeare, Goethe, Balzac, Tolstoy, Gorki are at the same time adequate presentations of distant great stages in the evolution of mankind, and signposts in the ideological struggle for the totality of man.[19]

As Lukács explains, a totalizing reading of *King Lear* would interpret the conflicts between the play's characters as arising from their author's historical location at the transition from feudalism to capitalism. Only by placing the play within the historical totality can we fully account for such individual foibles as Lear's rage or Edmund's guile. In similar fashion, Lukács compares Shakespeare's crowd scenes to the role of the chorus in Greek drama. The confused, multi-vocal hubbub of Shakespeare's crowds bespeaks a beleaguered, last-ditch effort to discern the social totality in an increasingly fragmented, capitalist world. As Stanley Mitchell summarizes Lukács's analogy:

> Shakespearean England is not the Athenian polis. But London is a focal city, drawing countrymen like Shakespeare to its urban culture. It has patricians, it has plebs. They are all there in the audience; they appear episodically, in crowd scenes, on the stage. The crowd scene, according to Lukács, is the aesthetic counterpart of the chorus in the Greek drama. It preserves, in a more chequered form, that same sense of totality, of a total world participating, of a total range of values, however fragile and self-contradictory these may be compared with those of the Greeks.[20]

Lukács was inspired by Hegel's account of history as the progressive manifestation and overcoming of 'alienation'. The forms taken by alienation vary with historical circumstances, but they all involve the illusory externalization of the human essence, whether in the form of gods, fetishes or money. In Lukács' view, capitalism involved an especially tenacious version of alienation, with its representation of human activity in symbolic, financial form. The conservative Hegelian T. S. Eliot tried to overcome the consequent fragmentation of experience, which he called the 'dissociation of sensibility', by poetic means. Eliot's work yoked disparate ideas together by the verbal violence of metaphor, in a conscious continuation of the English 'metaphysical' tradition. Lukács, in contrast, attempted to end alienation by direct participation in politics, first as a Marxist revolutionary, then as Minister of Culture in Hungary's short-lived communist Government in 1919, and again intermittently between 1946 and 1956.

Communists like Lukács and Brecht chose to pursue their practical politics behind the Iron Curtain. But the post-war capitalist democracies of Western Europe also produced a new emphasis on activism among Marxist intellectuals. In the 1980s, politicized Shakespeareans were divided by the question of whether the texts they studied produced 'subversion' or 'containment' among their audiences. Did they subtly, or even openly, undermine the hegemonic ideology of the aristocracy, as 'cultural materialists' like Jonathan Dollimore and John Drakakis claimed? Or did they bolster the dominant hierarchy by their apparent endorsement of monarchy and rank, as 'new historicists' like Stephen Greenblatt and Jonathan Goldberg argued? These discussions developed as the crisis of 'casino capitalism' called for an ethical critique of financial representation, which was increasingly acknowledged as analogous to (or even homologous with) literary forms of representation. This call was answered, after a fashion, by the 'new economic criticism', which we will discuss in the following chapter. Less overtly committed than Marxists to political practice, less interested in class conflict as the driving force of history, this critical tendency nevertheless contains the seeds of a moral critique of autonomous representation's role in the general economy.

5

Money as Metaphor: The New Economic Criticism

I

By the end of the second millennium, political Marxism was widely discredited. That was reasonable enough, given the world-wide collapse of Communist governments and the decline of labour movements throughout the Western world. But these political developments also convinced many people to dismiss philosophical Marxism, with far less justification. As late as 2009, many people still needed reminding that, in the words of Hugh Grady, 'the Marxist tradition... contained an extensive, appreciate archive of writings on the aesthetic.'[1] It is certainly true that Marx's confidence in both the inevitability and the desirability of communist societies has been refuted by history. However, the overwhelming preponderance of Marx's thought concerns not communism but capitalism – and capitalism shows no signs of following its erstwhile adversary onto history's scrapheap. Indeed, the rapid, dramatic extension of the capitalist ethos into every corner of public and personal life, the conquest of society by the economy, the burgeoning influence of market psychology on ethics, politics, aesthetics, even individual tastes and emotions, all suggest that a close philosophical study of capitalism is more badly needed now than ever before. Above all, Marx's pertinence to postmodernity derives from his analysis of political economy's historical and theoretical foundations, and Marx himself traces those foundations directly to Shakespeare.

Given the remarkable exfoliation that the economy is undergoing in the third millennium, it is unsurprising that twenty-first-century literary critics should find themselves attracted to economic issues in the works they study. Readers now tend to notice economic themes and imagery in places where they had previously gone unremarked. This is partly due to recent changes in our understanding of the economy. As the economy bursts the artificial bounds imposed on it by twentieth-century professional economists, it begins palpably to affect areas of experience that were once considered definitively beyond its purview. We seem to be returning to the situation described by Xenophon and Aristotle, in which economics unavoidably includes psychological and sociological considerations. Consequently, today's literary critics frequently point to the economic implications of texts that once seemed concerned with entirely different matters.

Under present circumstances, it was probably inevitable that *something* called the 'new economic criticism' would arise. Yet the conferences, collections and anthologies assembled under that name suggest that the 'new economic critics' share little in common except their interest in economics. In fact it is hardly an exaggeration to say that any non-Marxist who writes about economic issues in literature now qualifies as a 'new economic critic'. This diverse group is at least united, however, by their common interest in the formal parallels between aesthetics and economics. This interest was stimulated by recent changes in the nature of the economy. Until the 1970s, the economy was generally conceived as material. It was associated with production, heavy industry, trade unionism and class conflict. Literary historians frequently connect this kind of economy to aesthetic realism. The idea that signs refer, more or less transparently, to a real world beyond themselves seemed appropriate to a production-based economy, whose primary purpose was the manufacture of useful objects.

Since the mid-twentieth century, however, the production-based economies of the West have been supplanted by service-oriented, exchange-based economies dependent on a vastly expanded trade in stocks, shares, bonds and an array of complicated, symbolic, financial instruments. This is one of the ways historians distinguish our 'postmodern' era from the 'modern' age of the seventeenth through twentieth centuries. The 'economy' is now organized around exchange, rather than production. Its figurative financial devices are ontologically indistinguishable from linguistic signs. The twenty-first century has already seen an explosion of financial 'derivatives', known as 'futures', 'options' and so on. Derivatives are symbols representing ('derived' from) the already symbolic tokens traded on the stock market. The further removed such symbols become from any reference to reality – as happened when sub-prime mortgages were re-packaged and sold on to faraway banks with no knowledge of the original investors – the greater the potential for ethical and practical disaster. The postmodern economy, in short, is a system of autonomous representation, or rather a network of many such systems, and this opens a whole new world of intellectual opportunity for literary critics and economists alike.

The 'new economic criticism' is historicist in the sense that it interprets literature in its historical context. But it is also formalist, in the sense that it pays attention to patterns of formal similarity between the economic and the linguistic registers.[2] One of the earliest and most influential critics to approach economic issues from this perspective was Marc Shell. In *The Economy of Literature* (1978), Shell achieved the essential insight on which new economic criticism would be founded when he observed that literary texts are 'composed of small tropic exchanges or metaphors, some of which can be analysed in terms of signified economic content and all of which can be analysed in terms of economic form'.[3] The formal properties of literature and the formal properties of finance develop in lockstep, because they are two parts of a larger totality. Language and money are both forms of representation, and the connection between linguistic and financial representation is reflected etymologically. Shell observes that the Greek *seme* means both 'word' and 'coin', and as David Graeber points out:

> When Aristotle argued that coins are merely social conventions, the term he used was *symbolon* – from which our own word "symbol" is derived. Symbolon was originally the Greek word for "tally" – an object broken in half to mark a contract or agreement, or marked and broken to record a debt.

(28)

The other major precursor of the new economic criticism was Jean-Joseph Goux. In *Symbolic Economies* (1990). Goux concludes that '[t]he monetary metaphor that haunts discussions of language – not in accidental poetic incursions but quite coherently, in the site of substitutions – seems to betray an awareness, as yet veiled and embryonic, of the correspondence between the mode of economic exchange and the mode of signifying exchange'.[4] This 'monetary metaphor' was more than a simple symbol of money. Like Shell, Goux believes that the relation between literary meaning and financial value is too close for a mere analogy. Rather, the relation between the financial and the semiotic is described as a 'homology', a term which expresses a more fundamental kinship than a simple resemblance. Money and language are both systems of signs: one produces meaning, the other value. As Goux puts it in *The Coiners of Language* (1994): 'The parallel between language and money, literature and political economy, is not a mere juxtaposition, but is made possible and operative by processes at work simultaneously in both economies'.[5] This would become the basic, definitive and perhaps the only assumption shared by all new economic critics.

The new economic criticism did not acquire its sobriquet until the late 1990s. More than a decade earlier, however, books began appearing that fit the criteria later developed for membership of that school. They concentrated on economic matters, but from a perspective that downplayed class conflict and political practice in favour of examining newly-visible formal connections between semiotic and financial media of representation. In *The Economics of the Imagination* (1980), Kurt Heinzelman reminded his readers of the generalized, figurative valence of the term 'economy':

> In English usage, economy suggests both frugality and efficiency; by extension, it applies to the management of any structures, political and domestic, commercial and aesthetic. In its largest sense, the word asserts our capacity for creating intellectual structures and for imaginatively regulating them. It indicates our ability to distinguish between ends and means, and therefore, as a reflector of human choice, it represents the thoroughness of our self-consciousness.[6]

Like the general concept of the 'economy', the minutest of economic concepts inexorably expand beyond their merely financial significances. The irreducible metaphoricity of language makes this inevitable, as Heinzelman notes: 'Economic signifiers – words such as "labour," "price," "profit," "credit," and "cost" – necessarily point to semantic and philosophical values which are not simply or merely commercial' (x). The figurative nature of the medium in which it must be expressed guarantees that economic discourse will diffuse its significances, both explicit and implicit, throughout the rest of experience. Furthermore, as Goux observes, 'the borrowing between economics and literature goes both ways' (1994, 25). Just as literary critics were beginning to comment on the parallels between language and finance, some economists were starting to notice that their discipline also utilized rhetorical, semiotic and literary devices. As Deirdre McCloskey put it in *The Rhetoric of Economics* (1985):

> Figures of speech are not mere frills. They think for us.
> Someone who thinks of the market as an 'invisible hand'
> and the organization of work as a 'production function'
> and his coefficients as being 'significant', as an economist
> does, is giving the language a lot of responsibility.[7]

McCloskey's work angered many of her fellow economists by
suggesting that theirs was not a scientific discipline like physics
or chemistry, dedicated to the pursuit of objective truth, but
rather an aesthetic construction of subjective significances,
akin to music, painting or literature. She insists that economists
inevitably use rhetorical devices in their attempts to persuade
their readers, and she claims that 'Rhetoric is an economics
of language' (xviii). Challenging as they are to economists'
traditional understanding of their discipline, McCloskey's
ideas have also inspired many followers. In *Economics as
Literature* (1995), Willie Henderson refers to 'the cross-over
between literature and economics' in the work of McCloskey,
Shell and Heinzelman as an 'alternative tradition' whose
'concern is both with economic argument and the ways in
which the argument is presented in literary form'.[8]

II

The new economic criticism certainly draws on an ancient
'tradition' of connections between aesthetic and economic
representation, but those connections were largely invisible
during the modern era. The new economic criticism attempts
to make them visible again. The first book to announce
itself by name as an example of this movement was Mark
Osteen and Martha Woodmansee's extensive collection of
essays on a wide range of authors, periods and genres,
*The New Economic Criticism: Studies at the Intersection
of Literature and Economics* (1999). The volume collected
papers from a 1994 conference at Case Western Reserve

University in Cleveland, Ohio, which launched the term 'new economic criticism' on the academic world. As they explain in their Introduction, Osteen and Woodmansee had originally coined the phrase in 1991 in response to a 'perception of an emerging literary and cultural criticism founded upon economic paradigms, models and tropes' (3). Parallel developments in the United Kingdom included a conference at Exeter University in 1998, and a special issue of *New Literary History,* edited by Regina Gagnier in 2000.

Taking their theoretical lead from Shell, Goux and McCloskey, the participants in these projects set out to challenge the very existence of the 'economy'. As Aram Weeser observed in his Introduction to *The New Economic Criticism,* many of the contributors aimed to 'dismantle the dichotomy of the economic and the non-economic' (ix). With hindsight, in fact, this dichotomy looks like a specific characteristic of the high modern era. It has effectively collapsed in postmodernity, and it was also quite foreign in early modernity, as Sandra Fischer's *Econolingua* (1985) makes clear. Fischer's comprehensive glossary provides analysts of Renaissance literature with an indispensable tool, as her Introduction explains:

> the concepts of exchange-value, maximization of personal utility, and an extension of usury to the "use" or exploitation of humans were such fundamental and radical changes that they were of necessity explored in the drama. As dramatists acknowledged the inadequacy of the old economic theories, they also sought replacement values. Indeed, the drama for a time became a forum for the investigation of new economics, what Aristotle has termed "chrematistics" (pure acquisition for its own sake), as it conquered and usurped the old economy of household management and efficient allocation of resources.[9]

Fischer argues that English Renaissance drama developed as an aesthetic correlative of the new, chrematistic economy. Shakespeare was its most incisive analyst: 'In Iago and

Shylock... or even Edmund and Bolingbroke, he embodies the morality of chrematistics, characterized as violating nature's order of hierarchical relations and productivity' (16). Where a more traditional critic might have examined the plays primarily through the prism of psychology, Fischer shows that they can also be read in economic terms. Marxists would agree. But where a Marxist would understand the 'economy' as a matter of production and class relations, new economic critics like Fischer view it primarily as a matter of exchange and representation. Because language is 'economic by its very nature as an exchange medium' (17), economic questions are ubiquitous and unavoidable in any literature. But they are especially prominent in the Renaissance, when 'Economy begins to penetrate all human relations: money becomes the only way of assessing value, profit the only impetus for human action' (ibid.).

So pervasive is this influence that Fischer posits the emergence in the period's drama of 'a new language, econo-lingua' (ibid.). The extraordinary range of meaning and connotation that she finds in the early modern usages of such familiar terms as 'actor', 'agent' and 'angel', and many others, amply vindicates her claims. Her book was followed by a deluge of economically-oriented studies, which suggests that she achieved her declared intention 'to open up a new arena of inquiry and observation' (33). Many such works, like Jean-Christophe Agnew's *Worlds Apart* (1987), further explored the parallels between the theatre and the market-place. As a highly profitable, commercial enterprise, the theatre of Shakespeare and his colleagues was itself a part, as well as a symbol of the market. In Agnew's view it was a 'proxy form of the new and but partly fathomable relations of a nascent market society'.[10]

Part of the kinship that early modern audiences noticed between the theatre and the marketplace was doubtless purely empirical. Many ways of behaving were familiar from the marketplace and the stage alike: dissembling, shape-shifting, rhetorical manipulation. By representing such tendencies on the stage, the theatre both personified and reified them. As Agnew puts it, the Renaissance drama 'subsumed subjectivity within the objective' (xi). This was both an empirical and a theoretical union. Economic exchange-value is a man-made symbol imposed upon an object's natural, inherent use-value. With its invented identities and systematic pretence, the theatre appeared not only to illustrate, but also to endorse and even to propagate this kind of market value. After all, both the market and the theatre rely on 'credit'. As Agnew puts it:

The theater of late medieval and early modern England ... was a theater in and of the marketplace. And though the rules governing credit in the market stalls of those times may have differed in detail from the conventions governing credibility in the adjoining theatrical booths, the fact nonetheless remains that in either instance the customer's will to believe was a stipulated or conditional act, a matter less of faith than of suspended disbelief.

(x)

The theatre answered a public demand for art that could interpret the new forms of social interaction, and the new conceptions of personal identity, that were being thrown up by the growth of the market economy. The social mobility facilitated by the market seemed akin to the 'self-fashioning' of an actor playing a role. In an age before the economy had been differentiated from the rest of life, this meant that public hostility towards the disruptive effects of large-scale market exchange was frequently projected both against and onto the stage. Anti-theatrical campaigners like Stephen Gosson denounced theatres as 'markets of bawdry, where choice without shame hath been as free, as it is for your money in the Royal Exchange, to take a short stock, or a long, a falling bond, or a french ruffe'.[11] Thomas Dekker claimed: 'The theatre is your poets' Royal Exchange upon which their muses (that are now turned to merchants) meeting, barter away that light commodity of words'.[12] These polemicists saw in the public theatre a deplorable commercialization of aesthetics, and they were convinced that such commodified art must have regrettable moral consequences.

Both Gosson and Dekker were playwrights themselves, but they seem unconcerned about charges of hypocrisy. In fact, anti-theatrical sentiments were often expressed from the stage, as in Ben Jonson's prefaratory diatribes ironically warning his audiences that they may judge his play only by the price of admission. The well-known playwright Anthony Munday was also a well-known anti-theatricalist. One of the most notorious hacks of all time, Munday knew whereof he spoke when he condemned the aesthetic effects of commodification: 'Who writeth for reward, neither regardeth virtue, nor truth, but runs unto falsehood, because he flattereth for commoditie'.[13] This much of the anti-theatrical case was accepted by all sides of the debate. Differences arose mainly over practical issues such as public order, disease, or the anticipated consequences of closing the theatres. Agnew notes Shakespeare's 'ambivalence about the theatre's own theatricality' (127), and he takes Prospero's abjuration of magic to mean that:

> *The Tempest* appears to be a final gesture proffered against the offensive spectacle of the man-made self and the self-made man. Here, Shakespeare seems to have anticipated the more general alienation from public and private theaters that took hold in London after 1610.
>
> (145)

Agnew's book was immediately and widely influential. Several subsequent works, like Douglas Bruster's *Drama and the Market in the Age of Shakespeare* (1992), developed its thesis in productive directions. Bruster emphasized Renaissance drama's exploitation of 'the traditional links between sexual and economic transaction' and, anticipating the vogue for 'object-centred criticism', he notes the subtle effects of commodity fetishism on the relations between people and things:

> Props in Renaissance farce became markers of value and status, encoding identity into worth counters which, passed from hand to hand, often acted as reservoirs of erotic potential. Consciously or unconsciously, playwrights connected identity with ownership, rendering the relationship between property and person as one of almost complete interdependence.[14]

Early modern anti-theatricalists believed that the experience of watching plays inculcated such fetishistic attitudes in the audience. In the modern era critics tended to scoff at such claims, but the magical power of spectacles seems more plausible in postmodernity. The key theoretical analysis of this power is Guy Debord's *Society of the Spectacle* (1967), which rehearses ethical arguments against fetishized visual perception that date back at least to Tertullian's first-century diatribe, *De Spectaculis*. According to Debord, and later thinkers like Jean-François Lyotard and Jean Baudrillard, the 'spectacle' was the visible manifestation of commodity fetishism. In the 'spectacle', then, an originally economic phenomenon burst its bounds, and exerted its influence throughout the psyche.

In response to such developments, the 1990s produced several works of Renaissance literary criticism that explored the newly expanded, figurative senses of the 'economy'. In *Marlowe, Shakespeare and the Economy of Theatrical Experience* (1991), Thomas Cartelli used the term to designate a 'structure of exchanges – psychological, social and political',[15] indicating that its non-financial significances are at least as important as the traditional meaning. In *Shakespearean Pragmatism: Market of his Time* (1993), Lars Engle claims that Shakespeare viewed 'social interaction as an economy, a diffuse network of discursive transactions which hang together according to humanly established (and thus mutable) patterns of exchange'.[16] Engle's argument exhibits the archetypal new economic critic's transition from the restricted to the general sense of 'economy'. He concedes that the Henry plays do not deal with economics in the literal sense – they 'are not much concerned with marketplaces per se' – but he nevertheless argues convincingly that they deal with economics in an analogous, figurative sense: 'they elaborately document, in both festive and official settings, the particulars of supply and demand, of indebtedness or wealth' (122).

In *Theatre, Finance and Society in Early Modern England* (1999), Theodore Leinwand admits that his critical task is complicated by the fact that what we consider purely economic terminology was often applied to subjective feelings in Renaissance drama. This produces a paradoxical critical vocabulary in which:

> While my terminology throughout this volume – from credit crunch to nostalgia to venture capital – is often anachronistic, the economic categories and attendant affective responses that I describe are, I think, not ... Credit, debt, mortgages and venturing were fully within the realm of experience of early modern English people. Of course, so was affect.[17]

Leinwand's problem is that the texts he studies use the kind of language that we consider economic to discuss the kind of experience we consider emotional or affective. The new economic criticism developed as a means of assimilating such trans-discursive tendencies into a viable critical practice. The first work of self-declared 'new economic criticism' in Shakespeare studies was the essay collection *Money and the Age of Shakespeare: Essays in the New Economic Criticism* (2003). In her Introduction, Linda Woodbridge draws attention to the proliferation of economic themes and imagery in early modern drama, noting that 'Commercial language permeates even plays whose plots are not primarily money-oriented'.[18] In fact, the volume's contributors discuss such a wide variety of issues that the term 'economics' is rendered manifestly inadequate. Chapters are devoted to commodity fetishism, usury, use-value and exchange-value, risk, consumerism, poverty, double-entry book-keeping, trade, investment, gifts, dowries, insurance, money, social mobility and the birth of capitalism itself. The collection conclusively established the versatility of economic questions in early modern literature.

Woodbridge's monograph *English Revenge Drama: Money, Resistance, Equality* (2010) exemplified the keen insights made available by the new economic criticism. She accounts for the popularity of 'revenge plays' on the Shakespearean stage by connecting the avenger's 'devotion to bilateral symmetry' to commodity exchange. The artificial equivalence that commodification imposes on things provoked a mass obsession with 'getting even', and the issue of usury kept the theme of payback in the public mind. Thus the spread of commodity exchange influenced aesthetics. The word 'fair' began to mean 'equal' as well as 'beautiful' and, as Woodbridge notes, 'calibrating revenge to an offense is an accounting skill'. Theatre audiences became connoisseurs of 'condign' revenge. The art lay in constructing the most ironically appropriate mode of satisfaction, so that not only the degree but also the kind of injury inflicted matched the injury suffered. In George Chapman's *The Revenge of Bussy D'Ambois*, Clarmont questions the ethics of revenge: 'Shall we revenge a villainy with villainy?' Charlotte's answer encapsulates the spirit of the age: 'Is it not equal?' (3.2.89–90). As Shylock says when he asserts his right to revenge: 'If we are like you in the rest, we will resemble you in that … The villainy you teach me I will execute' (3.1.62–3, 66). In *Othello* Emilia advocates female revenge on men: 'The ills we do, their ills instruct us so' (4.3.102).

Woodbridge's work illustrates the aesthetic impact of originally economic phenomena. The rise and spread of the market economy were not only creating new sources of wealth, they were giving rise to new ways of thinking, and new forms of social arrangements. In the resulting disruption, many people were upset to find, like Iago, that 'Preferment goes by letter and affection / And not by old gradation, where each second / Stood heir to th'first' (1.1.35–7). The Elizabethan and Jacobean stages were full of such malcontents exacting their revenge, enforcing by nefarious guile the fairness and equality of which life has deprived them. Shakespeare often translates the concepts and terminology of revenge into the unfamiliar and initially ill-fitting terms of finance. Titus Andronicus inquires: 'Is she not then beholden to the man / That brought her for this high good turn so far?' (1.1.401–2). The response – 'Yes – and will nobly him remunerate' (1.1.403) – indicates that Tamora's mode of payback will be aristocratic in tone, even though it can be expressed using monetary concepts.

The new economic criticism's defining principle is neatly expressed in the Introduction to Stephen Deng and Barbara Sebek's edited volume, *Global Traffic: Discourses and Practices of Trade in English Literature and Culture from 1550 to 1700* (2008). The editors find a unity among the book's diverse chapters in their shared adherence to 'the critical axiom that economic practices must be understood as complex cultural and discursive phenomena'.[19] This conviction that the modern understanding of 'economy' is too narrow and restricted to be usefully applied to either the early modern or the postmodern eras is the new economic criticism's grounding assumption. That assumption has encouraged the new economic criticism in its disregard of established boundaries between disciplines. As a result, such criticism can reveal previously undreamt-of homologies between ostensibly disparate figurative registers. It discovers common projects and insights shared between discourses that the modern world had thought of as divergent, and it assimilates the realization that metaphorical associations can both reflect and create material relationships into its method of interpretation.

Jonathan Gil Harris's *Sick Economies: Drama, Mercantilism and Disease in Shakespeare's England* (2004) has achieved canonical status, with its startling but well-supported examples of the mutual influence, and even unconscious collaboration, between the early modern discourses of economics and medicine. Harris contends that '[e]conomic development helped writers imagine disease as a foreign body... in turn, the new vocabularies of contagious or exogenous disease provided writers with the imaginative resources for an emergent discourse of national or global economy'.[20] This kind of trans-disciplinary insight was obscured, during the modern era, by the disciplinary quarantine imposed by Eliot's 'dissociation of sensibility', which allegedly instigated a psychological divorce between reason and emotion, and a corresponding divergence between the arts and sciences. But perhaps such insights are now again becoming possible, with the postmodern dissolution of disciplinary borders. If so, the new economic criticism is well-placed to achieve them. For example, Bradley Ryner's *Performing Economic Thought* (2014) calls attention to previously un-noticed formal similarities between the early English mercantile treatises and the conventions of the contemporary drama. This kind of inter-disciplinary analysis has become the new economic criticism's stock-in-trade.

Peter Grav's article, 'Taking Stock of Shakespeare and the New Economic Criticism' (2012), emphasizes the movement's trans-disciplinary nature. Grav defines it as 'work that employs semiotics and historicism to consider literary dealings with the economic'.[21] This description applies well to his own monograph, *Shakespeare and the Economic Imperative* (2008), which argues for a progressive decline, over the course of Shakespeare's career, in his ethical evaluation of market society. According to Grav, Shakespeare's depictions of capitalism 'grow increasingly darker and, in the end, incarnate Marx's view that money is "the confounding and confusing of all human qualities."'[22] In the essay, Grav sums up his book's thesis: 'what is a benign condition in *The Comedy of Errors* becomes, fifteen years later, a malignant disease in *Timon of Athens,* and the book identifies a thematic thread that begins in comedies like *The Merry Wives of Windsor,* whose message is that affective ties are morally preferable to economic connections' (ibid.). In this view, Shakespeare grew increasingly concerned about the domination of his society by the economy. He expressed his worries in works like *The Merchant of Venice*, in which 'Portia views human volition as being predicated on economics' (99), and *Measure for Measure*, which presents the dire consequences of 'a relentless pattern of exchange born of a market mentality' (126).

Grav argues that this degeneration in Shakespeare's moral evaluation of the market 'culminates in *Timon of Athens*, with its vitriolic rejection of economically-based homosocial relations taken to the point that removal from society and death are portrayed as preferable to such manifestly worthless ties' (159). By thus attributing Timonesque views to Shakespeare, Grav takes issue with Frederick Turner's *Shakespeare's Twenty-first Century Economics* (1999), which provocatively suggests that the Bard's view of the market-place was happily enthusiastic. In fact, Turner claims that Shakespeare anticipates many of the rationalizations of capitalism made by the neo-classical economists of the late twentieth century. He identifies three main contentions in Shakespeare's economics:

> First, that human art, production and exchange are a continuation of natural creativity and reproduction, not a rupture of them. Second, that our human bonds with one another, even the most ethical and personal, cannot be detached from the values and bonds of the market. And third, that there is a mysterious dispensation according to which our born condition of debt can be transformed into one of grace. These three arguments may be taken as refutations of the three reproaches to the market offered by its critics: that the market necessarily alienates us from nature, from each other, and from God.[23]

Turner does not explain how Shakespeare might have acquired such anachronistic opinions in an age when, according to the vast preponderance of written evidence, people reviled capitalism's moral effects almost without exception. He does, however, offer a penetrating diagnosis of the political imperatives behind the new economic criticism:

> Money holds value as words hold meaning ... The analogy also explains why the disappointed critics of the capitalist market system turned to the deconstruction of verbal meaning after the failure of Marxist economics. Like Puritans smashing idolatrous stained glass and holy images in the pursuit of an unmediated contact with the divine, the Marxists and their postmodern successors sought to smash the currency and language that they believed alienated us from economic and textual reality.
>
> (81)

Perhaps it is unfair to describe new economic critics as seeking to destroy language. But Turner is certainly correct to note that many critics now work with the knowledge that money and language are analogous systems of representation. As his own book testifies, however, this insight can easily be extrapolated into support of capitalism, as well as opposition to it. In fact, it is not politics but a shared interest in the aesthetic, moral and psychological effects of capitalism that unites new economic critics. It is also what divides them from their predecessors.

III

Until the late twentieth century, politically conservative Shakespeareans generally applauded the Bard's nostalgia for feudal values and relations, because of their own antipathy to capitalism. This was something they shared with Marxists. Indeed, since many Marxists saw capitalism as a necessary, and thus almost a positive stage in the transition to socialism, conservative opposition to the market often exceeded the

Marxists in vehemence and tragic spirit. Some critics have gone so far as to argue that all opposition to capitalism is conservative, because it offends the allegedly pro-market sensibilities of the American working class. In *Class, Critics and Shakespeare* (2000), Sharon O'Dair argues that 'the demonization of capital functions in part to mystify the power of knowledge to impose hierarchy and inequality'.[24] Today many liberal critics openly favour market morals and mores, though they are not often bold enough to claim Shakespeare as a precursor. The optimistic views on the liberating power of the market shared by O'Dair and Turner are echoed in such studies as David Baker's *On Demand: Writing for the Market in Early Modern England* (2010). Unlike Turner, Baker does not suggest that Shakespeare anticipated his own enthusiasm for the market. On the contrary, he criticizes the playwright for failing to appreciate the copious bounty of capitalism. In *Troilus and Cressida* for example, 'demand was figured as self-consuming "appetite" and nothing more', as opposed to the 'subtle engine of incentive and information' that Baker assumes it actually is.

In the twentieth century, conservatives often elided Shakespeare's references to economics in favour of his allegedly universal reflections on human nature. Today, however, pro-capitalist critics often find their own opinions anticipated in early modern literature, while theoretical texts like Russell Berman's *Fiction Sets You Free* (2007) demonstrate that the convergence between economics and aesthetics can be interpreted to the ethical advantage of the marketplace.[25] Although their politics were apparently diametrically opposed to Berman's, this tendency can be traced back to French post-structuralists like Derrida and Deleuze, with their ludic celebrations of the 'free play' of representational 'différance'. In the 1960s, 'différance' was hailed on the *rive gauche* as the destroyer of repressive, essentialist identity. By the 1980s a commitment to post-structuralist theory was fast becoming *de rigueur* among the politically correct on both sides of the Atlantic.

The economic triumph of a clearly analogous philosophy of value has now cast considerable doubt on the political effects of such enthusiasm. Postmodern anti-capitalists share with their ostensible opponents the conviction that economic issues inexorably expand into poetics and psychology. This belief provides the major impetus behind the new economic criticism. Thus Aaron Kitch's *Political Economy and the States of Literature in Early Modern England* (2009) repudiates economic determinism, but only by stretching the concept of the 'economy' beyond any determinate boundary:

> In an age when the 'economy' was not yet imagined as an abstract system defined by mathematical models, economic policy about currency valuation, the regulation of imports, and customs' dues was deeply embedded in religious, cultural, political, and literary discourses and practices.[26]

Kitch's focus on 'the enduring presence of religious claims in early modern political economy' (188) produces commendably original readings of early modern texts on their own terms. David Landreth's *The Face of Mammon* (2012) treats metaphysical concepts with a similar seriousness, concentrating on the disconcerting figure of 'Mammon', through which early modern society filtered its encounter with muscle-flexing youthful capitalism. Landreth describes how the literary device of personification expresses the objectification of the human subject:

> 'Mammon' is an Aramaic word for meaning 'riches' that appears in two of Christ's sayings in the Gospels; it is the name of a demon who personifies those riches, who in Spenser's Faerie Queene calls himself 'God of the world and worldlings'; and we might define the relation of object to personification in Mammon as the principle that 'money talks'.[27]

Landreth shows how, through the figure of Mammon, as well as a host of other images, personifications and mobile metaphors, writers of the English Renaissance studied 'money's intrusion into literary contexts that otherwise ... don't seem directly motivated by the concerns we'd call economic' (5). The people of early modern England used such images to express an ethical critique of a money-based economy. Landreth evaluates that critique more positively than Baker or Turner, but he points out that Shakespeare and his contemporaries 'do not propose merely to repudiate Mammon, through ascetic retreat from the material and social world. Instead, they seek to understand why we have made him' (6). By that very act of understanding, however, Shakespeare, Donne, Spenser and similar thinkers were able to locate the birth of capitalism at a specific historical juncture, and so to neutralize its claims to be natural or inevitable. As Landreth concludes: 'Mammon may have tried to tell them his delusive secrets, to prophesy economy. But in listening to him they chose to hear other values, other truths' (238).

Stephen Deng's *Coinage and State Formations in Early Modern English Literature* (2011) reveals the implicit ethics and politics of numismatics, the study of coins. Following Shell and Goux, Deng examines the early modern economic debate 'between intrinsic and extrinsic value theories, between the value embodied in a coin's material and that ascribed by the state's stamp'.[28] Those political economists who held a 'metal' theory of money, believing that financial value is inherent in a coin's body, are known to history as 'bullionists'. Those who challenged them, advancing a 'sign' theory of money and arguing that financial value could survive and thrive independently of its physical incarnations, are known today as 'mercantilists'. In reaction against the 'bullionist' theory, mercantilist political economists like Thomas Mun recognized that financial value existed independently of the gold, jewels and silver in which it was represented. This involved a process of mental abstraction which also isolated economics from its discursive environment. Furthermore, the

separation of financial value from precious metals was part
of a wider, epochal shift in human consciousness, whereby
identity came to be defined relationally rather than essentially, the connection between sign and referent was revealed
as purely arbitrary, and meaning came to seem a function of
representation. As Michel Foucault comments:

> The relation so strictly laid down in the sixteenth century is
> forthwith reversed: money (and even the metal of which it
> is made) receives its value from its pure function as sign ...
> Things take on value, then, in relation to one another; the
> metal merely enables this value to be represented, as a name
> represents an image or an idea, yet does not constitute it.[29]

Valerie Forman's *Tragicomic Redemptions: Global Economics
and the Early Modern Stage* (2008) skilfully blends formalism
with historicism in a manner typical of the new economic
criticism. Forman describes the emergence and growth of
economic investment, by which apparent loss is a necessary
precursor of eventual profit. She argues that this economic
version of 'redemption' mingled with the theological sense
of the term in the literary genre of 'tragicomedy'. The
distinction between the literal and the figurative is deliberately
blurred in Shakespeare's last plays, and the Bard's late turn
to tragicomedy reflects his attempt to forge a syncretic
conception of redemption that would combine the economic,
religious and literary valences of the term. Thus *The Winter's
Tale* shows a transition 'from an interest in affective losses
to an interest in the exchange of commodities and the
accumulation of material wealth'.[30] Leontes banishes Perdita
like a trader 'carelessly and wastefully sending English bullion
abroad and thus producing losses' so that 'the play must work
to transform the effects of his loss-producing actions into
profits' (95).

The fluency with which Shakespeare moves between the
affective and the financial economies shows that they are
not yet entirely distinct for him. Since they still conceived of

experience as a totality, Renaissance minds understood that questions about financial value's morality applied to the ethics of representation as a whole. Early modern England produced revolutionary transformations in the religious, aesthetic, and psychological forms of representation, along with radical changes in the mode of financial significance. The postmodern age seems more receptive to such connections than the modern, and this is reflected in the number of recent critical studies that move easily between what were once considered divergent discursive spheres. This trans-disciplinary approach is arguably the new economic criticism's definitive characteristic. It does not diminish the influence of the economy over aesthetics, but rather expands it. In the postmodern era, as in Shakespeare's day, there is nothing outside the economy.

PART TWO

Economics in Shakespeare

6

'Going to the market-place': The Commons and the Commodity

I

In Part One, we looked at various economically-oriented approaches to the criticism and analysis of Shakespeare. In contrast, Part Two assays some economic readings of Shakespeare's own work. First however, we need to briefly remind ourselves of the key economic developments through which England was passing during his lifetime. The most significant of these was the spread of wage labour. In the sixteenth and seventeenth centuries, one of the main obstacles barring the way to capitalism's maturation was the visceral revulsion evoked by the prospect of working for a wage. In ancient and medieval times, the condition of a wage worker had been regarded as comparable, and if anything inferior, to that of a slave. Both groups were sold for money – slaves in their entirety, proletarians piecemeal – and both consequently suffered a degrading legal and psychological reification. But whereas slaves at least benefited from their owners' interest in keeping them alive, wage workers were simply abandoned to starvation the moment the market no longer required their services. Resistance to wage labour was sustainable throughout the feudal period because of the complicated network of traditional rights, privileges and mutual obligations collectively known as the 'commons', which meant that most English people could subsist without having to work for a wage.

Before masses of people could be persuaded to sell their labour on the market, a lengthy process of ideological indoctrination and systematic economic expropriation was called for. Customary rights to grazing, hunting, fishing and gathering were declared inimical to the proper functioning of the 'economy', and restricted or abolished wherever possible. Along with the enclosure of smallholdings, this confiscation of communal property drove hundreds of thousands of people into beggary. This happened suddenly enough for contemporaries to take notice. Karl Polanyi claims that 'It was in the first half of the sixteenth century that the poor first appeared in England' (104). William Harrison's *Description of England,* written in the 1570s, presents beggary as a recent phenomenon: 'it is not yet threescore years since this trade began: how it hath prospered since that time it is easy to judge, for they are now supposed, of one sex and another, to amount unto above ten thousand persons'.[1] Modern historians regard Harrison's estimate as too low, although it is apparently echoed by Westmoreland in *Henry V:* 'O that we now had here / But one ten thousand of those men in England / That do no work today!' (4.3.16–17). Michael Perelman describes the fork on which the English peasantry now found itself impaled:

Primitive accumulation cut through traditional lifeways like scissors. The first blade served to undermine the ability of people to provide for themselves. The other blade was a system of stern measures required to keep people from finding alternative survival strategies outside the system of wage labor. A host of oftentimes brutal laws designed to undermine whatever resistance people maintained against the demands of wage labor accompanied the dispossession of the peasants' rights, even before capitalism had become a significant economic force. For example, beginning with the Tudors, England enacted a series of stern measures to prevent peasants from drifting into vagrancy or falling back onto welfare systems. According to a 1572 statute, beggars over the age of fourteen were to be severely flogged and branded with a red-hot iron on the left ear unless someone was willing to take them into service for two years. Repeat offenders over eighteen were to be executed unless someone would take them into service. Third offenses automatically resulted in execution.[2]

As Braudel remarks, the Elizabethan Poor Laws 'were in fact laws *against* the poor' (40). Draconian measures were necessary to overcome people's natural reluctance to spend their lives engaged in activities they considered unpleasant. As Sylvia Federici puts it: 'In the 16th and 17th centuries, the hatred for wage-labor was so intense that many proletarians preferred to risk the gallows, rather than submit to the new conditions of work' (136).[3] Often, Federici reports, the expropriated peasants became 'beggars, vagabonds and criminals'. The most enterprising became 'pedlars', 'tinkers', or semi-criminal petty traders like Autolycus in *The Winter's Tale*. Such folk were only too willing to exploit the commodity fetishism fostered by nascent consumerism:

> Ha, ha! what a fool Honesty is! and Trust, his sworn brother, a very simple gentleman! I have sold all my trumpery: not a counterfeit stone, not a ribbon, glass, pomander, brooch, table book, ballad, knife, tape, glove, shoe-tie, bracelet, horn-ring, to keep my pack from fasting: they throng who should buy first, as if my trinkets had been hallowed and brought a benediction to the buyer ...

> (4.4.597–604)[4]

This is the company to which Parolles is accused of belonging in *All's Well That Ends Well*, when Lafew arraigns him: 'You are a vagabond and no true traveller' (2.3.259–60). The social dislocation resulting from mass unemployment was dramatic and, as R. H. Tawney memorably remarked, 'the sixteenth century lived in terror of the tramp' (268). In 1607, Shakespeare's home county of Warwickshire, along with its neighbours Leicestershire and Northamptonshire, was convulsed by the series of riots against enclosure known to posterity as the Midland Revolt. In 1656 John Moore was still claiming that the 'inclosers' of Leicestershire buy 'the poore for silver ... make chaffer and merchandize of them for gain and profit: they use them as they doe their beasts, keep them or put them off for advantage: they buy them, and sell them, as may best serve their turns to get by them'.[5]

This was the topical background to which Shakespeare alludes in figures like Autolycus who, finding himself 'out of service', takes to the road, only to discover that 'Gallows and knock are too powerful on the highway: beating and hanging are terrors to me' (4.3.28–30). This was the context that produced the army of ragged 'scarecrows' that Falstaff recruits for the wars, and Poor Tom 'who is whipped from tithing to tithing and stocked, punished, and imprisoned' (3.4.131–2). Tom is a pathetic figure who 'eats cow-dung for salads' (3.4.128–9), but when Jack Cade, leader of the peasant rebels in 2 Henry VI, commands his superiors to 'Look on me well: I have eat no meat these five days' (4.10.37–8), his tone is aggressive and threatening. One of his comrades has 'seen him whipped three market days together' (4.2.53–4), and the play's aristocrats are under no illusions about the desperate poverty that has driven Cade to extremities. As Clifford remarks, 'he hath no home, no place to fly to, / Nor knows he how to live but by the spoil, / Unless by robbing of your friends and us' (4.8.36–8). As Polanyi reminds us: 'the poor in the middle of the sixteenth century were a danger to society, on which they descended like hostile armies' (104).

The ferocity of the counter-revolution in 2 Henry VI can be explained as a response to the severity of the threat to the social order. The Earl of Gloucester's response to the pleas of a rebel's wife – 'Alas, sir, we did it for pure need' – reveals the attitude behind the Elizabethan Poor Laws: 'Let them be whipped through every market town / Till they come to Berwick, from whence they came' (2.1.150–1). After the Beadle has revived the fake beggar Simpcox by whipping him, the assembled crowd sarcastically proclaim 'a miracle!' (2.1.147) This treatment is immediately followed by the news of Cade's revolt, which is explicitly presented as class warfare. Cade makes a joke of his unemployment when he claims 'I am rightful heir unto the crown'. Stafford protests that 'thy father was a plasterer. / And thou thyself a shearman', but Cade responds by appealing to the natural rights of producers: 'And Adam was a gardener' (4.2.124–5). The disruption of the traditional rural economy was fraught with danger for the social hierarchy, as newly redundant peasants searched for legal markets on which to sell their labour-power. One of Cade's fellow rebels hints at the possible consequences: 'it is said "Labour in thy vocation"; which is as much to say as, "Let the magistrates be labouring men"; and therefore should we be magistrates' (4.2.15–17).

Generally speaking, people refused to work for others while they were able to live off the land by themselves. The 'commons' therefore presented a clear and present threat to the supply of labour. Shakespeare subjects the term 'commons' to a close analysis in 2 Henry VI, where it can refer to common land, as in the petition 'against the Duke of Suffolk, for enclosing the commons of Melford' (1.3.411) and also to ordinary people, as when Winchester exclaims: 'The commons hast thou rack'd' (1.3.20–1). The play sometimes personifies the 'commons' as the many-headed multitude. York plans his strategem to 'perceive the commons' mind' (3.1.373), while Queen Margaret condemns the flattery by which Gloucester 'hath won the commons' hearts' (3.1.28). To the noblemen the commoners appear bestial. The Earl of Warwick speaks of 'The commons, like an angry hive of bees' (3.2.125), while the Earl of Suffolk refers to 'the commons, rude, unpolish'd hinds' (3.2.271). Cade uses 'the commons' as a rallying cry for his class war:

> you that love the commons, follow me.
> Now show yourselves men; 'tis for liberty.
> We will not leave one lord, one gentleman:
> Spare none but such as go in clouted shoon,
> For they are thrifty honest men ...

> (4.2.173–7)

If the revolt succeeds, Cade tells the beggarly weavers, tanners and butchers, 'henceforward all things shall be in common' (4.7.16). It is a dream shared by Gonzalo in *The Tempest*, whose ideal commonwealth would also have 'All things in common' (2.1.160). In an age that was witnessing a rapid and unprecedented transfer of wealth from public to private hands, such manifestos did not express utopian fantasies of a remote future so much as nostalgia for the recent past. They were the more threatening as a result, as Shakespeare's frequent and uneasy depictions of rebellions suggest. We do not need to agree with Lee Bliss, who believes that 'Shakespeare doubtless had at least some personal knowledge of the rioters and their demands',[6] to conclude that the Midland Revolt of 1607 must surely have affected the Warwickshire landowner, encloser and usurer. In *2 Henry VI*, *Julius Caesar* and *Coriolanus*, the mob is a fearsome monster, driven by irrational appetite, and these plays positively quiver with class anxiety.

Coriolanus is particularly emphatic in its stress on class conflict. Volumnia curses the mob: 'the red pestilence strike all trades in Rome, / And occupations perish!' (4.1.12–13). This almost amounts to an anathema upon labour itself, an impression reinforced when Menenius denounces the tribunes: 'You have made good work, / You, and your apron-men; you that stood so much / Upon the voice of occupation and / The breath of garlic-eaters! ... You have made fair hands, / You and your crafts! You have crafted fair!' (4.6.96–9, 118–19). This play portrays a society in violent transition. In the words of Lars Engle, it features 'a social transformation towards an idea of a commonwealth as a market economy of competing interests, and away from an ancient idea of a *polis* as a people united by loved things held in common'.[7] In the eponymous hero's alienation from the commoners we find, as L. C. Knights noted, 'the patricians withdrawing into the closed circle of their caste, with its fixed and limiting assumptions' (42), as their aristocratic values begin to seem obsolete.

The reason for the plebeians' resentment of Coriolanus is succinctly identified by Brutus: 'He hath no equal' (1.1.248). Being exceptional is an aristocratic virtue, not a democratic one, and Shakespeare's mob has little respect for the warrior *ethos*. They may make egalitarian demands, but the play presents these as appeals for merely formal equality, analogous to the false equivalence imposed upon objects by commodification. To assert universal equality is to see human beings in quantitative rather than qualitative terms, to obscure their essence in favour of their numerical value. The act of commodification renders different things equivalent. For example, when one of Aufidius' serving-men looks forward to the war because 'I hope to see Romans as cheap as Volscians' (4.5.239–40), he refers to commodification's capacity to impose sameness upon difference. Romans may be qualitatively different from Volscians, but they can be regarded as equal in terms of their quantitative value, which depends on the fluctuations of the market rather than on their inherent qualities.

Shakespeare often dwells on this false equality produced by commodification. In *Titus Andronicus,* Tamora appeals to Titus to spare her sons' lives because of what she claims is an equivalence between Romans and Goths: 'if thy sons were ever dear to thee, / O, think my son to be as dear to me' (1.1.110–11). Of course, her logic does not impress the Romans. Later, Demetrius pointedly protests against such false equality when he answers Chiron's indignant expostulation 'Was never Scythian half so barbarous!' (1.1.134) with a disdainful assertion of qualitative difference: 'Oppose [i.e. compare] not Scythia to ambitious Rome' (1.1.135). A similar elitism leads Coriolanus to scorn democracy. He refers to his participation in elections as 'going to the market-place', alluding to the importance of the *agora* in the ancient *polis*, but also reminding the audience of the link between democracy and commodification:

> Mother, I am going to the market-place;
> Chide me no more. I'll mountebank their loves,
> Cog their hearts from them, and come back home beloved
> Of all the trades in Rome.

(3.2.131–4)

The citizens glory in the power of the mass, which they identify with the *polis* itself: 'The people are the city' (3.1.200). Coriolanus' heroic individualism is made to seem attractive in comparison. This goes some way towards justifying remarks such as the one made by Nigel Lawson, Chancellor of the Exchequer under Margaret Thatcher, who was convinced that *Coriolanus* was 'written from a Tory point of view'.[8] Similar comments are often made about *The Tempest*, because it depicts rebellion as merely comic. The revolutionary aspirations of Caliban and company stand no chance of success, and are represented as based entirely on irrational appetite. This gives Shakespeare another opportunity to denounce the false equality of the marketplace. Although Caliban hopes for liberation, what he receives is commodification. As Trinculo exults:

> Were I in England now (as once I was) and had but this fish painted, not a holiday fool there but would give a piece of silver. There would this monster make a man; any strange beast there makes a man. When they will not give a doit to relieve a lame beggar, they will lay out ten to see a dead Indian.

(2.2.27–33)

The assertion that Caliban would 'make a man' in England is ambiguous. He would 'make' Trinculo in the sense of making his fortune, but the price would be his own identity. The process of commodification would rob him of the capacity to 'make a man' in the sense of attaining the definitive characteristics of manhood, for in the act of reification – reduction to a thing – it would deprive him of the soul, the human essence itself. Caliban's condition after any successful revolt would be identical to the slavery in which he is kept by Prospero. He will always remain a 'property', he is in fact a study of objectification, and perhaps that helps to account for the modern fascination with his character. Slavery is illegal today, but almost everybody works for a wage, and must therefore conceive of themselves as properties, serving ends other than their own during work hours. Wage labour was spreading rapidly in Shakespeare's lifetime. It did not only involve completely landless, full-time proletarians. As they were deprived of traditional, communal sources of subsistence, many peasants were forced into piecemeal wage labour to make ends meet. James Fulcher estimates that 'over half the households in sixteenth-century England were at least partly dependent on wage labour'.[9] David McNally gives smaller numbers, but still contends that 40 per cent of English peasants were doing some wage labour by 1640.[10] New ideas about the self, labour and property developed as people struggled to come to terms with such an unprecedented shift in their relations to their environment.

II

Like 'commons', Shakespeare's usages of 'commodity' allow us to observe the word settling into its modern meaning.[11] The Latin root commod- meant both 'appropriate' and 'advantage', and early modern English retained both these senses. A 'commodity' is appropriate in the sense that it fulfils a need or answers a demand. It is an advantage because its possession brings comparative benefit, or marginal utility, to the possessor. As early modern English people cast around for a vocabulary to describe the development of the economy, the word 'commodity' lay ready to hand. As Shakespeare's extended consideration of its various meanings shows, however, it was not assimilated into the discourse of political economy without difficulty.

To begin with, the word retained a moral ambivalence: it implied an *illegitimate* advantage or an *illicit* benefit. Charles Whitney traces this connotation to its use by the sixteenth-century Commonwealth men to mean private as opposed to public interest (110). This pejorative sense remains prominent in Shakespeare, even when his use of the term approximates the modern. When Falstaff tells Hal: 'I would to God thou and I knew where a commodity of good names were to be bought' (1.2.81–2) he appears corrupt for his presumption that reputation can be purchased. In *2 Henry IV,* the fat knight plans to claim his gout is a war-wound: 'A good wit makes use of anything. I will turn diseases to commodity' (1.2.247–9). Here the word 'use' is employed in the economic sense: Falstaff will act as a usurer with regard to his disease, he will take advantage of it. Similarly in *1 Henry IV,* Falstaff is supposed to recruit soldiers, but acquires instead 'a commodity of warm slaves' (4.2.17–18) which he translates into money (today we might say 'monetizes') as they buy their way out of service.

The fetishistic aura that was attached to commodities reminded many people of magic. In *The Comedy of Errors,* Antipholus of Syracuse reports that, as he wanders around the foreign streets of Ephesus:

> Some offer me commodities to buy.
> Even now a tailor call'd me in his shop,
> And show'd me silks that he had bought for me,
> And therewithal took measure of my body.
> Sure, these are but imaginary wiles,
> And Lapland sorcerers inhabit here.

(4.3.6–11)

Alluring as they are, it seems, there is something supernatural about 'commodities'. The value, the meaning, of a commodity is not produced by nature, and this made it a source of unease. To be attracted to commodities was to be seduced, as Philip the Bastard indicates in his lengthy disquisition on 'Commodity' in *King John*. 'Commodity' is figured here as a force that can bypass reason and distort the conscious will: 'that same purpose-changer, that sly divel, / That broker, that still breaks the pate of faith, / That daily break-vow' (2.1.567–9). The word 'broker' came up frequently in germinal discussions of economics, where it generally designated a pawnbroker, but could also refer to usurers in general. Like any seducer, the 'smooth-faced gentleman, tickling Commodity' (2.1.573) appeals to desire, to appetite. By such means he 'wins of all' (2.1.569), presenting his interactions with every level of society as a competition from which he always emerges victorious.

In Philip's speech, then, 'Commodity' connotes 'advantage' in the pejorative sense that makes us think it morally wrong to 'take advantage'. This phrase originally meant taking interest on a loan, as when Shylock reminds Antonio that 'you neither lend nor borrow / Upon advantage' (1.3.69–70). Although Antonio indignantly replies 'I do never use it', in *King John* Philip argues persuasively that *everybody* 'uses it' – not necessarily because they practise usury in the restricted economic sense, but in the broader sense that they generally seek their own advantage in economic transactions. He anticipates Hobbes when he calls Commodity 'the bias of the world'. Despite being universal, however, this 'bias' is not natural. Indeed Shakespeare uses the word 'bias' to designate the inevitable but nonetheless sinful human fallibility that, as Philip claims, distorts the balance of natural creation:

> Commodity, the bias of the world,
> The world, who of itself is peised well,
> Made to run even upon even ground,
> Till this advantage, this vile drawing bias,

> This sway of motion, this Commodity,
> Makes it take head from all indifferency,
> From all direction, purpose, course, intent ...
>
> (2.1.574–80)

It is notable that Philip does not criticize Commodity for altering the purpose of particular things, but rather for disregarding *all* purpose. Because it appeals to appetite rather than to reason, the pursuit of Commodity is completely incompatible with rational teleology. Although he recognizes Commodity's destructive and reprehensible nature, Philip explicitly denies that his protest is principled. Instead he clinches his case by revealing that even he is pursuing Commodity in the very act of denouncing it. He rails against it only because it has not yet favoured him with its attentions. As soon as it does, he is resolved to change his tune. The speech's final line returns to the restricted meaning of the term, when the personification of 'Commodity' is replaced by 'Gain'. Philip's final resolution echoes the widespread view of commodification as a kind of religious idolatry: 'Since kings break faith upon commodity, / Gain, be my lord, for I will worship thee' (2.1.597–8).

Philip encapsulates the capacious early modern understanding of 'commodity' when he calls it 'This bawd, this broker, this all-changing word' (2.1.582). Commodity is an agent of transformation, a sign that alters the identity of its referents. It is a trope of usury (a 'broker') and also of pimping (a 'bawd'). The writers of Renaissance England focused on the intimate relationship between usury and prostitution with prurient interest, but also with intellectual consistency. Both were forms of concupiscence, diverting money and sex away from their natural purposes and 'taking advantage' of people's desire for both. The Fool in *Timon of Athens* delights in the riddling symmetry between usurers and prostitutes:

> I think no usurer but has a fool to his servant; my mistress
> is one, and I am her fool. When men come to borrow of

your masters, they approach sadly, and go away merry; but
they enter my master's house merrily, and go away sadly.

(2.2.103–7)

Timon himself alludes to this connection when he tells the
prostitute Timandra: 'Be a whore still. They love thee not that
use thee' (4.3.84). Prostitution functioned as an 'illustrative
synecdoche'[12] to convey the impact of commodification when
applied to a human being. In fact, the word 'commodity' was
a common synonym for 'prostitute', as in *2 Henry VI* when
one of the rebels demands 'when shall we go to Cheapside
and take up commodities upon our bills?' (4.7.119–20).
Shakespeare repeats the joke in *Much Ado About Nothing*,
where Borachio remarks: 'We are like to prove a goodly
commodity, being taken up of these men's bills' (3.3.1485).
In *The Taming of the Shrew,* having arranged the union of
Katherine and Petruchio for his own advantage, Baptista
Minola comments 'now I play a merchant's part, / And venture
madly on a desperate mart' (2.1.320–1). Tranio takes up the
analogy: ''twas a commodity lay fretting by you; / 'Twill bring
you gain or perish on the seas' (2.1.322–3). Katherine had
been 'fretting', or wasting away, her value depreciating like
an unused sum of money; but being put out on the market,
she will bring profit. Shakespeare returned regularly to this
parallel between concupiscent sexuality and usury, deploying
it as a guiding theme of the *Sonnets* and *Measure for Measure*
as well as *Timon of Athens* and *The Merchant of Venice*. He
evidently found that it revealed something of fundamental
importance to the great transformation that he was engaged
in chronicling.

III

As the use of 'commodity' for 'prostitute' suggests, prostitution was widely conceived as a didactic symbol of for

the commodification involved in wage labour. In several of Shakespeare's plays, the brothel stands for all systems of commercial exchange, as Lysimachus informs Marina in *Pericles:* 'the house you dwell in proclaims you to be a creature of sale' (4.6.74–5). Hence Elbow in *Measure for Measure* tells the pimp Pompey 'you will needs buy and sell men and women like beasts' (3.2.1–2). In *Pericles* the Pandar uses words like 'market' and 'mart' to designate the physical marketplace, but also the general economic climate, as he speaks in terms that could be echoed by any species of trader: 'Search the market narrowly; Mytilene is full of gallants. We lost too much money this mart by being too wenchless' (4.2.3–5).

Such simultaneously literal and figurative usages of 'market' arose in response to perceived empirical and conceptual links between prostitution and the new forms of economic behaviour. This connection was especially direct in the case of usury. Countless contemporary pamphlets warn young noblemen against dissipating their fortunes in either the stews or the usurer's house, while noting that habitual frequenters of the former usually end up at the latter. Referring to the recent repression of brothels and the simultaneous legalization of limited usury, *Measure for Measure*'s Pompey laments: 'Twas never merry world since, of two usuries, the merriest was put down, and the worser allowed by order of law' (3.2.5–7). When confronted with the inside of a debtor's prison he comments: 'one would think it were Mistress Overdone's own house, for here be many of her old customers' (4.3.2–4), going on to list the various usorious practices that have landed these unfortunate whoremongers in gaol. In *Pericles,* Gower describes the bawd as a kind of usurer, living off the interest from the whore's investment of labour. He observes that Marina does not lack for customers 'of noble race, / Who out their bounty on her; and her gain / She gives the cursed bawd' (4.6.9–11).

Neither the financial nor the sexual economy could be contained within linguistic limitations. Just as Shakespeare deploys economic terms and concepts in a huge variety of figurative contexts, so his sexual imagery also expands far beyond its original scope. A 'bawd' was originally a pimp, but Shakespeare uses the word to designate an intermediary or go-between of any kind, as *Measure for Measure*'s Isabella suggests when she denounces Pompey: 'Thy sin's not accidental, but a trade; / Mercy to thee would prove itself a bawd' (3.1.148–49). Anything, even mercy, she claims, can function as a 'bawd' to the right person – as Apemantus from *Timon of Athens* confirms when he describes a group of creditors as: 'Poor rogues, and usurers' men, bawds between gold and want!' (2.2.64–5). When *The Merchant of Venice*'s Bassanio calls silver 'thou pale and common drudge / 'Tween man and man' (3.2.103–4), when Troilus calls Pandarus a 'broker-lackey' (5.11.33), or when the pimp himself laments 'Thus is the poor agent despised' (5.10.36), the object of contempt is to be found in the 'general' as well as in the 'restricted' economy. Under the rubric of 'bawdry', Shakespeare condemns the commodification of mediation itself, whether in its financial, sexual or aesthetic manifestation.

Shakespeare was himself accused of practising an especially novel and pernicious species of 'bawdry'. Prostitution was not, of course, new to Shakespeare's England, but the public theatres were. The theatres and the brothels were located next to each other on the south bank of the Thames, in the 'liberties', an area nominally free from the control of the puritan-dominated London Corporation, and this empirical proximity served to emphasize the conceptual kinship between the two entertainment institutions.[13] Anti-theatrical pamphleteers like Stephen Gosson and Philip Stubbes pointed out that people received nothing material in return for their money in either place; instead, actors and prostitutes both appeared to simply sell themselves. The theatre and the brothel were both conceived as sensual temptations, with the spectacular allurement of the stage providing a handy metaphor for the fleshly inducements offered by its neighbour. Both places were believed to spread disease. There were even prostitutes touting for business in the theatres during performances, and the anti-theatrical campaigners hammered away obsessively at what seemed to them a clear causal connection between theatrical and venereal vice.

This gave particular poignancy to the many depictions of prostitution on the early modern stage. Many words in the erotic lexicon, including 'love' and 'dear', acquire an ironic ambiguity in such literature; they refer simultaneously to the range of subjective emotion and to the objective standards of financial evaluation. In Shakespeare, they often carry a disturbing suggestion that the two senses are inseparable, as when King Lear asks his daughters to say which 'loves' him most. Following Cordelia's refusal to speak, the word 'dear' shifts from an emotional to a financial significance in the space of two lines: 'When she was dear to us, we did hold her so, / But now her price is fallen' (1.1.197–8). Kurt Heinzelman places these lines in historical context:

> By Shakespeare's time, the meaning of "price" itself had changed in order to accommodate economic usage. Until well into the sixteenth century, price meant merely estimation or esteem, so that what was priceless was worthless. In the new language of nascent capitalist economics, however, what was priceless came to be understood as what was beyond measure, beyond mere price.
>
> (227)

To 'prize' something is to value it highly, as when Diomedes says of Cressida: 'To her own worth / She shall be prized' (4.4.132–3). However, to 'price' something is also to commodify it, and these meanings of 'prize' and 'price' tend to converge in Shakespeare. In *Antony and Cleopatra* Caesar reassures the Egyptian queen: 'Caesar's no merchant, to make prize with you / Of things that merchants sold' (5.2.182–3). Both 'price' and 'prize' frequently connote market value, the value of mere opinion, as when Cressida remarks that 'Men prize the thing ungained more than it is' (1.2.283), or when Troilus begs Hector not to 'Beggar the estimation which you prized / Richer than sea and land' (2.2.91–92). 'Price' means a false value when the First Citizen in *Coriolanus* demands: 'Let us kill him, and we'll have corn at our own price' (1.1.10–11), and it retains this sense of arbitrary significance when Coriolanus ironically demands: 'Well then, I pray, your price o'th'consulship?' (2.3.72–3). The Citizen's reply – 'The price is to ask it kindly' (2.3.71–2) – confirms the degeneration of politics to a marketplace. Shakespeare even uses 'praise' as a cognate of 'price' in *Pericles,* when Cerimon alludes to 'diamonds of a most praised water' (3.2.103). In *Love's Labour's Lost,* Berowne associates two kinds of unreliable signs in his encomium to Rosaline: 'Fie, painted rhetoric! O, she needs it not. / To things of sale, a seller's praise belongs; / She passes praise' (4.3.235–7). A commodity deserves only a 'seller's praise' because it possesses only exchange-value: a seller's price. Sonnet 21 repeats the pun: 'I will not praise, that purpose not to sell' (14). The kind of false praise, or price, imposed on something that one sells is different and inferior to real, authentic worth.

In *Troilus and Cressida,* Hector needs to combine 'precious' with 'dear' to find a superlative, as if the two words carry distinct meanings for him: 'Life every man holds dear, but the dear man / Holds honour far more precious-dear than life' (5.3.27–8). Shakespeare frequently plays with the moral conflicts raised by the dual significance of 'dear' as 'beloved' and 'expensive'. The word carried an affective significance in the general economy, and a different, conflicting meaning when used in the context of restricted economy. In similar fashion, *Antony and Cleopatra*'s Caesar shrewdly applies market methods of evaluation to popular affection when he accounts for the returning Pompey's popularity by observing that 'the ebbed man, ne'er loved till ne'er worth love, / Comes deared, by being lacked' (1.4.43–4). Democratic politics, like the economic marketplace, is determined by image, not substance, and must follow the law of supply and demand.

Shakespeare sometimes uses the word 'dear' to designate strong but hostile feeling, thus drawing attention to the influence of its quantitative connotations over its qualitative meaning. In such usages, 'dear' refers to the degree of emotion, not the kind. Thus Hamlet declares: 'Would I had met my dearest foe in heaven / Or ever I had seen that day' (1.4.182–3), while in *As You Like It* Celia recalls, 'my father hated his father dearly' (1.3.31). The bitter irony in the reproach offered to the patricians by *Coriolanus'* First Citizen – 'they think we are too dear' (1.1.18) – springs from the presence of 'dear' in the restricted economic sense of 'expensive' contrasted with the absence of 'dearness' in the general economic sense of 'beloved'. Sonnet 31 begins by attributing to the speaker's current beloved the value of all his past loves: 'Thy bosom is endeared with all hearts / Which I, by lacking, have supposed dead' (1–2). Such lines blend the financial and the emotional senses of 'dear' so closely that they become indistinguishable.[14]

In Shakespeare's work, this blurring of the distinctions between binary oppositions like subject and object, worth and value, or use and exchange constitutes an important ethical problem. In *Richard II,* John of Gaunt wryly repeats the word 'dear' to call attention to this change in England's customary mode of evaluation. His words carried a deep resonance in the era of enclosure: 'This land of such dear souls, this dear dear land, / Dear for her reputation through the world, / Is now leased out – I die pronouncing it – / Like to a tenement or pelting farm' (2.1.57–60). As Gaunt laments, this movement from 'dear' in the affective register to 'dear' in the commercial sense bespeaks the spirit of the age, as the economy begins its colonization of both society and the psyche.

Shakespeare was an important influence, at a formative stage, on the language and concepts through which we still interpret the economy to this day. By focusing microscopically on key terms like 'commodity', 'commons', 'price' and 'dear' he moulded them into shapes capable of accommodating the new meanings thrown up by the re-imagination of the world to which he bore witness. A way of life based on 'economics', as understood in ancient and medieval culture, was being displaced by one founded on the 'banausic' science known to the Greeks as 'chrematistics'. People were learning how to see the exchange-value of objects, and forgetting how to see their use-value. The concepts 'use-value' and 'exchange-value' are ancient, but they acquired their specific, modern inflections in Shakespearean English. Heinzelman notes that, in early seventeenth-century England: 'Words which had earlier signified the bonds of feudal loyalty lost their ethical overtones ... [words] acquired a singularly commercial, fiduciary significance' (14). In his gleeful, obsessive deployment of puns, Shakespeare took full advantage of the consequent linguistic quibbles, and in the process he created a vocabulary for the burgeoning discourse of political economy.

7

'The soul of trade': Worth and Value

I

On the first page of *Capital*, Marx offers an extraordinarily astute fragment of literary criticism: 'In English writers of the seventeenth century we still often find the word "worth" used for use-value and "value" for exchange-value. This is quite in accordance with the spirit of a language that likes to use a Teutonic word for the actual thing, and a Romance word for its reflection'.[1] Perhaps because of its literary provenance, the importance of this remark to Marx's economic theory has been sadly under-estimated. Marx's interpretation of the distinction between use- and exchange-value has determined the destinies of great nations, inspired entire social movements and produced whole schools of philosophy. Yet here he acknowledges the seminal influence of seventeenth-century English authors, among whom his clear favourite was Shakespeare, on the history of economic thought. Although Shakespeare did, as Marx notes, use 'worth' and 'value' in the literal sense of 'restricted' economy, he also employed these words in a wide variety of general, figurative senses. In such contexts we can observe the moral implications still attached to the terms – implications which were to be systematically excluded from the science of political economy.

In *Much Ado About Nothing*, for example, Friar Francis illustrates Marx's observation when he reflects: 'That what we have we prize not to the worth / Whiles we enjoy it, but being lacked and lost, / Why then we rack the value ...' (4.1.217–19). A thing's 'worth' here is its use-value, which we can only enjoy while in physical possession of the object. Having been deprived of that possession, we can only 'rack' – that is, both 'torture' and 'reck(on)' – its 'value'. Exchange-value, which can be reckoned in quantitative terms, is the only mode of estimation available to those who are not in physical possession of the object. Early modern English men and women were just growing accustomed to such subtle distinctions. They were the first Western Europeans since ancient times to be exposed to the effects of a large-scale market economy, so they were unavoidably struck by the divergence it instituted between real use-value and symbolic exchange-value. In the years before political economy was declared a specialist science, they discussed these two kinds of value, and other phenomena that we would consider 'economic', in common sense, everyday language. In large part, they discussed it in the language of Shakespeare, utilizing his idiomatic vocabulary to make sense of the unprecedented experiences of modernity. The legacy of this language gives Shakespeare a plausible claim to be ranked among the founders of political economy. In his work we can observe the conceptual and terminological framework of modern economics taking shape.

Of course Shakespeare was not the only one considering these matters, and Marx's claim is corroborated in the work of several other seventeenth-century writers. In the 1660s, Thomas Traherne's 'Misapprehension' declared that 'Men are not wise in their True Interest, / Nor in the Worth of what they long possest: / They know no more what is their Own / Than they the value of't have known'.[2] Traherne refers here to the ancient conundrum which Foucault has called 'the great paradox of value'. Since the dawn of civilization, people have observed that the most useful things, such as water, have very little financial value, while the monetary value of relatively useless objects, like gold or diamonds, is very great. Traherne elaborates on this paradox here, when he distinguishes between an illusory 'value' and an authentic 'worth'. Men have 'long possest' the latter, he asserts, but lately they have forgotten their ownership, because they have started to confuse it with financial value.[3]

Traherne's prose *Centuries of Meditation* subjects these concepts to closer scrutiny: 'Worthless and Useless go together. [But] a Piece of Gold cannot be Valued, unless we Know how it relates to Clothes, to Wine, to Victuals, to the Esteem of Men, and to the Owner' (1:143). Once again, 'worth' here means use-value, which is inherent in the physical body of an object, and 'value' is exchange-value, which is artificially imposed and relationally defined. The problem with contemporary England, as Traherne laments repeatedly, is that people are confusing 'worth' with 'value'. The result, as he puts it in two of his titles, is that 'Right Apprehension' is in danger of being permanently displaced by 'Misapprehension'. Traherne hopes to re-awaken a proper appreciation for natural phenomena in his readers: 'could we always be Sensible of their Use and Value; we should always be Delighted with their Wealth and Glory' (1:6). We need, in other words, to grasp the true meanings of 'Use' and 'Value', which means understanding the proper distinction and relation between them, in order to appreciate either of them.

The 'worth/value' dialectic also informs Andrew Marvell's 'Dialogue Between the Resolved Soul and Created Pleasure'. The soul responds to temptation by pointing to gold's financial function: 'Were't not a price who'd value gold? / And that's worth naught that can be sold' (61–2).[4] Marvell's soul does not say that gold is valuable because it has a price, but that it is valuable because it is a price. It is gold's function as money, not any of its natural qualities, that gives it this kind of 'value'. By the soul's standards, however, anything that 'can be sold' is 'worth naught'. Marvell does not of course suggest that commodities have no financial value but they do not, by definition, possess 'worth', because 'worth' designates use-value. Use-value is the essence of which money is the appearance. In this dialogue, Marvell deploys the distinction between apparent exchange-value and essential use-value to define the difference between the appearance of a human being – the body – and the human essence, or soul. John Donne's Elegy 19 considers the two ways of evaluating gold in similar terms:

> I, when I value gold, may think upon
> The ductileness, the application,
> The wholesomeness, the ingenuity,
> From rust, from soil, from fire ever free;
> But if I love it, 'tis because 'tis made
> By our new nature, use, the soul of trade.[5]
>
>   (11–16)

Donne constructs a witty paradox here, whereby the 'value' of gold is identified with its physical uses. If it evokes his 'love', however, it is because of a different kind of 'use'. This type of use is 'our new nature', it is part of custom, the 'second nature', which the Greeks called *nomos*. According to Donne's speaker, this 'second nature' has replaced the first, so that gold's exchange-value has become the essence, the 'soul', of the new, mercantile economy.[6]

Because use-value and exchange-value were two different kinds of wealth, they called for two ways of measuring wealth: the qualitative and the quantitative. Things could be evaluated either according to how useful they were, or according to how much money they might bring on the market. They could be measured by what they were, or by what they were worth – what they represented. In the words of Odd Langholm, measurement could be 'by need, according to nature, and by money, according to human convention'.[7] In Chapter 1, we saw how Socrates and Aristotle acknowledged only use-value as true wealth. This attitude remained constant throughout the Middle Ages. Langholm quotes the fourteenth-century Augustinian Henry of Friemar: 'human need is the true measure of value, while money is a measure instituted by law'.[8] But although the Scholastics remained convinced that use-value was 'truer', more authentic, than exchange-value, this opinion would not survive the Renaissance. The transition from evaluation by use to evaluation by exchange was historical as well as conceptual, and it led to a complete reordering of mankind's understanding of the world. Its most intensive phase coincided with Shakespeare's lifetime, and his plays are among the most perspicacious analyses of its social and psychological effects.

II

Like Donne, Traherne and Marvell, Shakespeare undertakes a concentrated investigation of both 'worth' and 'value'. His examination is protracted and insightful enough to suggest that he must have been among the seventeenth-century writers Marx had in mind when he mentioned their deployment of these terms in an economic context. In *Troilus and Cressida*, Helen of Troy provides a vehicle for the discussion of 'worth', 'value', and the relation between the two:

HECTOR
> Brother, she is not worth what she doth cost
> The holding.

TROILUS
> What's aught but as 'tis valued?

HECTOR
> But value dwells not in particular will;
> It holds his estimate and dignity
> As well wherein 'tis precious of itself
> As in the prizer. 'Tis mad idolatry
> To make the service greater than the god ...

(2.2.51–7)

To Hector's complaint that Helen is not 'worth' the 'cost' of keeping her, Troilus retorts that 'value' is subjective. It thus appears that Shakespeare is using 'worth' to mean inherent, natural, objective value, and 'value' to mean relational, customary, subjective value. But Hector's response introduces a more subtle refinement. He declares that the kind of 'value' that Troilus claims to find in Helen is actually objective, not subjective. Even relational value is not merely 'in the prizer'; a thing wins 'estimate' in part because it is 'precious of itself'. Hector believes that there ought to be a proportion between intrinsic worth and subjective evaluation because, as the Trojan war proves, there is in principle no limit to subjective evaluation, which is prey to 'mad idolatry' or fetishism, and can easily be induced to think a woman's face is worth a thousand ships, if it is not restrained by some reference to the objective world.

Later in the play, Ulysses draws one parallel between 'use' and 'regard', and another, opposing parallel between 'worth' and 'esteem'. The former pair suggests natural, inherent properties; the latter implies mere opinion: 'Nature, what things there are / Most abject in regard and dear in use! / What things again most dear in the esteem / And poor in worth!' (3.3.129–32). Many critics have found, like Lars Engle, that *Troilus and Cressida* shows a society with a 'rabid allegiance to market forces and an unrelieved economism' (148). But Ulysses' speech seems rather to suggest a society at a transitional stage between 'worth' and 'value', in which both concepts remain current. The obvious danger in such a society, as was confirmed by experience in seventeenth-century England, lay in confusing 'worth' with 'value', thus falling into the 'mad idolatry' of mistaking the sign for the referent. In *Henry V* the monarch fears that he has made this error with regard to the 'idol ceremony' (4.1.240). He suspects that the trappings of kingship are merely an external, artificial, nominal form of value, lacking in substance, 'soul' or real 'worth:'

And what art thou, thou idol ceremony?
What kind of god art thou, that suffer'st more
Of mortal griefs than do thy worshippers?
What are thy rents, what are thy comings in?
O ceremony, show me but thy worth!
What is thy soul, O adoration?

(4.1.236–41)

Worth is associated with the soul; value is associated with the body. We must guard against the 'mad idolatry' of the body, the adoration of appearance at the expense of essence. In *Troilus and Cressida*, religious, economic and sexual fetishism converge, as they have ever since Homer, on the figure of Helen of Troy. Paris' comment to Diomedes reveals the commercial terms in which Helen is assessed: 'you do as chapmen do, / Dispraise the thing that you desire to buy. / But we in silence hold this virtue well: / We'll not commend what we intend to sell' (4.1.77–80). Troilus's ultimate evaluation of Helen shows that he is well aware of her status as a commodity. The Trojans ought to keep her, he argues, because after all: 'We turn not back the silks upon the merchant / When we have soil'd them' (2.2.69–70). Nevertheless, he asserts that this admittedly commodified mode of value constitutes authentic worth: 'Is she worth keeping? Why, she is a pearl / Whose price hath launched above a thousand ships, / And turned crowned kings to merchants' (2.2.81–3). For Troilus, evidently, value has actually turned into worth.

At such moments Helen represents exchange-value itself, in pursuit of which even the monarchs of the earth willingly adopt the mercantile behaviour they affect to despise. As Matthew Gumpert explains: 'Helen does not mediate between designated antitheses; she is a figure for mediation itself … She is an emblem of ambivalence itself, a sign for self-difference, something close to what Jacques Derrida attempts to capture in a term like *différence*'.[9] Gumpert interprets the Judgment of Paris as a mythological account of exchange-value's origin.

The beauty that Hera asks Paris to identify is relative, not absolute. He is forced to rank the goddesses in relation to each other, and Helen is the bribe that Aphrodite gives him to ensure her victory. From the very start, as Gumpert observes: 'Helen always stimulates a chrematistic economy' (59):

> What Helen does ... is introduce an economy of *relative wealth*. Helen is always the most beautiful *comparatively speaking*. And to mention Helen is always to start speaking comparatively. Currency of comparison, Helen is the end and the means of an economy of desire or graft, a chrematistics. This is a currency that increases itself, reproduces itself, compounds itself, through metaphorical likenesses (*eidola*).
>
> (61–2)

Hector attempts to argue in terms that Troilus can understand, pointing out that Helen is not 'worth' the exchange, even if measured according to the quantitative standards of chrematistic 'value'. But Troilus wittily turns the tables, purporting to scorn such evaluation as foreign to his aristocratic world-view:

HECTOR
    If we have lost so many tenths of ours
    To guard a thing not ours, nor worth to us
    (Had it our name) the value of one ten,
    What merit's in that reason which denies
    The yielding of her up?

TROILUS
    Fie, fie, my brother!
    Weigh you the worth and honour of a king
    So great as our dread father in a scale
    Of common ounces? Will you with counters sum
    The past-proportion of his infinite?

(2.2.21–9)

Troilus insists that 'worth' is not subject to quantitative evaluation. He uses the word in a sense that anticipates *The Winter's Tale*, where it means 'blood' or 'breeding'. Leontes tells Florizel that he cannot marry a commoner: 'I am sorry ... Your choice is not so rich in worth as beauty, / That you might well enjoy her' (5.1.210, 213–14). Because of her low birth, Perdita lacks the inborn, essential 'worth' that would make her a fit spouse for a prince, in spite of the high value her physical appearance affords her. The revelation that Perdita is in fact of royal blood neatly abolishes the contradiction between 'worth' and 'value' in *The Winter's Tale*. But 'worth' acquires similar class implications in *Coriolanus*, when Volumnia scorns 'the rabble' as: 'Cats, that can judge as fitly of [Coriolanus's] worth / As I can of those mysteries which heaven / Will not have earth to know' (4.2.34–6). Once again, 'worth' is an exclusively aristocratic quality, inaccessible to the masses, who can only recognize quantitative value. In *Troilus and Cressida* Achilles' rage is stirred by his misunderstanding of 'worth'. He 'Grows dainty of his worth' (1.3.145), or jealous of the regard in which he is held by others. Achilles has confounded relative value with absolute worth. This mode of estimation produces what Ulysses later calls 'imagined worth' (2.3.171) – an oxymoron that emphasizes the inaccessibility of true worth in a society where reputation derives from public opinion.

The play's less astute characters are slow to grasp the implications of value's relativization. Achilles' convoluted expression catches the paradox when he laments being ignored by his fellow-Greeks 'who do, methinks, find out / Something not worth in me such rich beholding / As they have often given' (3.3.91–93). He knows that his 'worth' is something that should be 'in' him, but he feels deprived of it because it is not recognized publicly. His paranoia becomes self-fulfilling: naturally his comrades will not recognize his worth as inherent if he himself regards it as dependent on their evaluation. Achilles' scruples expose him as an anachronism, for *Troilus and Cressida* shows a world in which value is rapidly becoming relational. Troilus seems to grasp this when, impelled by his furious jealousy, his previous understanding of subjectivity breaks down – 'This is and is not Cressid' (5.2.153) – and he begins to describe his evaluation of her, and others, in purely comparative terms: 'as much as I do Cressid love, / So much by weight hate I her Diomed' (5.2.174–5). The idea of determining value by weight is a monetary metaphor, to which Shakespeare often returns when he wants to evoke relative value, rather than essential worth. In *Cymbeline,* for example, Iachimo observes that Posthumus' marriage to the king's daughter means that 'he must be weighed rather by her value than by his own' (1.5.15–16). Once convinced of a word's pivotal power to reveal the subterranean stirrings of the *Zeitgeist,* Shakespeare worried at it incessantly, punning and prodding at it from every possible angle. Timon of Athens shows the cynic Apemantus a jewel and inquires about its exchange-value: 'What dost thou think 'tis worth?' (1.1.216). The philosopher's answer redirects attention to its use-value: 'Not worth my thinking' (1.1.217). The jewel does not contain the kind of 'worth' he recognizes, though it does contain value. When *2 Henry VI*'s Lieutenant speaks of 'a worthless king, / Having neither subject, wealth, nor diadem' (4.1.81–2), the monarch is clearly understood to lack both the ability to reign usefully and financial wealth. Our attention is thus drawn to the convergence of the two meanings. Yet when, in the same play, Salisbury refers to Suffolk's victim as 'twenty times his worth' (3.2.268), the moral sense alone is intended. Like many of Shakespeare's favourite words, 'worth' and 'value' inhabit the restricted and the general economic registers simultaneously.

They also move easily between the two registers. When *Twelfth Night*'s Sebastian says he could 'pay' Antonio better 'were my worth, is as my conscience, firm' (3.3.17), the financial meaning seems to exclude the ethical. Yet the reverse is true in *The Merchant of Venice*'s opening scene. When Salerio politely tells Antonio that 'worthier friends'

(1.1.61) have arrived, he does not mean that Bassanio and the others are richer than he is. Antonio's reply emphasizes the bleeding of personal into financial qualities that forms the play's main theme: 'Your worth is very dear in my regard' (1.1.62). Shakespeare's dialogue is replete with such moments, when the economic and the affective registers merge and become indistinguishable. When, at the end of *Pericles,* Gower announces: 'In reverend Cerimon there well appears / The worth that learned charity aye wears' (*Epilogue* 9–10), Cerimon is praised for the correspondence between his appearance and his 'worth', his essence. But when *Troilus and Cressida*'s Nestor observes: 'Even so / Doth valour's show and valour's worth divide / In storms of fortune' (1.3.45–7), the opposite of 'worth' is 'show'. The 'worth' of valour is valour's essence; the 'show' of valour is its appearance. Through such quibbles Shakespeare depicts the rise of chrematistic value as the conquest of essence by appearance, a process that takes place throughout the general as well as the restricted economy.

III

In class terms, the conquest of essence by appearance is reflected in the decline of the nobility and the rise of the bourgeoisie. Aristocratic worth is based on blood, and is therefore conceived as natural, in contrast to bourgeois value, which derives from money and is therefore seen as artificial. In several of Shakespeare's plays an aristocratic character suffers a temporary relegation to the lower orders, and the plots hinge on the degree to which their true nature can be discerned beneath their apparently plebeian status. Miranda and Perdita are both easily recognized as too noble for their circumstances. Coriolanus' noble blood remains visible even after his expulsion from Rome, as the confusion among Aufidius' servants testifies:

2ND SERVINGMAN

Nay, I knew by his face that there was something in
him. He had, sir, a kind of face, methought – I cannot
tell how to term it.

1ST SERVINGMAN

He had so; looking as it were – would I were hanged,
but I thought there was more in him than I could think.

(4.5.158–63)

In *Troilus and Cressida*, Achilles shows his usual confusion
when he announces his intention to inspect Hector as if he
were a commodity. The Trojan corrects him, pointing out that
commercial evaluation is no way to discern true worth:

ACHILLES

I will the second time,
As I would buy thee, view thee limb by limb.

HECTOR

O, like a book of sport thou'lt read me o'er;
But there's more in me than thou understand'st.
Why dost thou so oppress me with thine eye?

(4.5.237–41)

The generalized understanding of the market's effects made
visible the kind of connections between apparently different
spheres of life that the political economists deliberately erased
when they restricted the meaning of 'economy'. In Hector's
question here, for example, commodification is conceptually
connected to the sense of sight. The rationale behind this link
was that the imposition of exchange-value obtruded a mere
image – which thus became an 'idol' – between the subjective
observer and the object observed. Instead of seeing the
thing-in-itself, the idolator perceives only the thing's image.
This in turn led to frequent comparisons between idolatry,

commodification and the irrational force of sexual attraction, as when *Much Ado about Nothing's* Benedick asks: 'Would you buy her, that you inquire after her?' (1.1.172). Their shared irrationality also connected the power of sexual desire to magic, and many words like 'glamour' and 'enchantment' connote both magical and erotic influence in Shakespearean English. The shift to chrematistic thinking opened the way for perception to replace reality in politics as well as in economics. Democracy is the political marketplace, as Coriolanus often remarks, in which men are evaluated in quantitative rather than qualitative terms. This produces the kind of image-based calculation that leads *Julius Caesar's* Metallus to urge Cicero's inclusion in the conspiracy: 'O let us have him, for his silver hairs / Will purchase us a good opinion, / And buy men's voices to commend our deeds' (2.1.143–5). Literal bribery is unnecessary when the mob's instinctive focus on appearances allows elections to be conducted like commercial transactions.

An economic view of the world, in the ancient sense, concerns itself with the qualities of things, while a chrematistic approach notices only their quantities. Traditional morality consists in the ability to restrict each of these respective modes of perception to the appropriate circumstances. In *King Lear* and *Antony and Cleopatra,* this morality is violated when characters are asked to quantify love.[10] Only objective things can be quantified; as a subjective phenomenon, love cannot be evaluated in the way that money can. To view love in quantitative terms is already, by that very act, to alter its nature, to degrade it to the level of exchange-value. As in many of Shakespeare's tragedies, events that take place at the microcosmic level of the individual psyche are replicated at the macrocosmic level of the state. Lear's quantification of subjective emotion leads directly to the expropriation of his feudal rights, which are also translated into numerical terms as he haggles with his daughters: 'Thy fifty yet doth double five and twenty, / And thou art twice her love' (2.2.451–2). As Richard Halpern points out: 'It is Lear himself who begins the dissolution of the "feudal" order in the play by means of one sweeping gesture: division of the kingdom'.[11] Although *King Lear* is often read as Shakespeare's most pessimistic play, Cordelia's overthrow of Goneril and Regan is a revolution against the tyranny of false value. It therefore holds up, however faintly, the prospect of the restoration of true worth. Thus Halpern finds in the play a protest against teleological history, calling it 'a fantastic but nonetheless coherent account of the transition from capitalism to feudalism' (247).

Cleopatra makes the same mistake as Lear with her misguided demand: 'If it be love indeed, tell me how much' (1.1.14). She anticipates a quantitative answer, but Antony informs her that to frame the question in financial terms is to reveal one's erotic deprivation: 'There's beggary in the love that can be reckoned' (1.1.15). It seems that Cleopatra has learnt this lesson when, in the final act, she denounces her treasurer Seleucus: 'O slave, of no more trust / Than love that's hired!' (5.2.153–4). But the irony is that Seleucus has given an objectively accurate account of her finances. The queen's displeasure arises from the fact that his account does not accord with her subjective desires: she is killing the messenger again. Understanding that love cannot be evaluated in financial terms, that 'it cannot be reckoned' or 'hired' because it is subjective, she mistakenly applies the same criterion to the genuinely objective sphere of finance itself.

In contrast, Prince Hamlet acknowledges the incommensurability of subjective emotion when he declares: 'I lov'd Ophelia. / Forty thousand brothers / Could not with all their quantity of love / Make up my sum.' (5.1.269–71) Hamlet denies that any number of brothers could equal his love. This is not so much because he loves Ophelia more than they could, as because love is not subject to quantitative evaluation. The frequency with which Shakespearean characters attempt to translate their emotions into quantitative terms suggests that the playwright saw this as a significant cultural problem. Even the *Sonnets* include warnings against the commodification of love, as the speaker cautions in number 102: 'That love is merchandised whose rich esteeming / The owner's tongue doth publish everywhere' (3–4). Whenever they are used in a subjective context, commercial metaphors like 'merchandise' are synonyms for whatever is inauthentic, insincere, merely superficial. As Shakespeare's erotic reflections in the *Sonnets* and elsewhere reveal, this moral resistance to the commercialization of subjectivity constituted a serious ideological problem for England's nascent capitalist society.

8

'Knaves of common hire': Wage Labour, Slavery and Reification

I

It is to be expected that Shakespeare's proletarian characters would be psychologically affected by wage labour. However the logic of the marketplace, the mode of thought appropriate to commercial transactions, was spreading at every level of society, and it also invades the minds of Shakespeare's aristocrats. In *Troilus and Cressida* the lordly Ulysses recommends: 'Let us, like merchants, show our foulest wares, / And think perchance they'll sell; if not, / The lustre of the better yet to show / Shall show the better' (1.3.360–3). Even 'noble Macbeth' (1.2.69) is pleased to reflect that 'I have bought / Golden opinions from all sorts of people' (1.7.32–3). Thersites uses commodification as a synecdoche for exploitation when he insults Ajax in *Troilus and Cressida*: 'thou art bought and sold among those of any wit, like a barbarian slave' (2.1.46–7). Ajax is not literally a slave or a wage labourer, but he is treated like one. The fact that he sees nothing amiss in this until Thersites points it out indicates that commercial considerations are in the process of becoming respectable.

We've seen that a capitalist economy requires the commodification of land, labour and money. Some critics have complained that it is anachronistic to apply terms like 'commodification' to processes that took place in the sixteenth and seventeenth centuries,[1] but surely the terms 'land', 'labour' and 'money' are far better candidates for anachronism. As we saw in Chapter 1, 'land' is an inadequate way of describing the plethora of plants and animals, the extents of earth, sea and sky that were rudely subjected to the laws of the market around Shakespeare's lifetime. Masses of peasants saw their surroundings 'enclosed', or stolen, by the wealthy few, whose exponentially increased fortunes were fast coalescing into masses large enough to form the foundations of capitalist imperialism. This process of 'primitive accumulation' facilitated capitalism by concentrating wealth sufficiently for it to be invested in corporate enterprises. Customary rights to graze animals, chop wood, or harvest nuts and berries were eroded or abolished, as the English environment was incrementally privatized. This was more than the commodification of 'land'; it amounted to the transformation of nature itself into exchange-value. When we speak of the 'commodification of land', we describe the means by which mankind's objective environment was engrossed[2] and put up for sale.

The measures by which the English peasantry was deprived of the means of independent subsistence were many and various, but during Shakespeare's lifetime a combination of force and fraud conspired to turn hundreds of thousands of smallholders off their land, impelling them to live by selling their labour for money. As David McNally puts it: 'From the late sixteenth century onwards, sections of the gentry took advantage of the weakened state of the village community to launch a sustained offensive against the rights of the small tenants ... By 1700 three-quarters of all enclosure had already taken place'.[3] Through enabling the formation of large conglomerations of capital, 'enclosure' simultaneously provided the requisite workforce for such capital's productive investment. To make a living, dispossessed peasants were forced to sell their labour-power as a commodity, with all the physical and psychological trauma that process invariably entails. Prominent among these was 'reification'. A proletarian has to learn to conceive of his or her time, which is to say his or her life, as a thing that he or she owned, and could sell.

Unlike the independent craftsman or the peasant with a surplus, the wage labourer does not own or sell the product of his or her labour. Rather, the wage laborer sells his or her capacity to work for a given amount of time. Wage labour makes a commodity of time, which is to say of life itself. For this reason, wage labour was identified with slavery until modern times. The idea of selling one's time to somebody else, submitting to a contractual obligation to do another's bidding for the duration of work hours, seemed intrinsically degrading. To say that wage labour involved a loss of freedom was considered tautological. Wage labour means giving up control over one's own life to an external authority, which was the very definition of slavery. It was therefore assumed that proletarians would think like slaves. Thus Coriolanus imputes servility to his looting troops on the grounds that they see time in terms of money:

> See here these movers, that do prize their hours
> At a crack'd drachma! Cushions, leaden spoons,
> Irons of a doit, doublets that hangmen would
> Bury with those that wore them, these base slaves,
> Ere yet the fight be done, pack up.

(1.5.4–8)

By evaluating their lives in financial terms, the soldiers announce their own slavery. Shakespeare draws here on the classical tradition that we discussed in Part One. Aristotle famously declared that 'all paid jobs absorb and degrade the mind'.[4] In the *Rhetoric* he remarked that '[t]he condition of the free man is that he not live under the constraint of another'.[5] As Moses Finley comments, 'it is clear from the context that [Aristotle's] notion of living under restraint was not restricted to slaves but was extended to wage labour and to others who were *economically* dependent' (41). William L. Westerman claims that 'It has not been sufficiently emphasized that both of these thinkers [i.e., Plato and Aristotle] have thrown free workmen into close proximity with slave labor by their attitude upon the "banausic" trades'.[6] In the *Politics* Aristotle opines 'the best state will not make a *banausic* workman a citizen'.[7] This attitude passed intact from Greece to Rome. In Cicero's *De officiis,* proletarians are degraded to the level of slaves on the grounds that they sell their time, rather than the products of their labour: 'Illiberal too, and mean, are the employments of all who work for wages, whom we pay for their labour and not for their art; for in their case their very wages are the warrant of their slavery'.[8]

According to David Graeber's recent, meticulous history of wage labour, 'an ancient Greek would certainly have seen the distinction between a slave and an indebted wage labourer as, at best, a legalistic nicety'.[9] He points out that, in the *Odyssey* (2.488–91), 'Achilles, when trying to invoke the lowest and most miserable person he can possibly imagine, invokes not a slave but a *thete*, a mere labourer unattached to any household' (418n.70). In sum, Graeber claims, 'capitalism, or at least industrial capitalism, has far more in common with, and is historically more closely linked with, chattel slavery than most of us had ever imagined'.[10] Elsewhere he argues that wage labour originates as a sub-species of slavery:

> wage labor contracts appear to have developed from within the institution of slavery in many times and places, from ancient Greece to the Malay and Swahili mercantile city states of the Indian Ocean. Historically, I think one can say wage labor, at least considered as a contractual arrangement, emerged from slavery.[11]

Graeber quotes Leon Battista Alberti from as late as the fifteenth century: 'to be subject to another's commands is nothing but slavery' (53). He argues that this historical connection between slavery and wage labour reflects a fundamental conceptual affinity. A proletarian, like a slave, is under the control of another's will:

> what one buys when one buys a slave is the sheer capacity to work, which is also what an employer acquires when he hires a labourer. It's of course this relation of command that causes free people in most societies to see wage labour as analogous to slavery, and hence to try as much as possible to avoid it.
>
> (79)

The opponents of early modern capitalism found the philosophical weapons for their battle in the *Politics* and *Ethics* of Aristotle. But they were also aware that the Romans had developed Greek ideas about economics into legal form. As we saw in Part One, legally speaking, to be a property was to be a 'thing', what Roman law called a *res*. 'Things' in this legal sense were not necessarily material. People could be legal things, as could their labour-power. As Diana Wood explains:

> In Roman law property was "things," and the law of "things" featured prominently in Justinian's textbook, the *Institutes*, although the law students were left to work out for themselves just what "things" were. In its simplest form, property was any "thing," material or immaterial, that was owned or possessed and had some economic value. The most obvious and important thing was immovable: it was land, the chief source of wealth, and, in a primitive economy, the means of production. But "things" also included the immovable buildings erected on that land, the moveable animals which grazed on it, the crops which grew on it, and an infinite variety of movable chattels. These might be natural raw materials or manufactured goods. A "thing" might even be intangible, such as the labor of one's own body. It might be a legal right, such as a right of way.

It might involve rights over someone, a master's rights over a slave, a husband's rights over a wife, a manorial lord's over a serf or villain.[12]

To be legally a thing was to be 'reified'. Only 'things' could be owned, only 'things' could be bought and sold. Thus to be reified was to be commodified, to be translated into exchange-value. This line of thought provided Roman law's rationalization of slavery. As a commodity, a slave could be biologically human without being legally so. Commodities may or may not be material, but they are always objects, always things. William Buckland observes that in Roman law 'a slave was a *Res,* and, for the classical lawyers, the only human *Res* ... From the fact that a slave is a *Res* it is inferred, apparently as a necessary deduction, that he cannot be a person. Indeed the Roman slave did not possess the attributes which modern analysis regards as essential to personality.'[13] Orlando Patterson makes the same point succinctly in *Slavery and Social Death*: 'the most common conception of the slave among the Romans became, by the end of the republic, that of a thing. The slave was above all a *res, the only human res*'.[14]

We can deduce commodification's reifying and equalizing effects by gauging its impact on human beings. Aristotle notoriously identifies some people as 'natural slaves'. Natural slaves, while biologically human, are empirically and legally distinct from people who are naturally free. Aristotle found the idea of a fully human being who was also a commodity contradictory. A person might be one or the other but not both. This was because the process of commodification robs anything of its nature, and imposes a merely conventional, artificial value upon it. This 'exchange-value' does not arise out of any of the commodity's inherent properties, it is imposed from outside. To the degree that anything is regarded as a commodity, its nature is obliterated. To the degree that a human being is commodified, it follows, his or her essential identity is occluded. This process is not limited to proletarians.

In the *Economic and Philosophic Manuscripts of 1844,*
Marx described the effects of psychological alienation on the
possessors of money:

> That which is for me through the medium of *money* – that
> for which I can pay (i.e., which money can buy) – that am *I*
> *myself,* the possessor of the money. The extent of the power
> of money is the extent of my power. Money's properties
> are my – the possessor's – properties and essential powers.
> Thus, what I *am* and *am capable of* is by no means deter-
> mined by my individuality.
>
> (167)

Money is the magical power that robs people and things alike
of their natural, essential qualities. In this fetishized medium
of exchange, subjective activity was represented in objective
form, and objective symbols took on an artificial, supernatural
agency.

II

In many of Shakespeare's plays, the rise to power of money is
identified with and abetted by plebeian or bourgeois characters,
while the old orders of meaning and power are defended by
aristocrats. In fact, the attitudes various characters express
towards wage labour are perhaps the clearest class markers in
Shakespeare. Several characters still express a feudal attitude
to service: they are personally loyal to their master and willing
to serve him without monetary reward. In *As You Like It,*
the faithful Old Adam happily gives away the 'thrifty hire' he
has saved for his old age, prompting Orlando to remark that
such attitudes are rare these days: 'O good old man, how well
in thee appears / The constant service of the antique world, /
When service sweat for duty, not for meed' (2.3.56–8). *King
Lear*'s Kent exhibits a similarly feudal sense of loyalty and

disregard of remuneration. In contrast, those who serve for wages are unreliable, like Iago who boasts that he offers mere 'shows of service' (1.1.51).

Wages are seen as suitable for characters who are both plebeian and unprincipled. In *1 Henry IV* Falstaff gives the drunken Bardolph a bottle 'for thy labour' (4.2.7), while *Measure for Measure*'s Elbow frankly responds to Escalus' inquiry concerning his dubious role as constable: 'I do it for some piece of money, and go through with all' (2.1.265–6). In contrast, when the virtuous Viola is offered wages in *Twelfth Night,* her response is indignant: 'I am no fee'd post, lady; keep your purse' (1.5.278). The idea that a given set of human actions can fairly be equated with a given sum of money provides an egalitarian standard of evaluation that does not depend on birth or blood. That is why Coriolanus rejects on principle any suggestion of an equivalence between his deeds and payment: 'I ... cannot make my heart consent to take / A bribe to pay my sword: I do refuse it' (1.9.37–8).

The Volscian aristocracy feel precisely the same contempt for wage labour and the mindset it fosters. Aufidius is insulted when: 'He wag'd me with his countenance, as if / I had been mercenary' (5.6.40–1). He attributes Coriolanus' clemency to the commercial mentality which he claims to have detected lurking beneath his heroic façade: 'At a few drops of women's rheum, which are / As cheap as lies, he sold the blood and labour / Of our great action' (5.6.46–8). In spite of his flirtation with the underworld, Prince Hal inwardly agrees with Coriolanus' conception of value. Rather than envisage himself performing valorous deeds and receiving fair recompense, Hal proposes to let Hotspur do all the work, collecting his valorous deeds for him, before he steps in to claim the accumulated honor:

> Percy is but my factor, good my lord,
> To engross up glorious deeds on my behalf;
> And I will call him to so strict account

That he shall render every glory up,
Or I will tear the reckoning from his heart.

(3.2.147–52)

Shakespeare frequently repeats the widespread contemporary denigration of 'hirelings', or wage labourers.[15] In *Othello,* Roderigo evinces the typical aristocrat's snobbery with his reference to 'a knave of common hire, a gondolier' (1.1.123). Coriolanus refuses to show the people his battle scars: 'As if I had receiv'd them for the hire / Of their breath only!' (2.2.148–9). He believes that his deeds are inherently valuable and do not need external validation: 'Better it is to die, better to starve, / Than crave the hire which first we do deserve.' (2.3.112–13). He flatly refuses to deal in commercial or democratic terms: 'I would not buy / Their mercy at the price of one fair word' (3.3.90–1). Thus Shakespeare uses the imagery of exchange-value to convey the quantified, egalitarian nature of political democracy.

In *Titus Andronicus,* Bassanius agrees to dismiss his armed retainers: 'And to my fortunes and the people's favour / Commit my cause in balance to be weighed' (1.1.57–8). But although Shakespeare uses the same metaphor to describe it, Coriolanus' attitude is very different. He appears to judge the people in the same manner as they would judge him, by quantitative standards: 'your people, / I love them as they weigh' (2.2.72–3). In fact however, he is using a quite different mode of evaluation. He is saying that he will judge the people according to *their* judgment. He will evaluate them based on how 'they weigh' his *own* cause, which he assumes to be inherently righteous regardless of the people's verdict. If and only if the people are wise enough to recognize his natural worth, to 'weigh' him correctly, Coriolanus is willing to extend them his approbation.

To understand how Shakespeare came to associate democracy with exchange-value, we must recall Aristotle's observation that 'All things that are exchanged must be somehow comparable. It is for this end that money had been introduced'.[16] For him, the function of money was to replace essence with equivalence, and this is the source of its egalitarian tendency. Aristotle was unable to see, however, that this 'exchange-value' must represent human labour-power. This blind spot was due to the fact that he did not conceive of human labour-power as valuable. For him, labour-power was not the kind of thing that had value. He could not imagine labour-power as a separate commodity to be traded in isolation from the rest of the person who performs it. Only as wage labour replaced slavery did it become clear that labour itself had a value.[17] Only as it became clear that exchange-value, in the symbolic form of money, represented alienated labour-power, did it become possible to understand that capital, the power that rules the world, is nothing more than human activity in externalized, objective form. As Moses Finley observes in *The Ancient Economy*:

> Neither in Greek nor in Latin was there a word with which to express the general notion of "labor" or the concept of labor "as a general social function." The nature and conditions of labor in antiquity precluded the emergence of such general ideas, as of the idea of a working class.

(81)

The vast majority of people in capitalist societies live by selling their time, their lives, their selves, on a daily basis: they are proletarians. According to Aristotle's canonical description, proletarians are piecemeal slaves. It is true that they sell their labour by the hour, not by the lifetime, and they may even experience this as a voluntary bargain. Nevertheless, they meet Aristotle's definition of slavery as human activity directed towards an end that is not proper to the actor but to another. The slave's actions are not carried out for the purpose of benefit to the slave, but for that of the master. As anyone who works for a wage knows very well, this is equally true of proletarians – and we are almost all proletarians today.

III

According to historians like Patterson and Finley, the condition of the slave prefigures the isolated atomic individual of modernity, being defined by what Finley calls 'natal alienation'. A slave was, in the words of Brent Shaw, 'a person who is systematically deracinated and kept in the status of an isolated being who has no roots, no kin or family claims'.[18] For David Brion Davis, this enforced individualism means that 'slaves were the first "modern" people'.[19] The individualism and 'self-fashioning' that characterizes Renaissance drama must be seen in this context. Although he is obviously not a slave in the literal sense, Coriolanus believes that his service to Rome has alienated him from the ties of blood and birth: 'Wife, mother, child, I know not. My affairs / Are servanted to others. Though I owe / My revenge properly, my remission lies / In Volscian breasts' (5.2.81–4). The only thing that belongs to him, his only property, is his revenge, and he knows that he can only enjoy that, only come into its possession, by means of the Volscians. He thus comes as close as an aristocrat can to the condition of *King Lear*'s Poor Tom: unaccommodated man. The terror of slavery in the ancient world lay in its reduction of a person to an unaccommodated individual. Far from revealing a moral gulf dividing our society from slave-holders, however, this gave the slave an affinity with the proletarian, whose labour was similarly *banausic* in nature, and whose economic position rendered him or her just as anonymous and fungible as the enslaved. As Davies notes:

Today, we automatically contrast slavery with free wage labour or with various modern ideals of individual autonomy. Throughout most of history such antonyms would have appeared absurd or contradictory ... In premodern societies the salient characteristic of slavery was its antithetical relation to the normal network of kinship ties of dependency, protection, obligation, and privilege.

(15)

We have seen how, in Roman law, the object of a commercial exchange was defined as *res,* a thing. We have also seen how this remained true even when the thing in question was a person, and how the Marxist concept of 'reification' derives from this logic. The main legal and psychological effect of enslavement was thus the transformation of the self into a thing: the objectification of the subject. This is why the vocabulary of corporeality, of fleshliness, saturates discussion of slavery from ancient times. Jennifer Glancy notes that the 'equation between slaves and bodies actually begins with the lexicon of slavery. The Greek word for body, *to soma,* serves as a euphemism for the person of a slave'.[20] In Rome as in Greece, observes Glancy, 'slavery was identified with the body ... Slaveholders in the first century characterized their slaves as bodies, and their treatment of their slaves was commensurate with that characterization. This was equally the case in the fourth century, when Constantine came to power, and a century after that' (3).

Aristotle's *Politics* unequivocally declares that the 'most slavish' forms of labour are 'those in which the body is most used' (1258bl). Slaves are purely sensual beings, 'wholly lacking the deliberative element' (1260al, 12). Like Plato, Aristotle draws an analogy between the relation between master and slave and that between soul and body. The former elements of these dichotomies should rule the latter for the good of both: 'that which can foresee with the mind is the naturally ruling and naturally mastering element, while that which can do these things with the body is the naturally ruled and slave' (1252bl). In the ancient world, and still in Shakespeare's day, this logic was understood as applying to wage labourers as much as to slaves, for the object of any financial exchange could only be a thing. Thus Coriolanus recalls how Volumnia 'was wont / To call them [i.e. the citizens] wooden vassals, things created / To buy and sell with groats' (3.2.8–10). The terms in which patricians insult plebeians dwell incessantly on objectification, as when *Julius Caesar*'s Murullus scatters the mob while calling them 'You blocks, you stones, you worse than senseless things!' (1.1.36).

Shakespeare's natural aristocrats define themselves by their distance from quantitative standards of evaluation. They can usually be identified by their scornful contempt for exchange-value. When Cominius reports that Coriolanus spurned his share of the battle's booty and 'look'd upon things precious as they were / The common muck of the world' (2.2.125–6), Menenius' response conveys admiration, certainly, but also a kind of pity at such cripplingly anachronistic innocence: 'He's right noble' (2.2.129). In the same spirit, once he has bankrupted himself by unrequited generosity, Timon of Athens remarks: 'Unwisely, not ignobly, have I given' (2.2.179). Coriolanus' jesting wager with Lartius provides an opportunity for both aristocrats to parade their indifference to money. Lartius refuses to return the horse that his friend has lost: 'I'll neither sell nor give him: lend him you I will / For half a hundred years.' (1.4.6–7) In *1 Henry IV* Hotspur displays a similarly ostentatious generosity and contempt for calculation: 'I'll give thrice so much land / To any well-deserving friend: / But in the way of bargain, mark ye me, / I'll cavil on the ninth part of a hair' (3.1.131–4). In *2 Henry VI,* Whitmore is so perplexed about the infectious potential of market values that he even scorns the impeccably aristocratic practice of negotiating ransoms: 'when merchant-like I sell revenge, / Broke be my sword, my arms torn and defaced / And I proclaimed a coward through the world' (4.1.41–3).

When considering the reasons behind this revulsion from the market, it is important to remember that what proletarians sell is not labour, or the products of labour, but time.

In other words, they sell their own lives: they sell themselves. In his commonplace book Ben Jonson remarks that labour is a commodity:

> The price of many things is farre above, what they are bought and sold for. *Life*, and *Health*, which are both inestimable, we have of the *Physician*: As *Learning*, and *Knowledge*, the true tillage of the *mind*, from our *Schoolemasters*. But the fees of the one, or the *salary* of the other, never answer the *value* of what we received; but serve to gratify their labours.[21]

Shakespeare often debates the morality of treating labour as exchange-value. After the jester Feste has been paid in *Twelfth Night*, Viola reflects that his professional skills deserve remuneration, on the assumption that labour is valuable: 'This is a practice / As full of labor as a wise man's art' (3.1.65–6). When Orsino offers him money 'for thy pains' (2.4.67), Feste rebukes his unwarranted presupposition: 'No pains, sir, I take pleasure in singing, sir' (2.4.68). But Orsino insists – 'I'll pay thy pleasure then' (2.4.69) – and his impulse is entirely in accordance with the basic presumption of wage labour: that work itself is unpleasant activity for which one deserves compensation. In *Troilus and Cressida*, Pandarus forces our attention onto the shifting significance of 'labour' when he complains: 'I have had my labor for my travail, ill-thought on of her, and ill-thought on of you; gone between and between, but small thanks for my labour' (1.1.69–70). The first kind of 'labour' here means 'trouble' or 'inconvenience'. The second usage carries a similar sense, but now Pandarus refers to something he has performed rather than to something he has received. The pun thus reveals the degradation of human activity in wage labour: because it needs to be compensated or recompensed, wage labour is conceived as expenditure, a loss, a 'pain'. The worker who constantly looks forward to five o'clock, willing time to pass more quickly, has entered into an alienated and antagonistic relationship with his or her own life. This is what Marx calls the psychological estrangement of humanity from its 'life-activity' or 'species-being'.

The keenest observers of early modern English society noticed that subjective human activity was being commodified under the title of 'labour', just as the objective pole of experience was being commodified under the name of 'land'. That is why the terms 'land' and 'labour' are inadequate and anachronistic in this context. The third precondition of a fully-functioning market economy is the commodification of money. Yet the word 'money' is also unnecessarily narrow here. The commodification of money involved the legalization of usury, which makes the medium of exchange into an object of exchange. This phenomenon affected the general as well as the restricted economy. Money was only one medium of representation among several, and what was really being offered for sale through the incremental legitimization of usury was mediation, or representation itself. The age of 'primitive accumulation' thus involved the necessarily simultaneous commodification of that which experiences (subjectivity), that which is experienced (objectivity), and that which mediates between subject and object (representation). This meant that people were forced to re-conceptualize their entire experience, to re-evaluate their whole world according to new standards. This is the process depicted in Shakespeare's work, and the perspicacity of his depiction surely explains his unwaveringly broad appeal to audiences throughout the modern era.

9

'Unkind abuse': The Legalization of Usury

I

A remarkably high proportion of late sixteenth- and early seventeenth-century English writers were personally involved in the practice of usury. That is some indication of usury's ubiquity in early modern England, but perhaps it also suggests a parallel between the ability to manipulate the linguistic system of representation and involvement in usury's complicated system of financial semiotics. Early modern writers could be borrowers, lenders, or both at the same time. Shakespeare, Milton, Herrick and Middleton were the sons of usurers, and practised varying degrees of usury themselves, while Thomas Dekker spent six years in debtors' prison. Many of the English language's seminal architects were heavily invested in usury, and their work shows that they were often profoundly conflicted about their involvement. It is no surprise to find that many words and phrases now used to describe debt, redemption, confidence, credit and other 'economic' phenomena develop their modern, restricted senses in the poetry, prose and drama of Renaissance England.

The era's horror of usury lay in its violation of the border between subject and object. Usury made an objective entity behave in a subjective fashion, and it confronted people with their own subjective activity in the form of a reified commodity. By allowing money to breed, usury bestowed upon it the definitive characteristic of life. This gave rise to copious jokes in early modern literature. In *Twelfth Night* the Fool holds up a coin: 'Would not a pair of these have bred, sir?' Given the economic assumptions of the age, Viola's answer is predictable: 'Yes, being kept together, and put to use' (3.1.50–1). Usury was understood to replace actual life with an objectified representation of life. This is why Shakespeare deemed it appropriate for Shylock to seek a literal pound of flesh: he has already sought to possess human life in symbolic form, simply by means of money-lending. Marx surely had Shylock in mind when he wrote:

> In the credit system man replaces metal or paper as the mediator of exchange. However, he does this not as man but as the existence (*Dasein*) of capital and interest. The substance, the body, clothing, the spirit of money is not money, paper, but instead it is my personal existence (*Dasein*), my flesh and blood, my social worth and status. Credit no longer actualises money-values in actual money but in human flesh and human hearts.

(165)

When concepts like 'credit', 'confidence', or 'goodwill' are expressed in financial terms, a properly subjective experience is rendered in objective form. As Emmanuel Levinas observed, money 'is an element in which the personal is maintained while being quantified'.[1] In the form of money, human beings are transformed from qualitative essences – use-values – into quantified symbols: exchange-values.

In Part One we saw how, in Roman law as in Greek philosophy, exchange-value was defined in relation to its dialectical opposite, use-value, which was conceived as a kind of wealth that could not be alienated or exchanged. The medieval scholastics also differentiated between 'natural' wealth, by which they meant use-value, and what Aquinas calls '[a]rtificial wealth [which] comprises the things which of themselves satisfy no natural need, for example, money'.[2] This was one of the logical reasons behind the ban on usury: since use-value was identical with wealth, it was impossible to separate use from ownership. When the usurer sold the 'use' of his money, it followed, he also gave up ownership of it and had no further claim upon it. As Aquinas put it: 'when we grant to someone the use by that very fact we grant also the thing, and for this reason to lend things of this kind is to transfer the ownership'.[3] Wood cites the English didactic pamphlet *Dives and Pauper* to this effect: 'The usurer selleth together the thing that he lendeth and the use of the thing and therefore *usury* cometh of selling the use'.[4]

As 'selling the use' grew widespread, in violation of all established moral precepts, people also began to remark on a growth in the autonomous reproduction of signs beyond the economy. Braudel remarks on the sinister convergence between finance and linguistics, which was presaged by the rise of 'credit money': 'this type of money, money that was not money at all, and this interplay of money and mere writing to a point where the two became confused, seemed not only complicated but diabolical' (357). In the days before the economy had been cordoned off as a discrete area of experience, usury's fetishistic vivification of signs was recognized as a species of idolatry. In *The Ruinate Fall of the Pope Usurie, Derived from the Pope Idolatrie* (1580), Nicholas Sander remarked that coins loaned out at usury:

> be no where at al. For in one moment they were consumed and spent by him that borrowed them, and in place of them an Idoll is conceaved, which Idoll doth remain constantly, not any where in nature and truth, but in name and imagniation. For it is feyned, that the ten crownes lie still in a certaine bancke, and there do begat little ones, which again have other little ones ... See ye not this Idol, which the Devill hath consercrated in the world?[5]

Usury assumes that money, which is in reality only a sign, has an essential value in itself. On this basis it can be made to 'breed' without reference to anything in the physical world. Usury elides and ignores referentiality, and it bestows determining power on surface representation. As Appleby notes, the philosophical assumptions implicit in the medieval, feudal economy were 'Platonic, with essences, forms, and a hierarchical structure' (1978, 247). The modern, chrematistic economy, by contrast, collapses the distinctions between essence and appearance, sign and referent, reality and representation. Signs replace what they had originally represented, as Appleby explains: 'The removal of key links in production and consumption from the range of tactile experience promoted the creation of symbolic representations. Price, rate, and credit began to stand in place of the bargain, the payment, the contract they represented' (ibid.). The legitimization of usury thus instituted the rise of what postmodernist philosophers call 'hyper-reality'.

Several of Shakespeare's characters mention that usury is a topical issue. Lear laments that he lives at a time when 'The usurer hangs the cozener' (4.6.159). In *Cymbeline*, Belarius tells his son that he would be less eager to re-join civilization: 'Did you but know the city's usuries, / And felt them knowingly' (3.3.45–6), and the First Citizen in *Coriolanus* complains that the senators 'make edicts for usury, to support usurers' (1.1.80–81). Shakespeare's original audiences would have recognized these as allusions to contemporary debates. The legalization of usury was a gradual process, with the law generally trying to catch up with already established practices. Because cash was in short supply, most small-scale transactions were conducted through the medium of credit throughout the early modern period. Carl Wennerlind reports that 'Historians have estimated that during the second half of the sixteenth century demand for money grew by approximately 500 percent, while the supply of coins expanded by only 63 percent'.[6] As a result, early modern England developed 'an

elaborate credit network based on personal agreements'
(ibid.). This meant that the issue of usury was extremely
personal, as well as extremely topical. Craig Muldrew
describes how usury's growth forced the household-oriented
economics of the feudal era to yield before the finance-
oriented chrematistics of modernity:

> Each individual household had to earn profits on the
> market, whether it was merely to survive or to become
> wealthy, and establishing a reputation for reliability
> was needed to do this. But, at the same time, because of
> the serial nature of credit, it was also in the interest of
> households to be concerned with the trustworthiness of
> other households to which they were extending credit.
> … [A] person's or household's trustworthiness … would
> not have been the concern of a few individual associates
> only, but of whole towns and villages because of the
> extensiveness of credit and the potential domino effect of
> defaults.[7]

The earliest tracts of political economy, composed in the
1620s, ask whether money is a commodity that must be
invested or lost. This question was fundamental to the
distinction between 'bullionists', for whom money was
identical with precious metal and hoarding was the logical
way to wealth, and 'mercantilists', who understood money as
a sign, and therefore urged that it must be 'put out to use' or
waste away. This debate enters Shakespeare's work in a wide
variety of figurative contexts, many of which are ostensibly far
removed from economic matters. In fact, Shakespeare's usages
remind us how recent, and how arbitrary, is our delimitation
of 'economic' themes. When the Pandar in *Pericles* laments
that 'our credit comes not in like the commodity, nor the
commodity wages not with the danger' (4.2.28–9), the
layers of punning and *double entendre* are so thick that the
economic and sexual significances interpenetrate, and must be
understood together or not at all.

II

The conceptual connection between usury and barren, or 'concupiscent', sexuality was firmly established in seventeenth-century England. Usury took money, which was naturally barren, and made it fruitful. Concupiscence took sex, which is naturally fruitful, and perverted it to the unnatural end of barren pleasure. Shakespeare often deploys this argument ironically, as a deceitful seducer's trick. In 'Venus and Adonis', the goddess of love tempts the beautiful youth with the injunction 'Be prodigal' (755). She draws an analogy between failure to use sexuality and failure to practise financial usury: 'Foul cank'ring rust the hidden treasure frets, / But gold that's put to use more gold begets' (767–8). Adonis' reply shifts the discussion onto the level of language. He suggests that Venus' choice of financial metaphor reveals the truth about her sexuality: 'I hate not love, but your device [i.e. metaphor] in love / That lends embracements unto every stranger. / You do it for increase' (789–91). The 'increase' he has in mind is financial, not the natural propagation of children. As Kurt Heinzelman comments:

> Venus's "device in Love" is her monetary metaphor, her economic reasoning. In hinting that her sexuality is self-interested and usurious – a commercial "increase" – Adonis identifies Venus in her Venetian aspect as a love merchant, "lend[ing] embracements to every stranger."
>
> (309n.8)

Even when employed as a straightforward synonym for sex, the verb 'to use' suggests unnatural, or non-procreative behaviour. In *Pericles*, Gower finds it appropriate to describe the incestuous relations between Antiochus and his daughter: 'But custom what they did begin / Was with long use account'd no sin' (*Prologue* 29–30). When the Bawd in the same play inquires 'will you use him kindly?' (4.5.55–6), she makes a joke based on the contrast between the unnatural pleasure implied by 'use' and the association of 'kind' with 'natural'. In *All's Well That Ends Well*, Parolles discusses Helena's virginity in terms that anticipate political economy's theory of trade. The humour arises from the contrast between his economically sound mercantilist advice and conventional sexual morality: 'Keep it not; you cannot choose but lose by't. Out with't! Within the year it will make itself two, which is a goodly increase, and the principal itself not much the worse. Away with't!' (1.1.146–50). Like food or wine (and, as many were beginning to argue, like money), a human body decays with time. If its productive value is to be realized, virginity must not be hoarded. As Parolles explains: ''Tis a commodity will lose the gloss with lying; the longer kept, the less worth. Off with't while 'tis vendible' (1.1.154–6).

The opening procreation sequence of the *Sonnets* depends on the same conceit. At first, the speaker urges his young male lover to reproduce in a natural fashion, by procreating with a woman. The witty paradox is that he does so in a vocabulary drawn from usury, which was conventionally figured as an unnatural form of reproduction. The first twenty poems contend that, as the couplet of number 4 puts it, 'Thy unused beauty must be tombed with thee, / Which used, lives th'executor to be' (13–14). The speaker reproaches his lover for his failure to 'lend' his beauty to others, calling him a 'profitless usurer' who, although possessed of a great fortune, fails to profit by it, due to his insistence on hoarding. This was a common seducer's line, employed by many contemporary villains. Milton's Comus also tells his intended victim that 'Beauty is nature's coin, must not be hoarded / But must be current' (739–40). In the Sonnets though, it is deployed by an older man for the purpose of convincing a younger man to have sexual intercourse with a woman. Nor is this the only time Shakespeare uses it in this context. In *Romeo and Juliet*, Friar Laurence reproaches Romeo in identical terms: 'Fie, fie, thou sham'st thy shape, thy love, thy wit, / Which, like a usurer, abound'st in all, / And usest none in that true use

indeed / Which should bedeck thy shape, thy love, thy wit'
(3.3.122–5).

The narrative of the *Sonnets* is driven by the conventional
analogy – or rather the homology – between usury and
'sodomy', which meant any form of non-reproductive or
'concupiscent' sexuality. In Sonnet 4, the speaker warns his
young male lover that his beauty does not belong to him. It
is merely a loan from nature: 'Nature's bequest gives nothing,
but doth lend, / And being frank, she lends to those are
free' (3–4). 'Frank' and 'free' both mean 'generous', so that
the youth is urged to match nature's bounty by lending out
his beauty. But 'free' also means 'at liberty', and connotes
freedom from usury, which is associated with bondage,
compulsion and literal imprisonment. This sense is included
in the lament of *Timon*'s Steward about his master's tendency
to expect disinterested generosity from his friends. Such a
'thought is bounty's foe; / Being free itself, it thinks all others
so' (2.2.229–30).

As the sonnet sequence continues, we find that the speaker
does not expect the youth to lend himself *gratis*. Sonnet 6
alludes to the 10 per cent maximum legal rate of interest
when the speaker tells the youth: 'That use is not forbidden
usury / Which happies those that pay the willing loan; / That's
for thyself to breed another thee, / Or ten times happier, be it
ten for one' (5–8). Here the speaker envisages himself in the
role of usurer, loaning his lover out to a woman. He imagines
that he can retain ownership of his lover's affections, while
the female reaps a usurious profit in the form of children.
As he puts it in Sonnet 20: 'Mine be thy love, and thy love's
use their treasure' (14).[8] Just as in *The Merchant of Venice*,
Shakespeare appears to construct a coherent defence of usury
here. Indeed, *Measure for Measure*'s Duke Vincentio employs
a similar argument to convince Angelo that his inward virtues
must be expressed in external action: '... nature never lends /
The smallest scruple of her excellence / But, like a thrifty
goddess, she determines / Herself the glory of a creditor, / Both
thanks and use' (1.1.36–40).

The Duke claims that we must 'use' our virtues, meaning that they must be externalized to truly exist; otherwise: 'twere all alike / As if we had them not' (1.1.34–5). This is the relational, relativist morality that arises along with exchange-value, as when Aufidius acknowledges in *Coriolanus* that 'our virtues / Lie in th'interpretation of the time' (4.7.49–50). In *Measure for Measure*, however, the Duke's plans go seriously awry, and so does the scheme of the *Sonnets*' narrator. He plots to loan his beloved to a woman, but by Sonnet 134 the tables have been turned. The youth's female lover has taken possession of him, and the speaker now merely borrows what he once loaned out to her. Thus he reproaches his rival: 'Thou usurer, that put'st forth all to use, / And sue a friend, came debtor for my sake: / So him I lose through my unkind abuse' (10–12). The speaker, who originally aspired to play the usurer, finds out that he has been robbed of that role, and with it his proprietorial right over the young man.

Timon of Athens suffers from a similar misunderstanding of what it is to 'use' money. He reassures his Steward that, since he has many friends, he will have no difficulty finding cash. He is convinced that, if he so wished: 'Men and men's fortunes could I frankly use / As I can bid thee speak.' (2.2.183–4). Once again, the word 'frankly' here means 'freely'. Timon is claiming that his friends will gladly allow him to 'use' their money, in the sense that they will put it at his disposal. Unbeknown to him however, the meaning of the word 'use' has shifted since he last had cause to encounter it. His supposed friends will indeed allow him to 'use' their money, but only in the sense that he can borrow it at interest – and only then if he proves credit-worthy. Timon's tragedy is that he expects his friends to evaluate him in qualitative terms, as an individual, but in keeping with the *Zeitgeist*, they actually evaluate him in quantitative terms, as a bad credit risk.

By the fourth act, rejected by his friends and exiled outside the city walls, Timon has accumulated enough bitter experience to instruct Apemantus in the nature of gold. The philosopher comments, with unwonted naivete, that 'Here is no use for gold' (4.3.293). Timon corrects him, pointing out that unminted gold is not yet exchange-value. It is not yet 'hired', and so it remains in its natural, subordinate place: 'The best and truest; / For here it sleeps, and does no hired harm' (4.3.294–5). Much of Shakespeare's meaning is lost if, as many editors still do, we neglect the 'restricted' economic significance of the word 'use'. In his footnote to the Pandar's remark in *Pericles*: 'If there be not a conscience to be us'd in every trade, we shall never prosper' (4.2.11–12), Roger Warren comments: 'I don't under- stand why some editors attack the Pander's "twisted" idea of *conscience* here: why is it wrong to give value for money?'[9] But surely what is objectionable is the idea that conscience can be commodified, alienated, loaned out or, in other words, 'used' in the restricted, financial sense of the word.

The same delicate ambiguity informs the king's criticism of the Dauphin in *Henry V*: 'he comes o'er us with our wilder days, / Not measuring what use we made of them' (1.2.268–9). Unknown to the Frenchman, Prince Hal has 'used' his apparently wasted youth, in the sense that he has invested it wisely, and is now reaping the interest in the form of experience and wisdom which will enable him, as he says in *I Henry IV,* to 'pay the debt I never promised' (1.2.204). Coriolanus draws on the same sense of 'use' as productive investment when he advises Aufidius to 'so use it / That my revengeful services may prove / As benefits to thee' (4.5.91–1). This recalls the point made by Xenophon's Socrates, which we discussed in Chapter 1: even a man's enemies can be counted among his wealth, provided he knows how to use them to his own advantage. There is another financial pun in 'prove', which refers to the process by which gold was evaluated on the touchstone. Shakespeare often returns to this image, as when the Shepherd in *The Winter's Tale* tells his son: 'This is fairy gold, boy, and 'twill prove so' (3.3.119).

In *Measure for Measure,* Escalus asks the disguised Duke where he comes from. He replies: 'Not of this country, though my chance is now / To use it for my time' (3.2.211–12). The

Duke means that he will 'use' his country to elicit information, but he also refers to his disguise as a merchant, under which he can be presumed to 'use it' in the financial sense. Expressed through this extended financial conceit, the ideas of debt and redemption motivate erotic and political behaviour alike. In *1 Henry IV* Hotspur warns against 'this proud King, who studies day and night / To answer all the debt he owes to you, / Even with the bloody payment of your deaths' (1.3.181–3). Worcester agrees that 'The king will always think him in our debt, / And think we think ourselves unsatisfy'd / Till he hath found a time to pay us home' (1.3.280–3). In spite of Brutus' warning that Coriolanus 'intends to use the people' (2.2.155), Volumnia is forced to remind her son about the potential advantages of psychological usury: 'I have a heart as little apt as yours, / But yet a brain that leads my use of anger / To better vantage' (3.2.29–31).

The words 'vantage' and 'advantage' were regularly applied to money-lending, as when Shylock observes that Antonio never lends 'upon advantage', or Richard III imagines his mother's tears: 'Advantaging their loan with interest / Of ten times double gain of happiness' (4.4.323–4). Volumnia urges Coriolanus to follow her example and 'use' his anger to his 'vantage', but according to the king in *Henry V*, his former follower Scroop has required no such instruction. The king accuses him as one who 'knewst the very bottom of my soul, / That almost might'st have coined me into gold / Would'st thou have practiced on me for thy use?' (2.2.97–9). Henry declares that Scroop's knowledge of his innermost essence, 'the very bottom of my soul', nearly enabled him to 'coin me into gold', to function as a royal surrogate, an efficacious image of the king. He archly inquires whether Scroop planned to exploit this ability for his own advantage, or 'use'.

When Hamlet remarks that 'use almost can change the stamp of nature' (3.4.170), he alludes to usury's unnatural power to pervert things away from their essences. However, the phrase 'stamp of nature' already contains an oxymoron, since it compares nature to the artificial 'stamp' that bestows value on a coin. As Stephen Deng has recently noted, James I used stamped gold coins in his magical cure for scrofula, 'the King's evil'. Building on Shakespeare's mention of this practice in *Macbeth*, Deng cites this ritual as evidence for the capacity of 'objects to move in and out of the commodity phase across their life cycles' (7). James was using an originally financial object in a non-financial manner, thus suggesting that the meaning of objects varies with cultural context. But James' fetishistic deployment of money is in perfect accordance with its economic function. Money was perceived as quite literally magic, and this was as true of its financial as its medicinal properties. The people of early modern England were watching money come alive, and Renaissance poetry and drama is packed with its personifications. George Herbert addresses money directly in 'Avarice':

> thou hast got the face of man; for we
> Have with our stamp and seal transferr'd our right:
> Thou art the man, and man but drosse to thee.
> Man calleth thee his wealth, who made thee rich ...
>
> (10–13)

Shakespeare often employs such role reversals of subject and object to heighten moments of dramatic tension. In *2 Henry IV* Prince Henry describes how:

> I spake unto this crown as having sense,
> And thus upbraided it: "The care on thee depending
> Hath fed upon the body of my father;
> Therefore thou best of gold art worst of gold.
> Other, less fine in carat, is more precious,
> Preserving life in medicine potable ...
>
> (4.3.157–62)

Henry addresses the crown as if it were alive. He is consciously indulging in fetishism: he subjectifies an object to deplore its incitement of ambition in other subjects. In doing this he has recourse to two different notions of what is 'precious'. In financial terms, the gold of which the crown is made is extremely valuable. But Henry still prefers to think of gold in alchemical terms, which celebrate the natural, useful properties of the metal rather than its symbolic significance and which, in his wistful disillusion, Henry judges 'more precious' than exchange-value. By the standards of Shakespeare's England, he thus signals his obsolescent ideology and unfitness to rule. The future belonged to finance.

III

The people of early modern England understood that exchange-value, or money, was a sign rather than a thing. But they also understood that this sign had attained an autonomous, independent power. In *The Taming of the Shrew,* Hortensio declares Katherine is so 'shrewd' (1.2.89) that 'I would not wed her for a mine of gold' (1.2.91). But Petruchio answers in the spirit of the age, by suggesting that gold has the power to alter character: 'Thou knowst not gold's effect' (1.2.75). To the extent that it is allowed to reproduce independently, in the manner of a living creature, money becomes a performative or efficacious sign, as opposed to a referential one. It achieves the same kind of practical power that Coriolanus attributes to verbal signs: 'oft, / When blows have made me stay, I fled from words' (2.2.71–2). In *The Merchant of Venice,* Antonio conveys this sense of financial value as an active agent when he vows to 'Try what my credit can in Venice do' (1.1.180).

The ethical and pragmatic implications of semiotics had been established in the liturgical debates that had roiled Europe since the start of the sixteenth century. The Sacramental controversies, and especially the disputes over the Eucharist, concentrated on the ethics of representation. One of the most widely influential theologians in Shakespeare's Britain was John Calvin, whose *Institutes of the Christian Religion* provided the doctrinal basis of the Church of Scotland and various Puritan sects. Calvin accused Catholics of taking Christ's words at the Last Supper – 'this is my body'– at an absurdly literalistic level. To account for the miraculous Mass, they had developed the irrational theory of transubstantiation, whereby the bread's essence could be transformed while its appearance remained the same. In response, Calvin pointed out that Christ generally spoke in extended metaphors or parables. He insisted that Christ had been speaking figuratively at the Last Supper, and had meant: 'This represents my body'.

Crucially however, Calvin denied that the metaphorical status of Christ's words was any bar to their efficacy. The Sacrament was objectively efficacious, even though it was merely a sign of His flesh, not the substance. Calvin's position on the Eucharist thus acknowledged and assimilated the newly independent, performative power of representation. For Calvin, of course, the efficacy of signs was strictly limited to the Sacraments, which were unique points of contact between the divine and the human. To attribute autonomous agency to man-made signs was idolatry. An idolatrous response to an image regards it as a fetishistic end in itself, not as a sign pointing to an ulterior referent. Such idolatry revealed magical thinking, for magic is the attempt to alter the objective condition of the world by the manipulation of images. The people of Renaissance and Reformation Europe believed that both idolatry and magic were increasingly widespread and dangerous forces, palpably active in the contemporary world, and directly inspired by Satan. The iconoclasm of the Protestant Reformation, and the ferocity of the great European witch hunts, both reflected a visceral fear of autonomous representation.

Idolatry and magic share one definitive characteristic: they misconstrue the nature of representation, by mistaking the sign for the referent. In the Christian tradition, furthermore, idolatry and magic are both associated with slavery, because they are forms of hermeneutic literalism. The main source of the link between literalism and servility is Paul's Epistle to the Galatians:

> For it is written, that Abraham had two sons, the one by a bondmaid, the other by a freewoman.
>
> But he who was of the bondwoman was born after the flesh; but he of the freewoman was by promise.
>
> Which things are an allegory: for these are the two covenants; the one from the mount Sinai, which gendereth to bondage, which is Agar.
>
> For this Agar is mount Sinai in Arabia, and answereth to Jerusalem which now is, and is in bondage with her children.
>
> (4.22–5)

According to the complex pattern of imagery developed by Christian typology, the Jews erred by taking the story of Abraham and Sarah literally. Paul insists that Old Testament story must be read as an 'allegory' prefiguring the liberation from the law available to believers in Christ. It must not be read according to the objectified 'flesh', but according to the figurative 'spirit'. This reading was ratified extensively in Patristic commentary, and summarized in Augustine's *Of Christian Doctrine:* 'there is a miserable servitude of the spirit in this habit of taking signs for things'.[10] In the economic context of Renaissance England it inevitably reinforced the association of Jews with usury, which was assumed to result from a literalistic reading of the Deuteronomic injunction to lend to 'strangers' but not to 'brothers'. Christian commentators rejected the tribal interpretation of this verse, arguing that since all men are figuratively brothers, the Deuteronomic prohibition amounts to an absolute ban on interest.

The Hellenic tradition also describes exchange-value as legalistic, ascribing it to the sphere of *nomos,* which meant 'law' as well as 'custom'. Aristotle explained that money 'has become by convention a sort of representative of demand, and this is why it has the name "money" [*nomisma*] – because it exists not by nature but by law [*nomos*]'. George Herbert exploits this linkage between usury, legalism and literalism in his characterization of 'The Jews': 'Who by not keeping once, became a debtor; / And now by keeping lose the letter' (5–6). According to Herbert's logic, which was typical in Renaissance England, the very literalism of 'the Jews' reveals their ignorance, and enslaves them in a manner analogous to the usury they themselves practise. From this perspective, Judaism, usury, slavery, literalism and legalism were all forms of illegitimate objectification. This reasoning drives the plot of *The Merchant of Venice*. The letter of the law 'killeth' according to Paul, and this explains Shylock's preoccupation with death and the flesh. As we have seen, slavery was typically described as a living death, and Shylock himself notes the parallel between usury and slavery in his stunningly incisive indictment of the court:

> You have among you many a purchased slave,
> Which (like your asses, and your dogs and mules)
> You use in abject and in slavish parts,
> Because you bought them, -- shall I say to you,
> Let them be free, marry them to your heirs?
> Why sweat they under burthens? let their beds
> Be made as soft as yours, and let their palates
> Be season'd with such viands? You will answer
> 'The slaves are ours,' -- so do I answer you:
> The pound of flesh which I demand of him,
> Is dearly bought, 'tis mine and I will have it ...

(4.1.90–100)

Like the slave-owner, the usurer makes other human beings his property by his possession of exchange-value, and Shylock claims that this renders the two kinds of ownership legally and morally equivalent. Many critics have found his argument convincing, and it is often suggested that Portia's question in the courtroom – 'Which is the merchant here, and which the Jew?' (4.1.172) – indicates a fundamental kinship between Antonio and Shylock. After all, they both live by trade. For Shakespeare however, the salient point is that Shylock trades in the commodity of money, which is the symbolic equivalent of human life. He makes the medium of exchange into an object of exchange, thus both facilitating and personifying the cultural transition from economics to chrematistics. As Simon Critchley and Tom McCarthy argue:

> If *The Merchant of Venice* is one large economic system, then its central drama is the conflict between two coexisting yet contradictory conceptions of economy itself. We might call these the *Antonian* and the *Shylockean,* and we would like these two meanings of economy to overlay... a distinction inherited from Aristotle between *oikonomia* and *techne chrematisike,* between natural economy and the art of money-making. Crudely stated, this is the distinction between the good, Antonian natural economy of the *oikos* and the bad, Shylockean artificial economy that arises when money (*to khrema*) appears on the scene.[11]

Shylock's faith in the law, his absurd literalism, and his insistence on his 'bond' are construed as inseparable from his usurious approach to life in general. Above all, as he himself points out, Shylock's usury aligns him with slave-owners, who also profit from the commodified exchange of human beings. As Amanda Bailey remarks: 'The connection Shylock forges between the defaulted debtor and the slave has rhetorical force and speaks to an association alive and well for those watching Shakespeare's play'.[12] She cites examples including Henry Wilkinson's *Debt Book:* 'It is a servile thing to be indebted ... By debt a man's states and person are in a manner mancipated to the lender' (18). The creditor held power over the body of defaulting debtor, who he could and frequently did consign to prison, and this strengthened the association between usury and slavery. This pattern of association is especially clear in *The Merchant of Venice*, but along with similar relations of analogy and homology, it subtly informs the rest of Shakespeare's *oeuvre* as well.

10

'Lear's shadow': Identity, Property and Possession

I

During Shakespeare's lifetime, and in no small part through his efforts, the English language mutated to accommodate the requirements of the new market economy. Stephen Greenblatt asserts that in Shakespeare 'status relations ... are being transformed before our eyes into property relations'.[1] Birth and accomplishment, the traditional sources of natural worth, were diminishing in social significance compared to the strange, unnaturally fertile form of wealth known as 'money'. Responding to the concomitant displacement of use-value by exchange-value, many words shifted from a qualitative to a quantitative sense. The word 'property' entered the English language in the fourteenth century, when it meant 'quality'.[2] A 'property' of something was a part of its nature, one of its qualities. In the seventeenth century, however, the word was used more and more in the sense of 'possession'. It stopped being something one was, part of one's essence, and mutated into something one owned.

We have seen that, for Aristotle, a slave was his master's 'property' in the sense that he belonged to him, but also in the sense that the slave was a part of the master's whole: an attribute belonging to him, one of his qualities. As Aristotle explains, 'the slave is a part of the master, a living but separated part of his bodily frame'. As we should use our bodies to serve the purposes of our souls, and as our appetite is properly a servant to our reason, so the *telos* of the slave is not his own purpose but that of his master, to which end he is merely a means:

> The master is only the master of the slave; he does not belong to him, whereas the slave is not only the slave of his master, but wholly belongs to him. Hence we see what is the nature and office of a slave; he who is by nature not his own but another's man, is by nature a slave; and he may be said to be another's man who, being a human being, is also a possession. And a possession may be defined as an instrument of action, separable from the possessor.[3]

To be 'by nature a slave' is to be a 'possession' and to be a possession is to be the instrument of an alien purpose. This definition of a slave has nothing to do with legal ownership, for Aristotle famously differentiates between 'legal' and 'natural' slaves. The category of *legal* slave refers to people who are actually, empirically enslaved. The category of *natural* slave refers to the objective characteristics of slavery: the slave *qua* slave. Because he does not follow the proper end of a human being, and because a human being is defined by his or her proper end, the slave *qua* slave is not fully human. He is rather a 'possession' and a 'property' of his master, and so his identity is subsumed within his master's. This loss of identity entails the loss of *telos*, and thus the slave *qua* slave does not employ his rational faculties: 'he who can be, and therefore is, another's and he who participates in rational principle enough to apprehend, but not to have, such a principle, is a slave by nature' (7).

As the process of reification moves inward, the human subject experiences itself as a property, a thing. The subject is no longer an end in itself; it becomes a means to the external end of earning money. In a system of virtually universal wage labour, everybody's activity becomes a thing that they own and must sell by the hour. As Marx put it in *Capital*: 'The capitalist epoch is therefore characterized by the fact that labor-power, in the eyes of the worker himself, takes on the form of a commodity which is his property' (1976, 274n.4). Two centuries earlier John Locke made a similar point: 'every man has a "property" in his own "person"... The "labour" of his own body and the "work" of his own hands, we may say, are properly his'.[4] Even earlier, Hobbes had outlined the theory that C. B. Macpherson calls 'possessive individualism' with its 'conception of the individual as essentially the proprietor of his own person or capacities'. Hobbes observed that '[a] man's Labour also, is a commodity exchangeable for benefit, as well as any other thing'.[5] Exchange-value represents labor-power in symbolic form so that '[t]he Value, or Worth of a man is, as of all other things, the Price; that is to say, so much as would be given for the use of his Power' (151). A human being's 'power' can be used by somebody else if it is represented in the form of money. Money is transferable power, congealed human activity, the force of which can be stored and released because it has been encapsulated in symbolic form. In symbolic form, human activity can become transferable property.

Once something is conceived as a 'property', it becomes a part of a greater whole. It loses its independent identity and belongs to something else. Its nature is defined by its relation to something other than itself, just as the slave takes his identity from his relation to the master. In the ancient world the *oikos,* including its human members, was an inseparable part of its owner's identity. This idea extended into the feudal household, which explains why Lear experiences the loss of his feudal retainers as the dissolution of his personal identity. 'Who is it that can tell me who I am?' (1.4.221) exclaims the former king, only to receive the Fool's reply: 'Lear's shadow' (1.4.222). To be property was to be deprived of identity. In *The Merry Wives of Windsor,* Fenton tells Anne Page that her father, knowing he needs her money to pay his debts, has declared "tis a thing impossible / I should love thee, but as a property'. (3.4.9–10) When one person is another's 'property', when one person 'belongs to' another, the identity of the owned is assimilated into the identity of the owner. A slave is his master's property in the same way that, as Corin says in *As You Like It,* 'the property of rain is to wet and fire to burn' (3.2.25). Wetness is a 'property' of rain, thus wetness is part of rain's identity: wetness belongs to rain. This is the sense in which, according to Aristotle and Xenophon, a slave is the 'property' of his master.

The ancient conception of slavery was applied to wage labour throughout the early modern period, when hundreds of thousands of Englishmen and women chose to become beggars rather than sell themselves in this way. People were also reluctant to conceive of their natural environment – or 'land', in the reified form of expression – as something that could be bought and sold with money. The proprietorial rights acquired by money were still shockingly new in Shakespeare's day. They flew in the face of centuries-old tradition. Shakespeare was born into a society as yet unfamiliar and uncomfortable with the idea that money alone bestowed rights of possession, particularly over land or labour. As recently as 1525 the Ploughman, a sturdy peasant character in John Rastell's 'Of Gentylnes and Nobylyte', took it as a matter of course that

> All possessions began furst of tyranny
> For when people began furst to encrese
> Some gafe them self all to Idylnes
> And wold not labour but take by vyolence
> That other men gat by labour & dylygence
> Than they that labouryd were fayne to gyfe
> Them {per}t of theyr getting{is} in peas of lyfe
> Or ell{is} for theyr landis money a porcyon
> So possessyons began by extorcyon[6]

The Ploughman does not distinguish between theft 'by vyolence' and giving 'for theyr landis money a porcyon'. Both are forms of 'extorcyon', and both are illegitimate. As Diana Wood explains, medieval law recognized two forms of ownership, '*dominium directum,* the lord's ultimate legal ownership of the land, and *dominium utilis,* the dominion of use of the tenant, which involved the right to "use, have, and enjoy"'.[7] The user of the land had legal rights on a par with its owner:

> Feudal tenure has been described as the "antithesis of private ownership." A tenant could not sell his holding without the consent of his lord, he could not leave it by will, nor did his family have any legal right to succeed to it. All that he had was "seisin," or possession. The lord had lordship, or dominion, but unless he was the king, he was himself a tenant.
>
> (35)

The lord's dominion was in practice reduced to no more than the right to exact dues. It was a purely financial right; the right to use the land belonged to the tenant. Shakespeare employs this distinction in *Timon of Athens,* when the Poet remarks that Timon's 'large fortune... / Subdues and properties to his love and tendance / All sorts of hearts' (1.1.56–9). The hearts are not Timon's property in the sense of *dominium directum,* he does not own them. They are his property in the sense of *dominium utilis,* he enjoys their 'tendance' and is free to use them as he will. But the play records the dissolution of this kind of property. The 'enclosure' of the 'commons' involved the abolition or disregard of *dominium utilis* and, as Timon soon discovers, the new chrematistic order acknowledged only the right of money to bestow dominion.

II

David Armitage's comprehensive study of Shakespeare's treatment of 'property' concludes: 'A brief survey of the word "property" and its cognates in Shakespeare's works yields two consistent clusters of meaning: anything that is one's own and something (or somebody) that can be used or instrumentalized'.[8] This is an instructive observation, which reminds us that in early modern England the term 'property' did not designate ownership alone, but also exploitation. When *Twelfth Night*'s Malvolio complains, 'They have here propertied me' (4.2.91), he does not mean that anyone has taken ownership of him, he means that he has been deprived of his volition, treated as a thing: reified. When Julius Caesar says of Lepidus: 'Do not talk of him / But as a property' (4.1.39–40), he does not mean that he owns him legally. Lepidus is a natural slave, not a legal one. Caesar means that Lepidus can be made to serve ends other than his own. Since Lepidus is a 'barren-spirited fellow' (4.1.36), he is unfit to pursue the proper end of a human being, which is the cultivation of the soul. Just as the end of the body is to serve the soul, and just as the purpose of a slave is to serve his master, so Lepidus' natural role is to serve the ends of someone other than himself: 'His corporal motion governed by my spirit' (4.1.33), as Caesar puts it.

Lepidus is thus best regarded not as an independent essence in himself, but as an attribute, a capacity, a 'property' belonging to Caesar. Unlike Caesar, whose identity is essential, Lepidus' identity is relational. He is defined by his relation to Caesar, just as a slave's identity is defined in relation to his master. Shakespeare depicts a world in the process of abandoning essentialism in favour of a relational conception of identity. He understands that this is also a shift from an aristocratic to a bourgeois class perceptive. In *King John* the Dauphin declares: 'I am too high-born to be propertied, / To be a secondary at control, / Or useful serving-man and instrument / To any sovereign state throughout the world' (5.2.79–82). As a natural nobleman, he refuses to be 'used' by any external power, even the power of the state. He assumes that to be treated as use-value by an alien force implies servility. He recognizes no ends higher than his own, and therefore he can never be 'propertied'.

The taint carried by the word 'property' when applied to human beings even carries over into its ostensibly positive cognates. In *Othello* we hear that 'Cassio's a proper man' (1.3.390), and also that 'Lodovico is a proper man' (4.3.34), but to judge by the objects of the appellation it seems to mean 'adequate' at best. In *King Lear*, Kent attempts to reassure Gloucester about the consequences of his youthful lust: 'I cannot wish the fault undone, the issue of it being so proper' (1.1.16–17). But since the illegitimate son so described is plotting the death of his father, the word 'proper' here suggests the false appearance of propriety. The 'proper false' (2.2.29), as *Twelfth Night*'s Viola puts it, is a seducer, and seducers were consistently characterized as taking ownership of their victims. To 'enjoy' or to 'possess' somebody was to have sex with them. When it was first used in English in the fourteenth century, the verb 'to possess' meant to 'occupy' or 'reside in'. It acquired two new significances in the sixteenth century: 'to own as property' and, 'to be mastered by a demon'. The idea of possession necessarily implies alienation. A possession belongs to its owner alone. It is alienated from everyone else and it evidently seemed natural to Shakespeare to employ the same word to describe being controlled by an external, supernatural influence.

Shakespeare's usages of 'possession' convey a typically subtle meditation on its connotations. When *Much Ado about Nothing*'s Benedick suggests that a lady is 'possessed with a fury' (1.1.183), or when *2 Henry VI*'s Lord Say wonders whether Cade is 'possessed with devilish spirits' (4.7.70), the demonic sense is clearly intended. Elsewhere however, the word merely means an overwhelmingly strong impulse, as when *Measure for Measure*'s Vincentio responds to frantic knocking at the door by reflecting: 'That spirit's possessed with haste' (4.2.88). Shakespeare also uses the word to mean 'make aware of', or 'inform'. 'Is the senate possessed of this?' (2.1.131) asks Menenius in *Coriolanus*. 'Possess us, possess us, tell us something of him' (2.3.136–7) exclaims Sir Toby in *Twelfth Night*. When about to introduce Diomede to Cressida, Troilus promises to 'possess thee what she is' (4.4.111), which suggests that he will both tell him of her nature and bestow her on him as a gift. Shakespeare also uses the word to designate ownership in the straightforward sense, as when the parricidal son in *3 Henry VI* wonders if his victim is 'possessed with some store of crowns' (2.5.57). Property ownership and demonic possession are suggested simultaneously when Hamlet laments the world's decline: 'things rank and gross in nature / Possess it merely' (1.2.136–7). In several instances, knowledge and ownership are completely indistinguishable, as when *Titus Andronicus*'s Bassanius declares that he is 'possessed of that is mine' (1.1.413), or *The Merchant of Venice*'s Antonio asks 'is he yet possess'd / How much you would?' (1.3.62–3).

Through such concentrated clusters of ambiguity, Shakespeare focuses on the nexus of financial and psychological processes. The independence of financial value from precious metals was teaching English people that a power could be simultaneously subjective and objective. How could something be both a 'property' belonging to somebody, and a 'possession' in the sense of an alien force that invaded the human mind from outside? Non-metallic, non-material financial value was precisely such a force. It had no existence outside the human mind, yet it was beyond the control of any human mind, and in fact frequently seemed to control them. In short, when it first achieved practical autonomy from any physical incarnation, financial value appeared to be a supernatural, magical power.

Anthropologists report similar reactions to the introduction of a money economy throughout the postcolonial world today.[9] Societies suddenly exposed to market forces tend to respond with witch hunts. In money-based economies people achieve power and influence by mysterious, invisible, non-traditional means, often attracting suspicion and resentment in the process. This is happening in much of today's postcolonial world, and it also took place in Shakespeare's England. The period's literature leaves no doubt about the centrality of witchcraft to the concerns of ordinary people, or the intimate relations they perceived between money and magic. In Dekker, Ford and Rowley's *The Witch of Edmonton,* Elizabeth Sawyer is accused of being a witch. 'A witch!' she replies, 'who is not?' There are outwardly respectable people who:

> by enchantments can whole lordships change
> To trunks of rich attire, turn ploughs and teams
> To Flanders mares and coaches, and huge trains
> Of servitors to a French butterfly.
> Have you not city-witches who can turn
> Their husband's wares, whole standing shops of wares,
> To sumptuous tables, gardens of stolen sin;
> In one year wasting what scarce twenty win?
> Are not these witches?

> (4.1.111–19)

Most of Shakespeare's contemporaries would have answered with a resounding affirmative. They frequently observed that, like magic, sexual attraction worked by exploiting the power of performative appearances. An attractive body exerts an irrational influence on susceptible viewers, and this force was seen as analogous to the power of semiotic representation. In *Troilus and Cressida,* Ulysses scolds the eponymous heroine: 'Fie, fie upon her! / There's language in her eye, her cheek, her lip, / Nay, her foot speaks' (4.5.55–7). This conceit of the speaking body takes a grotesque form when Titus Andronicus vows to Lavinia, after her tongue and hands have been cut off: 'Thou shalt not sigh, nor hold thy stumps to heaven, / Nor wink, nor nod, nor kneel, nor make a sign, / But I of these will wrest an alphabet / And by still practice learn to know thy meaning' (3.2.42–5). Although Rosalind claims to be 'a magician' in *As You Like It,* David Schalkwyk correctly notes that 'The beneficial "magic" that Rosalind claims to possess at the end of the play is no more than the magic of the performative – the transformative magic of words'.[10] Sexual, verbal, financial and magical power were conceptually connected because they all worked through efficacious appearances. Much sixteenth- and seventeenth-century literature evinces the kind of popular fears expressed by Antipholus in *The Comedy of Errors*:

> Upon my life, by some device or other
> The villain is o'erraught of all my money.
> They say this town is full of cozenage,
> As nimble jugglers that deceive the eye,
> Dark-working sorcerers that change the mind,
> Soul-killing witches that deform the body,
> Disguised cheaters, prating mountebanks,
> And many suchlike liberties of sin ...

> (1.2.95–102)

Some of Shakespeare's references to magic provide ammunition for the 'charity denied' theory of witchcraft, which views it as a weapon used by the desperate and dispossessed to revenge their marginalization. Having been beaten by Achilles in *Troilus and Cressida,* Thersites – the spokesman of the morally and socially base – expresses his *ressentiment:* 'Would it were otherwise – that I could beat him whilst he railed at me. 'Sfoot, I'll learn to conjure and raise devils but I'll see some issue of my spiteful execrations.' (2.3.4–7). In *1 Henry IV* the rebel Glendower is a 'great magician' (1.3.82), and in *2 Henry VI* Buckingham cautions the king that he has discovered 'A sort of naughty persons' (2.1.158) who:

> Have practiced dangerously against your state,
> Dealing with witches and with conjurers,
> Whom we have apprehended in the fact,
> Raising up wicked spirits from underground,
> Demanding of King Henry's life and death ...

> (2.1.162–6)

James I was highly receptive to such warnings, having convinced himself that he had been the victim of a witches' conspiracy while king of Scotland. In reaction, James had composed *Daemonologie*, a learned study of witchcraft, to arm himself against any further supernatural assaults. Shakespeare appealed directly to the royal author's preoccupation in *Macbeth*, of course, but he also laced many of his other works with references to witchcraft and magic. Magic is generally characterized as a species of performative representation, and the signs, rituals and incantations of witchcraft are compared to the semiotic ambiguities of language. Thus Macbeth is deceived by 'juggling fiends ... That palter with us in a double sense' (5.8.19–20). In *2 Henry VI*, Cade responds to the news that his captive has 'a book in his pocket with red letters in't' (4.2.85) with a peremptory verdict: 'Nay, then, he is a conjuror' (4.2.86). In the same play the Cardinal cautions against Gloucester's rhetorical trickery: 'Look to it, lords: let not his smoothing words / Bewitch your hearts' (1.1.155–6). As movements like the witch hunts and the popular iconoclasm of the Reformation testify, this was a world living in fear of the efficacious sign.

III

As a professional manipulator of words, Shakespeare was in a particularly good position to reflect upon the similarities between moral, verbal and financial value. He was far from alone, however. George Herbert commented on the analogy between metaphor and commodification in 'Jordan (II)' when he criticizes his own earlier poetry for: 'Curling with metaphors a plain intention, / Decking the sense, as if it were to sell' (5–6). Francis Bacon deplored the autonomous power of liturgical, economic and verbal signs simultaneously when he declared: 'The Idols of the Market-place are the most troublesome of all, idols which have crept into the understanding through the alliances of words and names. For men believe that their reason governs words, but it is also true that words react upon the understanding'.[11] The problem for Bacon is the misleading yet ineradicable influence of mediation on human experience, which he calls the 'idols of the marketplace' – a concept that transcends the distinctions between linguistics, economics and theology.

The convergence of ethics, semiotics and finance that fascinated Shakespeare was thus unavoidable in early modern England. It was forced upon people in the most mundane economic transactions of their daily life. The 'clipping' of coins to extract some of their *specie,* along with the great sixteenth-century inflations and debasements of the currency, helped to establish the idea that value was independent of the coins that represent it. The separation of financial value from precious metals opened upon new practical, poetic and epistemological possibilities that were both disturbing and exciting. If value was not inherent in the metal, then the symbolic 'stamp' by which the state authenticated metal and made it into legal tender could be conceived as an alternative source of value. People began to understand that money was a performative sign. As Frederick Turner explains:

> The moment that rulers began to mint and stamp coins with an inscription guaranteeing their weight, the value of those coins began to change from the barter value of the precious metal they contained to the credit value of the promise – the bond – implied in their inscription.

> (4–5)

Shakespeare's economic observations suggest his developing awareness of a disjunction between essence and appearance. Timon of Athens' faithful Steward attempts to convey the insubstantiality of financial value by comparing it to verbal signifiers: 'O my good lord, the world is but a word: / Were it all yours, to give it in a breath, / How quickly were it gone!' (2.2.157–8). The idea that a coin's true value was essential, and thus different from its appearance, informs the Duke's exclamation in *Measure for Measure*: 'O, what may man within him hide, / Though angel on the outward side!' (3.2.264–5). He refers to the possibility of hypocrisy in people, but of course an 'angel' was a golden coin, so that he also alludes to the immense potential for forgery if financial value were produced by the 'stamp' rather than inhering in the metal. That seems to have been the opinion of Shakespeare's exact contemporary and rival playwright Christopher Marlowe, who was convicted of criminal forgery, and was reputed to have claimed 'as good a right to coin as the Queen of England'. This financial image provides an appropriate vehicle by which Shakespeare reflects on human hypocrisy. Angelo employs it in *Measure for Measure*, when he warns the Duke that he may not possess the internal character to match the authority with which he is about to be invested: 'Now, good my lord, / Let there be some more test made of my metal, / Before so noble and so great a figure / Be stamp'd upon it' (1.1.46–9). Unless it corresponds to his inherent worth, Angelo realizes, the image of the Duke's authority will be an empty idol. Agamemnon uses the same metaphor in *Troilus and Cressida* when he claims that Jove sends us trials to test the 'fineness' of our 'metal' (1.3.22). The topical question of how the face of a coin related to its value had obvious potential as a source of figures by which to study human hypocrisy, and Shakespeare exploited it to the full.

The Elizabethan and Jacobean theatre was well-placed to represent and debate the new social mobility, and the consequent 'self-fashioning',[12] made possible by the market's flourishing. 'Hypocrite' is Greek for 'actor', and the theatre's many critics enjoyed extemporizing on the word's implications. The potential for profitable hypocrisy also flourished beyond the theatre, when London's goldsmiths began to issue the first forms of paper money, thus explicitly making 'credit' the object of their transactions. The possibilities for counterfeiting grew exponentially as a result, and the theme of fake money fills the period's literature. The notion that representation, be it financial, liturgical or verbal, was getting out of control is frequently mentioned. In *Twelfth Night* Feste, the self-described 'corrupter of words' (3.1.37) suggests the ambiguity of verbal meaning is a topical problem: 'To see this age! A sentence is but a chev'ril glove to a good wit – how quickly the wrong side may be turned outward!' (3.1.11–13). In his corrupt time, he laments, 'words are very rascals, since bonds disgraced them' (3.1.21). As Anne Barton's note explains, 'bonds' has a dual significance here: 'sworn statements (in place of a man's plain word or promise); (2) fetters (betokening criminality)'.[13] Although Barton does not say so, the usury debate provides a connection between these two senses. The word of a debtor is 'disgraced' when he defaults, and as a result he suffers the disgrace of literal bonds, or fetters.

This passage also suggests that words have become untrustworthy 'rascals' since, disgracefully, they are used to default on financial obligations, or 'bonds'. When Viola demands 'Thy reason, man?' (3.1.22), Feste's response indicates that autonomous representation evades the confines of rationality: 'Troth, sir, I can yield you none without words, and words are grown so false, I am loathe to prove reason with them' (3.1.23–5). The word 'prove' calls attention to the financial pun; Feste is comparing unreliable words with counterfeit coins. The word 'counterfeit' derives from the French *contre fait,* to 'make against'. It designates anything that is deliberately manufactured as an illusion. As Will Fisher has shown, in the discourse of Renaissance England, this included the 'artificial' (because 'unnatural') form of sexuality known as 'sodomy': 'Many early modern texts link counterfeit coins with counterfeit coitus'.[14] But 'counterfeit' is not necessarily pejorative. Timon of Athens seems to intend a compliment when he congratulates the Painter: 'Thou draw'st a counterfeit / Best in all Athens; th'art indeed the best; / Thou counterfeit'st most lively' (5.1.79–80). There is a palpable hint of irony in his overstatement, but in *The Merchant of Venice,* Bassanio is unequivocally overjoyed to find that his casket contains 'Fair Portia's counterfeit' (3.2.115). Apparently then, a 'counterfeit' might be any realistic representation, regardless of ethical status.

The word 'counterfeit' could also refer to representation in the abstract. In *1 Henry IV* Falstaff defines the term by contrasting it to inherent essence. He instructs Prince Hal: 'Never call a true piece of gold a counterfeit: thou art essentially mad without seeming so' (2.4.485–7). Falstaff believes that Hal's madness is his true nature but, as he eventually discovers, he is deceived. Hal is not 'essentially mad'; in fact like Hamlet's his madness is an 'antic disposition', a counterfeit. Falstaff's misreading of Hal is surprising, for he usually speaks wittily on the subject of counterfeits. Having survived the battle by playing dead he ruminates: 'Counterfeit? I lie, I am no counterfeit: to die is to be a counterfeit, for he is but the counterfeit of a man, who hath not the life of a man: but to counterfeit dying, when a man thereby liveth, is to be no counterfeit, but the true and perfect image of life indeed' (5.4.114–18). In Greek philosophy the body is the appearance to the soul's essence, so by dying Falstaff would have become a mere image or 'counterfeit' of a man. Having cheated death, however, the fat knight has retained the essence of life, and thus he can claim to be 'no counterfeit' in spite of his blatant play-acting.

In this speech, Shakespeare makes a distinction between a 'counterfeit' and a 'true and perfect image'; he is thinking of a counterfeit in the modern sense of a forgery. Unlike Falstaff, embodiments of aristocratic virtue like Coriolanus consider it humiliating to be counterfeit, though he admits it as a pragmatic necessity in the marketplace of democracy: 'I will practise the insinuating nod, and be off to them most counterfeitly; that is, sir, I will counterfeit the bewitchment of some popular man, and give it bountiful to the desirers' (2.3.97–101). To Coriolanus' noble sensibility, electioneering is both witchcraft and forgery. He must 'counterfeit' his true identity to participate in it. The uneducated masses understand only rhetoric, not reason, and they can be manipulated through images and bought for money. Coriolanus views democracy, the market-place and magic as various means to the same nefarious end of eliminating essential identity and imposing a false equivalence throughout the world.

Like most of Shakespeare's aristocrats, Coriolanus understands the danger posed by such autonomous representation to his class position, which rests upon the presumption of essential superiority. In *Antony and Cleopatra* the Egyptian queen perceives rhetorical manipulation as a similar threat to her aristocratic identity: 'He words me, girls, he words me, that I should not / Be noble to myself' (5.2.190–1). Cleopatra's sexualized imagery evokes the illicit reproduction of non-referential semiosis. Linguistic meaning looks disconcertingly fertile when employed rhetorically rather than referentially. When verbal significance is not restricted by referent, but emerges instead from the interstices of language, coining meaning out of the differences between words rather than deriving it from the words themselves, identity itself becomes relational and performative. This is a direct threat to the aristocratic ideology that derives worth from birth, blood and breeding.

Shakespeare tends to characterize counterfeiting, or 'coining', in terms of illicit sexual reproduction. In *Cymbeline*, Posthumus describes his illegitimate birth in financial terms. The man he called his father 'was I know not where / When I was stamp'd. Some coiner with his tools / Made me a counterfeit' (2.4.156–8).[15] The image recurs in *Measure for Measure*, when Angelo attacks sexual libertines who 'do coin heaven's image / In stamps that are forbid' (2.4.45–6). Gold itself becomes a coiner, as well as a begetter, in *Titus Andronicus*, when Aaron the Moor rejoices 'that this gold must coin a stratagem / Which, cunningly effected, will beget / A very excellent piece of villainy' (2.2.5–7). In *Timon of Athens* coining mixes natural with financial reproduction: 'steal but a beggar's dog / And give it Timon – why, the dog coins gold' (2.1.5–6). King Lear asserts the continuity of his essential identity when he declares 'they cannot touch me for coining. I am the king himself' (4.6.83–4). But of course he is not the king, having given away the title, any more than a coin is legal tender without an authenticating stamp. Lear's claim is not even legally accurate for, as Richard Halpern points out, 'royal abuses of coining had been notorious for some time' (258).

In fact it is not so much forgery as coining in general that Shakespeare associates with deception. When Gertrude tells Hamlet: 'This is the very coinage of your brain' (3.4.139), she means that he sees something that it not there. To 'coin' here is to create an artificial, supernatural apparition. Shakespeare reminds us that customary value and man-made significances are ethically inferior to the natural order of creation. This is also the assumption that informs Ben Jonson's caution: '*Custome* is the most certain Mistresse of Language, as the publicke stamp makes the current money. But wee must not be too frequent with the mint, every day coyning'.[16] Jonson's analogy between words and coins is echoed when Shakespeare's Henry V advises Katherine to 'take a fellow of plain and uncoined constancy, for he perforce must do thee right, because he hath not the gift to woo in other places' (5.2.152–5). The putative lover's constancy should be akin to bullion, which is conceived as authentic and natural before it has been stamped with a coin's artificial image of worth. If the lover had 'the gift to woo', he would be 'coining', letting his words flow for their outward impression, without regard for their inner worth. When *Troilus and Cressida*'s venerable Nestor refers to 'Thersites / A slave whose gall coins slander like a mint' (1.3.193), the low-born malcontent's words are likened to coins because of their lack of inherent worth. The metaphor of coining suggests a mindless reproduction of empty signs, as when Coriolanus remarks that 'my lungs / Coin words' (3.1.77–8). The kind of words that are coined are not products of reason. They do not emanate from the mind or the soul, but are linked instead to purely physical causes.

Despite his biographical investment in nascent capitalism, then, and in spite of the clear and cogent consideration he gives to pro-market arguments like Shylock's, it seems that Shakespeare never abandoned his conservative suspicion of autonomous financial value. We should be grateful to him for that suspicion. It gave him a critical perspective on the early stages of market society, and allowed him to achieve insights and sound warnings that seem more apposite than ever to the human predicament at the dawn of the third millennium.

Conclusion: Magic and Alienation

In ancient Greece and Rome, we recall, a slave was not a fully human being. A person who was a property of someone else was an attribute of his owner, an extension of an alien will, and not an autonomous actor. The salient, definitive characteristic of slavery was that the slave served the ends of his master, and this was also true of the wage labourer, or proletarian, whose condition was conceived as akin to slavery in the ancient and feudal worlds. As wage labour replaced peasant farming as English people's primary means of subsistence, people began to acquire a slave mentality. They started to think of themselves, and of each other, as pieces of property. They grew accustomed to translating their subjective activity into the objective, symbolic medium of money and, with the legitimization of usury, money began to breed, to proliferate, and to act in its own interests with an apparently autonomous volition.

In this book I've suggested that Shakespeare saw two significant psychological consequences following from the spread of wage labour and usury. First, the human subject was objectified and conceived as a thing. Shakespeare's work reflects the early stages of a tendency that would soon issue in the outright materialism of Hobbes and Rochester. Second, the media of representation were attributed practical power over the subjective mind and the objective world. This tendency lies behind the power of both magic and money, which Shakespeare analyses in close detail. The objectification of the subject and the subjectification of the object are two ways of regarding the same process. Shakespeare watched as human beings became reified and as, simultaneously, money came alive. His work documents the consequent changes in English psychology, culture and society.

At the end of his career, Shakespeare encapsulated his ideas about magic, labour and money in a prophetic parable of colonialist capitalism. *The Tempest*'s opening scene shows the ship's microcosmic society apparently threatened by the power of natural forces, in the shape of the eponymous storm. In this desperate situation, labour-power is the only source of value. The humble boatswain dismisses the aristocrats with the injunction 'You mar our labour' (1.1.13). He mocks the suggestion that his physical labour might be trumped by the power of lordly command: 'You are a counselor', he tells Gonzalo, 'if you can command these elements to silence and work the peace of the present, we will not hand a rope more' (1.1.20–3). When Sebastian arrogantly tries to interfere the boatswain dismisses him: 'Work you, then' (1.1.41). On the ship, the use-value of labour has displaced the artificial authority of words.

But we soon learn that the apparently natural storm has been artificially manufactured by Ariel, the agent of Prospero's magically efficacious spells. Prospero's 'art' consists in his ability to command the labour-power of others: Ariel's illusions, Caliban's physical work, and Ferdinand's 'wooden slavery'. Shakespeare uses these three characters to forge a distinction between slavery and wage labour. We first encounter both Ariel and Caliban as they bemoan Prospero's exploitation of their labour. 'There's wood enough within' (1.2.315) are Caliban's opening words, while Ariel first appears complaining 'Is there more toil?' (1.2.242). He describes the tasks with which Prospero loads him as 'pains' (ibid.). But Shakespeare carefully differentiates between the kind of labour performed by Ariel and that performed by Caliban, and this difference serves to assimilate alienated labour into the traditional moral economy.

Prospero's magic can turn appearance into reality, producing hallucinations that exercise objective power. His supernatural strength is irresistible, as Caliban knows: 'I must obey; his art is of such power / It would control my dam's god Setebos, / And make a vassal of him' (1.2.372–4). It gives him control of Caliban's useful labour: 'he does make our fire, / Fetch in our wood, and serves in offices / That profit us' (1.2.311–13). To Stephano and Trinculo, however, Caliban's value does not reside in his useful labour but in his 'marketable' (5.1.267) price. Shakespeare depicts the development of the chrematistic, 'popular rate' of evaluation through their plot to exhibit this 'monster' for cash. Stephano expresses the emergent form of value with his repetitive response to the new discoveries on the island, 'What things are these ... Will money buy 'em?' (5.1.265–6).[1]

While Caliban is addressed as 'earth', Ariel is an 'apparition', who embodies a non-material yet efficacious form of power. This distinction is reflected by a difference in their relations to Prospero. Caliban is a slave, but Ariel is an indentured servant. His servitude is temporary and measured by the clock, as Prospero indicates when he tells Ariel that 'The time 'twixt six and now / Must by us both be spent most preciously' (1.2.240–1). Ariel's initial reluctance reveals that his labour is alien to him, being directed towards Prospero's purposes rather than his own. But the temporary nature of his bondage transforms his attitude towards it. Prospero reminds Ariel of the distinction between permanent and temporary servitude when he recalls his subjection to the witch Sycorax: 'Thou, my slave, / As thou report'st thyself, wast then her servant' (1.2.270–1). He recalls how Sycorax commanded Ariel to perform 'earthy', material labour, but that he refused, being 'a spirit too delicate' (1.2.272). Ariel achieves practical effects by magical, symbolic means rather than through physical labour of the kind performed by Caliban.

Shakespeare continues the debate about the nature of labour through the figure of Ferdinand.[2] We have seen how sixteenth- and seventeenth-century English people identified certain types of labour as alienated on the basis of natural teleology. Labour was hostile, irksome and alien when it was directed towards an alien purpose. When directed towards its proper end, by contrast, labour served as the means of manufacturing virtue, as the Stoics had argued. Since the pursuit of virtue was the *telos* of a human being, this kind of labour could be considered an end in itself. Aristotle condemns labour performed for the purpose of making money as 'banausic', while labour that is carried out for its own sake is 'autotelic'. The former is degraded and servile, while the latter is exalted and free:

> if some activities are necessary and desirable for the sake of something else, while others are so in themselves, evidently happiness must be placed among those desirable in themselves, not among those desirable for the sake of something else; for happiness does not lack anything, but is self-sufficient. Now those activities are desirable in themselves from which nothing is sought beyond the activity.[3]

In the Aristotelian tradition, unalienated labour was directed to the fulfilment of one's own potential, identified with the rational 'activity of the soul in accordance with virtue'. In Christian Europe, the pursuit of virtue became a means to the ultimate end of salvation. The specific content of labour was irrelevant to its ethical status; labour was defined by its *telos*. For George Herbert, this was 'the elixir' that 'makes drudgery divine' (18).[4] However, this virtuous freedom faces constant threats, both external and internal. We have seen how Shakespeare often connects the force of sexual attraction to both slavery and magic, depicting erotic sympathy as an irrational appetite that threatens to usurp the reign of reason. Here, Prospero redeems sexual appetite from its magical taint by making it the product of labour, 'lest too light winning / Make the prize light' (1.2.452–3). Miranda's love is Ferdinand's wage, and the value of his 'prize' arises from his labour:

> There be some sports are painful, and their labour
> Delight in them sets off. Some kinds of baseness
> Are nobly undergone; and most poor matters
> Point to rich ends. This my mean task
> Would be as heavy to me as odious, but
> The mistress which I serve quickens what's dead,
> And makes my labours pleasures.
>
> (3.1.1–7)

Ferdinand's labour is not autotelic, in Aristotle's terms; it is not performed as an end in itself. But neither is it banausic; it is not performed for money. In Ferdinand, Shakespeare outlines a third term, a secularized version of Herbert's Christian teleology. The romantic remuneration he receives bestows value on his labour, it makes his 'drudgery divine'. This is the play's answer to Gonzalo's utopian proposal to abolish labour altogether, so that 'All things in common nature should produce / Without sweat or endeavour' (2.1.160–1). In the figure of Ferdinand, Shakespeare redeems wage labour from its traditional association with servility.[5] He also redeems magic from the aspersions of the witch-hunters. Prospero practises black magic, or as he calls it 'rough magic'. He commands the labour, not only of Ariel, Caliban and Ferdinand, but also of the 'elves' and 'demi-puppets' who manufacture 'green sour ringlets' and 'midnight mushrooms'. He even practises necromancy, boasting that 'graves at my command / Have waked their sleepers, op'd, and let 'em forth / By my so potent art' (5.1.48–50). By the standards of the early seventeenth century, Prospero is a sorcerer, and his real-life counterparts would still be subjected to criminal prosecution for much of the coming century.

However, *The Tempest* raises the prospect of a very different evaluation of practical magic. Prospero describes his art as 'prescience', hinting that its time has not yet arrived. Over the century following the composition of *The Tempest*, those who possessed the ability to manipulate alienated labour-power by translating it into symbolic form would learn to exploit the entire world for their own benefit, just as Prospero exploits the little world of his island, and by the same means. As a result of exchange-value's triumph over use-value, people would soon stop noticing the reality lurking beneath representation. They would, in other words, cease to 'believe in magic'. But magic was not eliminated by the witch hunts of the sixteenth and seventeenth centuries. Just as alchemy disappeared because its aim of creating financial value out of nothing was finally realized by the legalization of usury, so magic ceased to be a crime when the performative power of symbols became a necessary element of economic life. As Shakespeare shows in *The Tempest*, the autonomy of representation, and the concomitant objectification of subjective labour-power, are magical beliefs. But magic is no longer an activity practised only by specialists. When Prospero doffs his cape and burns his books, he declares that his art has finally achieved its end – in every sense – for we are all magicians now.

NOTES

Chapter 1

1 Moses Finley, *The Ancient Economy* (Berkeley, 1973), 21.

2 Xenophon, *The Economist* in *The Socratic Writings* trans. H. G. Dakyns (Digireads, 2009), 140.

3 Michel Foucault, *The Use of Pleasure: Volume 2 of The History of Sexuality* trans. Robert Hurley (New York, 1985), 175. With regard to Aristotle's *Politics* Foucault notes that 'in economics one is more concerned with persons than with inanimate property' (1.13.1259b).

4 Aristotle, *Economics* trans. E. S. Foster (Oxford, 1920), 1343a21–4.

5 Karl Polanyi, *The Great Transformation* (New York, 1944), 46.

6 See Michael McKeon, 'The Origins of Aesthetic Value', *Telos* (1982), 62–83.

7 Karl Marx, 'Debating the Freedom of the Press' (1842), in *Marx and Engels on Literature and Art: A Selection of Writings*, eds Lee Baxandall and Stefan Morawski (St Louis, 1973), 61.

8 Jacques Derrida, *Given Time: 1. Counterfeit Money* trans. Peggy Kamuf (Chicago, 1992), 158.

9 Plato, *The Republic* trans. B. Jowett (New York, 1892), 291.

10 4.10.18–23. All Shakespeare quotations will be from *The Arden Shakespeare Complete Works* eds Richard Proudfoot, Ann Thompson and David Scott Kastan (London, 1998).

11 See David Hawkes, *Ideology* (London, 2003), 98–9.

12 Joyce Oldham Appleby, *Economic Thought and Ideology in Seventeenth-century England* (Princeton, 1978) 15, 246.

13 Fernand Braudel, *Capitalism and Material Life, 1400–1800* trans. Miriam Kochan (New York, 1974), 328.

14 Karl Polanyi, *The Great Transformation: The Political and Economic Origins of Our Time* (Boston, 1944), 71–2.

Chapter 2

1 Cit. Odd Langholm, *The Legacy of Scholasticism in Economic Thought* (Cambridge, 1998), 20.

2 David McNally, *Political Economy and the Rise of Capitalism* (Berkeley, 1988), 8.

3 John Higgins, *Huloet's Dictionarie* (London, 1572).

4 Pietro Martire Vermigli, *Common places of … Doctor Peter Martyr* trans. Anthonie Marten (London, 1572).

5 Loys Le Roy, *Aristotles politiques*, (London, 1598)

6 Richard Braithwaite, *The Scholar's Medley* (London, 1614).

7 Matthew Kellison, *The Right and Jurisdiction of the Prelate and the Prince* (London, 1621).

8 Samuel Torshell, *The Three Questions of Justification* (London, 1632).

9 Henry Hawkins, *Partheneia Sacra* (London, 1633).

10 James Hart, *Klinik, or the Diet of the Diseased* (London, 1633).

11 Cit. Joyce Appleby, *The Relentless Revolution: A History of Capitalism* (New York, 2011), 96.

12 Diana Wood, *Medieval Economic Thought* (Cambridge, 2002), 1.

13 In *Idioms of Self-interest: Credit, Identity, and Property in English Renaissance Literature* (New York, 2006), Jill Phillips Ingram finds that this changed by the early seventeenth century: '[i]n 1623, Edward Misselden suggested that it was appropriate for merchants to seek their private gain' (6). For a classical Marxist debate on the transition from feudalism to capitalism, see Maurice Dobb, *Studies in the Development of Capitalism* (London, 1946), and Paul Sweezy's response in 'The Transition from Feudalism to Capitalism', *Science and Society* 14:2 (Spring 1950), 134–57.

14 Anthony Parel, review of *The Aristotelian Analysis of Usury* by Odd Langholm, *Journal of the History of Philosophy* 26:1 (January 1988), 139.

15 Oswald Spengler, *The Decline of the West* trans. Charles Francis Atkinson (Oxford), 38.

16 Neal Wood, *Foundations of Political Economy: Some Early Tudor Views on State and Society* (Berkeley, 14), 1.

17 See Max Weber, *The Protestant Ethic and the Spirit of Capitalism* (London, 2001, orig. 1904).

18 John Calvin, *Institutes of the Christian Religion* (2.1.9), cit. Charles Partee, *The Theology of John Calvin* (London, 2008), 128.

19 C. B. Macpherson, *The Political Theory of Possessive Individualism: Hobbes to Locke* (Oxford, 1970), 22, 29.

20 Immanuel Wallerstein, *The Capitalist World-economy* (Cambridge, 1979), 47.

21 Joseph Lee, *A Vindication of a Regulated Inclosure* (London, 1653), 9. Cit. Appleby (1978), 62.

22 Bernard Mandeville, 'The Grumbling Hive' in *The Fable of the Bees and Other Writings* ed. E. J. Hundert (Indianapolis, 1997), 27.

23 Timothy Mitchell, 'Dreamland', in *Evil Paradises: Dreamworlds of Neoliberalism* eds Mike Davis and Daniel Bertrand Monk (New York, 2007), 1.

24 Asger Sorenson, 'On a Universal Scale: Economy in Bataille's General Economy', *Philosophy and Social Criticism* 38:2 (2012), 169.

25 Georges Bataille, *The Accursed Share: An Essay on General Economy, Volume I: Consumption,* trans. Robert Hurley (New York, 1988), 25.

26 Georges Bataille, cit. Jacques Derrida, 'From Restricted to General Economy: A Hegelianism without Reserve', in his *Writing and Difference*, trans. Alan Bass (Chicago, 1978), 270.

27 Douglas Bruster, 'On a Certain Tendency in Economic Criticism of Shakespeare', in Linda Woodbridge (ed.), *Money and the Age of Shakespeare: Essays in the New Economic Criticism* (New York, 2003), 74.

28 David Hawkes, 'Exchange-value and Empiricism in the Poetry of George Herbert', in Woodbridge (ed.) (2003), 83.

29 Silvia Federici, *Capitalism and the Witch: The Body and Primitive Accumulation* (New York, 2004), 21–2. For cogent challenges to the idea that capitalism represents an advance on feudalism, see: André Gunder Frank, 'The Myth of Feudalism', in *Capitalism and Under-Development in Latin America* (New York, 1967), 221–42, and Ernesto Laclau, 'Feudalism and Capitalism in Latin America', *New Left Review,* 67 (May–June 1971), 37–8.

Chapter 3

1 Cit. Peter Stallybrass, '"Well grubbed, old mole": Marx, *Hamlet* and the (un)fixing of Representation', in Jean Howard and Scott Cutler Shershaw (eds), *Marxist Shakespeares* (London, 2001), 20.

2 Paul Lafargue, *Reminiscences of Marx* (1890) https: / /www. marxists.org /archive /lafargue /1890 /xx /marx.htm (accessed 31 August 2014).

3 S.S. Prawer, *Karl Marx and World Literature* (Oxford, 1978), 20.

4 Prawer, 210.

5 Prawer, 72.

6 Prawer, 215.

7 Friedrich Engels, from letter to Ferdinand Lasalle, 18 May 1859. http: / /www.marxists.org /archive /marx /410.htm (accessed 31 August 2014).

8 David Armitage, 'Shakespeare's Properties', in David Armitage, Conal Condren and Andrew Fitzmaurice (eds), *Shakespeare and Early Modern Political Thought* (Cambridge, 2009), 29.

9 Richard Levin, 'Reply to Michael Bristol and Gayle Greene', in *Shakespeare Left and Right* ed. Ivo Kamps (New York, 1991), 53.

10 Georg Lukács, 'Shakespeare and Modern Drama', in Paul A. Kottman (ed.), *Philosophers on Shakespeare* (Stanford, 2009), 136.

11 Sharon O'Dair, *Class, Critics and Shakespeare: Bottom Lines on the Culture Wars* (Ann Arbor, 2000), 46–7.

12 Victor Kiernan, *Eight Tragedies of Shakespeare: A Marxist Interpretation* (London, 1996), 34.

13 R. H. Tawney, *Religion and the Rise of Capitalism* (New York, 1954), 38.

14 See Isaiah 2:8, 17:8, 37:19.

15 Karl Marx, *Economic and Philosophic Manuscripts of 1844* trans. Martin Milligan (New York, 1993), 167–8.

16 Eduardo Ibarra-Colado, Stewart R. Clegg, Carl Rhodes and Martin Kornberger, 'The Ethics of Managerial Subjectivity', *Journal of Business Ethics* 64:1 (March 2006) 45–55, 46. For continuities between modern management techniques and slavery, see N. McKendrick, 'Josiah Wedgwood's Factory Discipline', *Historical Journal* 4:1 (1961) 30–55; Keith Thomas, 'Work and Leisure in Pre-industrial Society', *Past and Present* 29 (1964) 50–62, and E. P. Thompson, 'Time, Work-Discipline and Industrial Capitalism', *Past and Present* 38 (December 1967), 56–97.

17 Cit. Margot Heinemann, 'How Brecht Read Shakespeare', in Dollimore and Sinfield (eds), 207. But as Heinemann correctly notes: '[w]hile he consistently analyses Shakespeare in terms of the class situation, however, Brecht's is not the kind of "Marxist" criticism that stops at that point' (209).

18 Ernst Bloch, 'Alienation, Estrangement', in *Literary Essays* trans. Andrew Joron and Others (Stanford, 1998), 244.

19 Paul Delany, '*King Lear* and the Decline of Feudalism' in Ivo Kamps (ed.), *Materialist Shakespeare: A History* (London, 1995), 21.

20 A. A. Smirnov, *Shakespeare: A Marxist Interpretation* (New York, 1936) https: //www.marxists.org /subject /art /lit_crit / works /shakes.htm#a18 (accessed 31 August 2014).

21 L. C. Knights, *Drama and Society in the Age of Jonson* (New York, 1937), 83.

22 Irena R. Makaryk and Joseph G. Price, *Shakespeare in the Worlds of Communism and Socialism* (London, 2006), 30.

23 Makaryk and Price, 33.

24 See Shuhua Wang, 'From Maoism to (Post) Modernism: *Hamlet* in Communist China', in Makaryk and Price, 283–302.

25 Yang Zhouhan, 'Shakespeare's Life and His Major Works', in Makaryk and Price, 286.

26 *Pravda*, 23 April 1964, Makaryk and Price, 3.

27 Elliot Krieger, *A Marxist Study of Shakespeare's Comedies* (London, 1979), 6.

28 Georg Lukács, 'Realism in the Balance', in *Aesthetics and Politics* (London, 1977), 32.

29 Louis Althusser, *For Marx*, trans. Ben Brewster (New York, 1971), 111.

30 See David Hawkes, 'Against Materialism in Literary Theory', in Paul Cefalu and Bryan Reynolds (eds), *The Return of Theory in Early Modern English Studies: Tarrying with the Subjunctive* (New York, 2011), pp. 237–57.

31 Levin, 58n.1.

Chapter 4

1 Karl Marx, from the Preface to *A Contribution to the Critique of Political Economy* (1859), in Robert Tucker (ed.), *The Marx-Engels Reader* (New York, 1978), 5.

2 Friedrich Engels, letter to Franz Mehring, 14 July 1893. https: / /www.marxists.org /archive /marx /works /1893 /letters /93_07_14.htm (accessed 31 August 2014).

3 Doug Brown, 'Karl Polanyi's Influence on the Budapest School', in *The Life and Work of Karl Polanyi: A Celebration* (Montreal, 1990), 44–5.

4 Georg Lukács, *History and Class-consciousness* trans. Rodney Livingstone (London, 1971), 27.

5 Arnold Kettle, 'Introduction' to *Shakespeare in a Changing World* ed. Arnold Kettle (London, 1964), 11.

6 Louis Althusser, *Lenin and Philosophy and Other Essays*, trans. Ben Brewster (New York, 1971), 168.

7 Terry Eagleton, *Marxism and Literary Criticism* (Berkeley, 1976), 2.

8 Terry Eagleton, *Criticism and Ideology: A Study in Marxist Literary Theory* (London, 1978), 16–17.

9 Ivo Kamps, 'Introduction' to Ivo Kamps (ed.), *Materialist Shakespeare: A History* (New York, 1995), 1.

10 Jonathan Dollimore and Alan Sinfield, 'Introduction', in Dollimore and Sinfield (eds), *Political Shakespeare: New Essays in Cultural Materialism* (Manchester, 1985), viii.

11 Cit. Michael Bristol, 'Where does Ideology Hang Out?' in Kamps (1991), 31–46, 36.

12 L. C. Knights, 'Shakespeare', in *Public Voices: Literature and Politics with Special Reference to the Seventeenth Century* (London, 1971), 34.

13 Samuel Johnson, *A Short History of Shakespearean Critics,* ed. Arthur Eastman (New York, 1968), 21.

14 Eastman (1968), 112.

15 Daniel Vitkus, in Stephen Deng and Barbara Sebek (eds), *Global Traffic: Discourses and Practices of Trade in English Literature and Culture from 1550 to 1700* (New York, 2008), 20. See also William Ingram, *The Business of Playing: The Beginnings of the Adult Professional Theatre in Elizabethan London* (New York, 1992) and Melissa Aaron, *Global Economics: An Institutional Economic History of the Chamberlain's/King's Men and Their Texts 1599–1642* (New York, 1998).

16 H. Rick Smith, '*Henry VI Part 2:* Commodifying and Recommodifying the Past in Late-Medieval and Early-Modern England', in Thomas A. Pendleton (ed.), *Henry VI: Critical Essays* (New York, 2001), 10.

17 Cit. A. L. Morton, 'Shakespeare's Idea of History', *Our History* 33 (Spring 1964), 5.

18 Karl Marx, *Introduction to the Critique of Political Economy* (1857), 134–5.

19 Georg Lukács, *Studies in European Realism,* 5. Roy Pascal, 'Georg Lukács: The Concept of Totality', in G.H.R. Parkinson (ed.), *Georg Lukács: The Man, his Work and his Ideas* (New York, 1970), 155.

20 Stanley Mitchell, 'Lukács's Concept of "The Beautiful"', in Parkinson (ed.) (1970), 231.

Chapter 5

1 Hugh Grady, *Shakespeare and Impure Aesthetics* (Cambridge UP, 2009), 2.

2 Theodor Adorno argues that social and political issues are most clearly expressed in literary form rather than content: 'Social ideas should not be brought to works from without but should, instead, be created out of the complete organized view of things present in the works themselves', in 'Lyric Poetry and Society', trans. Bruce Mayo, *Telos* 20 (1974), 57.

3 Marc Shell, *The Economy of Literature* (Baltimore, 1978), 8.

4 Jean-Joseph Goux, *Symbolic Economies: After Freud and Marx,* trans. Jennifer Gage (Ithaca, NY, 1990), 96.

5 Jean-Joesph Goux, *The Coiners of Language* trans. Jennifer Curtiss Gage (Norman, OK, 1994), 77.

6 Kurt Heinzelman, *The Economics of the Imagination* (Amherst, 1980), ix.

7 Deirdre McCloskey, *The Rhetoric of Economics* (Madison, 1985), xvii.

8 Willie Henderson, *Economics as Literature* (London, 1995), 2.

9 Sandra Fischer, *Econolingua: A Glossary of Coins and Economic Language in Renaissance Drama* (Newark, DE, 1985), 15.

10 Jean-Christophe Agnew, *Worlds Apart: The Market and the Theater in Anglo-American Thought* (Cambridge, 1986), ix.

10 Stephen Gosson, *Plays Confuted in Five Actions* (London, 1582), G6.

12 David Hawkes, *Idols of the Market-place: Idolatry and Commodity Fetishism in English Literature, 1580–1680* (New York, 2001), 80.

13 Anthony Munday, *A Second and Third Blast of Retrait from Plaies and Theaters* (London, 1580), 109.

14 Douglas Bruster, *Drama and the Market in the Age of Shakespeare* (Cambridge, 1992), xi.

15 Thomas Cartelli, *Marlowe, Shakespeare and the Economy of Theatrical Experience* (University of Pennsylvania Press, 1991), xiii.

16 Lars Engle, *Shakespearean Pragmatism: Market of His Time* (Chicago, 1993), 3.

17 Theodore Leinwand, *Theatre, Finance and Society in Early Modern England* (Cambridge, 1999), 3.

18 Linda Woodbridge, Introduction to *Money and the Age of Shakespeare: Essays in the New Economic Criticism* (New York, 2003), 10.

19 Sebek and Deng, (2008), 1.

20 Jonathan Gil Harris, *Sick Economies: Drama, Mercantilism and Disease in Shakespeare's England* (University of Pennsylvania Press, 2004), 18.

21 Peter Grav, 'Taking Stock of Shakespeare and the New Economic Criticism', *Shakespeare* (8.1, 2012), 112.

22 Peter Grav, *Shakespeare and the Economic Imperative* (London, 2008), 158.

23 Frederick Turner, *Shakespeare's Twenty-first Century Economics: the Morality of Love and Money* (Oxford, 1999), 14.

24 Sharon O'Dair, *Class, Critics and Shakespeare* (Ann Arbor, 2000), 69.

25 See my review of Berman's book in the *Times Literary Supplement* (10/24/2008), 24–5.

26 Aaron Kitch, *Political Economy and the States of Literature in Early Modern England* (Burlington, VT, 2009), 29.

27 David Landreth, *The Face of Mammon: The Matter of Money in English Renaissance Literature* (Oxford, 2012), 3.

28 Stephen Deng, *Coinage and State Formations in Early Modern English Literature* (New York, 2011), 1.

28 Michel Foucault, *The Order of Things: An Archaeology of the Human Sciences* (New York, 1970), 176.

30 Valerie Forman, *Tragicomic Redemptions: Global Economics and the Early Modern Stage* (Philadelphia, 2008), 87.

Chapter 6

1 Gamini Salgado, *The Elizabethan Underworld* (New York, 1992), ix.

2 Michael Perelman, *The Invention of Capitalism: Classical Political Economy and the Secret History of Primitive Accumulation* (Durham, NC, 2000), 14.

3 See also Christopher Hill, *Change and Continuity in Seventeenth-century England* (Cambridge, MA, 1975), 219–39. For an interpretation of the commons in the light of ecological theory, see Charles Whitney: 'Green Economics and the English Renaissance: From Capital to the Commons', in Cary DiPietro and Hugh Grady (ed.) *Shakespeare and the Urgency of the Now: Criticism and Theory in the 21st Century* (New York, 2013), 103–25.

4 In 'Scene Stealers: Autolycus', *The Winter's Tale* and Economic Criticism', Barbara Correll observes that 'while characters like the Shepherd enjoy or suffer changes in their fortunes, Autolycus is most closely associated with the social mobility of market economy in which selling and stealing are integral activities' (Woodbridge, 2003), 58.

5 John Moore, *A Scripture-word against Inclosure* (1656), cit. Appleby (1978), 63. Crystal Bartolovich has explored the effects of enclosure on subjectivity, concluding that 'a certain enclosure, or limiting of historical possibilities, along with spatial ones, prepares the way for the enclosure of the modern subject', in 'Travailing Theory: Global Flows of Labor and the Enclosure of the Subject' in *A Companion to the Global Renaissance: English Literature and Culture in the Era of Expansion* ed. Jyotsna G. Singh (Oxford, 2009), 50. See also Paul A. Cefalu, 'Rethinking the Discourse of Colonialism in Economic Terms: Shakespeare's *The Tempest,* Captain John Smith's Virginia Narratives and the English Response to Vagrancy', *Shakespeare Studies* 28 (2000), 85–119.

6 Lee Bliss, Introduction to *Coriolanus* (Cambridge, 2010), 19.

7 Lars Engle, *Shakespearean Pragmatism: Market of His Time* (New York, 1993), 164.

8 Heinemann, in Dollimore and Sinfield (1994), 227.

9 James Fulcher, *Capitalism: A Very Short Introduction* (Oxford, 2004), 22.

10 McNally (2011), 150. See also McNally (1993), 17–18.

11 In this section I am indebted to the research of Heather Ackerman, currently a doctoral student at Arizona State University, and her forthcoming PhD dissertation, *The Accommodation of Commodities in Early Modern England.*

12 I believe this useful term is originally Jean Howard's. She uses it to refer to the theatre in *The Stage and Social Struggle in Early Modern England* (London, 1994), 23.

13 See Stephen Mullaney, *The Place of the Stage* (Chicago, 1988) and Howard (1994).

14 On Shakespeare's use of quantification to express affection, see Woodbridge (2003), 11. As Barbara Correll has recently shown, such combinations of affective and financial value are also characteristic of John Donne's poetry: 'In their poetic strategies of mixed discourses and the estranging meanings that ensue from them, Donne and Shakespeare signal an awareness of the alienating and plurally signifying potential of early modern market and material culture ... The coined speaker in Donne, the indeared bosom in Shakespeare are constitutive poetic metaphors moving between financial and affective signification' ('Terms of "Indearment": Lyric and General Economy in Shakespeare and Donne', *ELH* 75:2 [Summer 2008], 255).

Chapter 7

1 Karl Marx, *Capital*, vol.1, trans. Ben Fowkes (London, 1976), 126n.4.

2 Thomas Traherne, *Centuries, Poems and Thanksgivings*, 2 vols, ed. H. M. Margoliouth (Oxford, 1966), 2:118.1–4.

3 See David Hawkes, 'Thomas Traherne: A Critique of Political Economy', *The Huntington Library Quarterly* 62:4 (Spring 2000), 369–88.

4 *The Poems of Andrew Marvell* ed. Nigel Smith (London, 2006).

5 John Donne, *The Complete English Poems* (London, 1976).

6 For Donne on value, see John Carey, 'Donne and Coins', in his *English Renaissance Studies Presented to Dame Helen Gardener in honour of her Seventieth Birthday* (Oxford, 1980), 151–63, and Coburn Freer, 'John Donne and Elizabethan Economic Theory', *Criticism: A Quarterly for Literature and the Arts* 38 (1996), 497–520.

7 Odd Langholm, *Economics in the Medieval Schools: Wealth, Exchange, Value, Money and Usury according to the Paris Theological Tradition, 1200–1350* (Leiden, 1992), 230.

8 Langholm (1992), 545.

9 Matthew Gumpert, *Grafting Helen: The Abduction of the Classical Past* (Madison, WI, 2001), xiii.

10 See Woodbridge (ed.), (2003), 11.

11 Richard Halpern, *The Poetics of Primitive Accumulation: English Renaissance Culture and the Geneology of Capital* (Ithaca, NY, 1991) 218.

Chapter 8

1 See Blair Hoxby, letter to *TLS*, 30/042004.

2 'Engrossing' typically referred to outright theft, as opposed to the nominally or semi-legal 'enclosing'. See Joan Thirsk, 'Engrossing and Enclosing 1500–1640', in *Chapters from the Agrarian History of England and Wales*, vol. 3, ed. Joan Thirsk (Cambridge, 1967), 54–124.

3 David McNally, *Political Economy and the Rise of Capitalism: A Reinterpretation* (Berkeley, 1988), 7.

4 Cit. Roland Paulson, *Empty Labor: Idleness and Workplace Resistance* (Cambridge, 2014), 173.

5 Aristotle, *Rhetoric,* 1367a32.

6 William L. Westerman, *The Slave Systems of Greek and Roman Antiquity* (Philadelphia, 1955), 26.

7 Westerman, 27.

8 Jeremiah J. Sullivan, *The Future of Corporate Globalization: From the Extended Order to the Global Village* (Santa Barbara CA, 2002), 145. David Graeber points out that in ancient China, slavery and wage labour were 'two phenomena that, as so often in the ancient world, largely overlapped: the common phrase for workers used in texts from the period was (dasa-karmakara), 'slave-hireling', with the assumption that slaves and laborers worked together and were barely distinguishable'. *Towards an Anthropological Theory of Value* (New York, 2001), 428n.38.

9 David Graeber, *Debt: The First 5,000 Years* (New York, 2011), 211.

10 David Graeber, "Turning Modes of Production Inside Out: Or, Why Capitalism is a Transformation of Slavery", *Critique of Anthropology* 26: 1 (March 2006), 61 (accessed 15 February 2012).

11 David Graeber, *Possibilities: Essays on Hierarchy, Rebellion and Desire* (AK Press), 2007. Graeber also cites Friedman's conclusion that 'slavery in Classical Greece is a complex affair involving wage, interest and profit in an elaborate market system that appears to have had cyclical properties of expansion and contraction. This was, in other words, a form of capitalism that is not so different from the more obvious varieties in the modern world' (68). In present-day Madagascar, claims Graeber, the legacy of slavery means that 'wage labor, forced labor, military service – any relation based in the giving and taking of orders – are considered so many refractions of slavery'. This has a notable impact on social relations in general: 'The reluctance openly to command others is part of a more general aversion to any relationship in which one party is seen as directing the actions of another', in David Graeber, in *Lost People: Magic and the Legacy of Slavery in Madagascar* (Bloomington, 2007), 49.

12 Diana Wood, *Medieval Economic Thought* (Cambridge, 2002), 18.

13 William Warwick Buckland, *The Roman Law of Slavery* (orig. 1908, reprinted Cambridge University Press, 2010), 3.

14 Orlando Patterson, *Slavery and Social Death* (Cambridge MA, 1982), 32. See also Keith Bradley, 'Animalizing the Slave: the Truth of Fiction', *Journal of Roman Studies* 90 (2000), 110–25. Bradley notes that 'the common Greek term for slave, *andeapodon*, "man-footed creature," was built on the foundation of a common term for cattle, namely, *tetrapodon*, "four-footed creature"' (110).

15 See David Hawkes, 'The Concept of the "Hireling" in Milton's Theology', *Milton Studies* (2004).

16 Aristotle, *Nicomachean Ethics*, 1133a15–20.

17 As Marx explains in *Capital*:

> There was, however, an important fact which prevented Aristotle from seeing that, to attribute value to commodities, is merely a mode of expressing all labour as equal human labour, and consequently as labour of equal quality. Greek society was founded upon slavery, and had, therefore, for its natural basis, the inequality of men and of their labour powers. The secret of the expression of value, namely, that all kinds of labour are equal and equivalent, because, and so far as they are human labour in general, cannot be deciphered, until the notion of human equality has already acquired the fixity of a popular prejudice. This, however, is possible only in a society in which the great mass of the produce of labour takes the form of commodities, in which, consequently, the dominant relation between man and man, is that of owners of commodities. The brilliancy of Aristotle's genius is shown by this alone, that he discovered, in the expression of the value of commodities, a relation of equality. The peculiar conditions of the society in which he lived, alone prevented him from discovering what, "in truth," was at the bottom of this equality.

18 Brent Shaw, 'Introduction' to Moses Finley, *Ancient Slavery and Modern Ideology* (Princeton, 1998).

19 David Brion Davis, *Slavery and Human Progress* (Oxford, 1984), 14.

20 Jennifer Glancy, *Slavery in Early Christianity* (Oxford, 2002), 9.

21 Heinzelman, 14.

Chapter 9

1 Emmanuel Levinas, *The Ego and Totality,* in *Collected Philosophical Papers,* trans. Alphonso Lingis (Dordrecht, 1987), 45.

2 Thomas Aquinas, *Summae Theologiae* 1a2ae, 2, 1, vol.41, p. 33, in Wood (2002), 73.

3 Wood (2002), 75.

4 Wood (2002), 76.

5 Nicholas Sander, *The Ruinate Fall of the Pope Usurie, Derived from the Pope Idolatrie* (London, 1580).

6 Carl Wennerlind, *Casualties of Credit: The English Financial Revolution, 1620–1720* (2011), 18.

7 Craig Muldrew, *The Economy of Obligation: The Culture of Credit in Early Modern England* (New York, 1998), 150.

8 In *Outlaw Rhetoric: Figuring Vernacular Eloquence in Shakespeare's England* (Ithaca, NY, 2012), Jenny C. Mann reminds us that Sonnet 20 is titled 'The Exchange' in John Benson's 1640 edition. The allusion to London's centre of commerce thus becomes inescapable. See also Neal Dolan, 'Shylock in Love: Economic Metaphors in Shakespeare's Sonnets', *Raritan: A Quarterly Review* 22.2 (2002), 26–51; Peter C. Herman, 'What's the Use? Or, The Problematic of Economy in Shakespeare's Procreation Sonnets', in *Shakespeare's Sonnets: New Essays,* ed. James Schiffer (New York, 1999), 263–83, John B. Mischo, '"That Use is Not Forbidden Usury:" Shakespeare's Procreation Sonnets and the Problem of Usury', and David Hawkes: 'Sodomy and Usury in Shakespeare's *Sonnets',* *Renaissance Studies* 14:3 (September 2000), 344–61.

9 Roger Warren et al. (eds), *The Oxford Shakespeare* (2008), 180.

10 Cit. Joseph Kearney, *The Incarnate Text: Imagining the Book in Reformation England* (Philadelphia, 2009), 118.

11 Simon Critchley and Tom McCarthy, 'Universal Shylockery: Money and Morality in *The Merchant of Venice'*, *Diacritics* 34:1 (Spring 2004), 7. For other economic readings of *The*

Merchant of Venice, see especially Stephen Greenblatt,
'Marlowe, Marx, and Anti-Semitism', *Critical Inquiry 5*
(1978), 291–307; Marc Shell, 'The Wether and the Ewe: Verbal
Usury in The Merchant of Venice', in *Money, Language and
Thought* (Berkeley, 1982), 47–83; Paul Stevens, 'Heterogenizing
Imagination: Globalization, *The Merchant of Venice,* and
the Work of Literary Criticism', *New Literary History* 36:3
(Summer 2005), 425–37, and Aaron Kitch, 'Shylock's Sacred
Nation', *Shakespeare Quarterly,* 59:2 (Summer 2008), 131–55.
For a gendered reading of Shakespeare on usury, see Natasha
Korda, 'Dame Usury: Gender, Credit and (Ac)counting in the
Sonnets and *The Merchant of Venice*', *Shakespeare Quarterly* 60
(2009), 129–53.

12 Amanda Bailey, 'Shylock and the Slaves: Owing and Owning in
The Merchant of Venice, Shakespeare Quarterly 62:1 (Spring
2011), 12.

Chapter 10

1 Stephen Greenblatt, 'Murdering Peasants: Status, Genre and
the Representation of Rebellion' in Stephen Greenblatt (ed.),
Representing the English Renaissance (Berkeley, 1988), 25.

2 http://www.etymonline.com

3 Aristotle, *Politics* trans. B. Jowett (Stilwell, KS, 2005), 6.

4 John Locke, *Of Civil Government* (Toronto, 1924), 130.

5 Thomas Hobbes, *Leviathan* ed. C. B. MacPherson (London,
1985), 295.

6 John Rastell, 'Of Gentylnes and Nobylyte' (London, 1525).

7 Wood (2002), 36.

8 David Armitage, 'Shakespeare's Properties', in David Armitage,
Conal Condren and Andrew Fitzmaurice (eds), *Shakespeare and
Early Modern Political Thought* (Cambridge, 2009), 34.

9 See for example Peter Geschiere, *The Modernity of Witchcraft:
Politics and the Occult in Postcolonial Africa* trans. Peter
Geschiére and Janet Roitman (Charlottesville, 1997).

10 David Schalkwyk, *Speech and Performance in Shakespeare's Sonnets and Plays* (Cambridge, 2002), 51.

11 *The Works of Francis Bacon* (7 vols) ed. James Spedding, R. L. Ellis and D. D. Heath (London, 1857–9), 1.86.

12 The term is of course taken from Stephen Greenblatt's *Renaissance Self-Fashioning: From More to Shakespeare* (Chicago, 1980).

13 Anne Barton (ed.), *Twelfth Night* in *The Riverside Shakespeare* ed. Harry Levin et al. (Boston, 1974), 423n. 21.

14 Will Fischer, 'Queer Money', *ELH* 66 (1999), 1.

15 Ros King notes that Posthumus exhibits a commodified attitude to personal relations throughout the play: 'Posthumus sees his marriage as a form of commodity exchange (typified by the exchange of jewels) ... Since Posthumus so absolutely equates Imogen as a person with a thing, her rich jewel, and therefore with the bodily, muscular vaginal ring that embodies her sexuality, he is too easily persuaded of her lack of faith.' *Cymbeline: Constructions of Britain* (London, 2005), 138.

16 Cit. Heinzelman 15.

Conclusion

1 James Kearney points out that Trinculo and Stephano are fascinated by the false value of 'trumpery', which Caliban urges them to resist: 'Mocking the European propensity to decry the fetishism of the savage other, *The Tempest* stages the overvaluation of the "enchanted trifle" as a European (albeit, in this instance, a lower-class European) problem' ('The Book and the Fetish: The Materiality of Prospero's Text', *Journal of Medieval and Early Modern Studies* 32:3 [Fall 2002], 446).

2 On the general question of labour and the early modern stage, see Tom Rutter, *Work and Play on the Shakespearean Stage* (Cambridge, 2008), and Michelle Dowd, *Women's Work in Early Modern English Literature and Culture* (New York, 2014).

3 Aristotle, *Nicomachean Ethics* in *Works vol. IX*, trans. W. D. Ross, 1176b 1–5.

4 George Herbert, 'The Elixir', in *The Complete English Poems* ed. John Tobin (London, 1991).

5 See William Rockett: 'Labor and Virtue in *The Tempest*', *Shakespeare Quarterly* 24:1 (Winter 1973), 77–84.

BIBLIOGRAPHY

Aaron, Melissa D., *Global Economics: A History of the Theatre Business, the Chamberlain's/King's Men, and Their Plays, 1599–1642* (Newark, DE, 1995).

Agnew, Jean-Christophe, *Worlds Apart: The Market and the Theater in Anglo-American Thought* (Cambridge, 1986).

Althusser, Louis, *For Marx*, trans. Ben Brewster (New York, 1971).

Althusser, Louis, *Lenin and Philosophy and Other Essays*, trans. Ben Brewster (New York, 1971).

Appleby, Joyce Oldham, *Economic Thought and Ideology in Seventeenth-century England* (Princeton, 1978).

Appleby, Joyce Oldham, *The Relentless Revolution: A History of Capitalism* (New York, 2011).

Aquinas, Thomas, *Summae Theologiae*, in Wood (2002).

Aristotle, *Economics*, trans. E. S. Foster (Oxford, 1920).

Aristotle, *Nicomachean Ethics* in *Works*, trans. W. D. Ross, vol. 9.

Aristotle, *Politics*, trans. B. Jowett (Stilwell, KS, 2005).

Armitage, David, 'Shakespeare's Properties', in *Shakespeare and Early Modern Political Thought*, eds David Armitage, Conal Condren and Andrew Fitzmaurice (Cambridge, 2009), 25–43.

Bacon, Francis, *The Works of Francis Bacon*, 7 vols., ed. James Spedding, R. L. Ellis and D. D. Heath (London, 1857–9).

Bailey, Amanda, 'Shylock and the Slaves: Owing and Owning in *The Merchant of Venice*', *SQ*, 62 (2011), 1–24.

Bartolovich, Crystal, 'Travailing Theory: Global Flows of Labor and the Enclosure of the Subject' in *A Companion to the Global Renaissance: English Literature and Culture in the Era of Expansion*, ed. Jyotsna G. Singh (Oxford, 2009).

Bataille, Georges, 'Consumption', in *The Accursed Share: An Essay on General Economy*, trans. Robert Hurley (New York, 1988), vol. 1.

Bliss, Lee, Introduction to *Coriolanus* (Cambridge, 2010).

Bloch, Ernst, 'Alienation, Estrangement', in *Literary Essays,* trans. Andrew Joron et al. (Stanford, 1998), 239–45.

Bradley, Keith, 'Animalizing the Slave: The Truth of Fiction', *Journal of Roman Studies,* 90 (2000), 110–25.

Braithwaite, Richard, *The Scholar's Medley* (London, 1614).

Braudel, Fernand, *Capitalism and Material Life, 1400–1800,* trans. Miriam Kochan (New York, 1974).

Bristol, Michael, 'Where Does Ideology Hang Out?', in *Shakespeare Right and Left,* ed. Ivo Kamps (London and New York, 1991), 31–43.

Brown, Doug, 'Karl Polanyi's Influence on the Budapest School', in *The Life and Work of Karl Polanyi: A Celebration* (Montreal, 1990), 43–51.

Bruster, Douglas, *Drama and the Market in the Age of Shakespeare* (Cambridge, 1992).

Bruster, Douglas, 'On a Certain Tendency in Economic Criticism of Shakespeare', in Woodbridge, 67–78.

Buckland, William Warwick, *The Roman Law of Slavery* (orig. 1908, reprinted Cambridge, 2010).

Calvin, John, *Institutes of the Christian Religion* (Louisville, 2006).

Carey, John, 'Donne and Coins', in his *English Renaissance Studies Presented to Dame Helen Gardener in Honour of her Seventieth Birthday* (Oxford, 1980), 151–63.

Cartelli, Thomas, *Marlowe, Shakespeare and the Economy of Theatrical Experience* (Philadelphia, 1991).

Cefalu, Paul A., 'Rethinking the Discourse of Colonialism in Economic Terms: Shakespeare's *The Tempest,* Captain John Smith's Virginia Narratives and the English Response to Vagrancy', *Shakespeare Studies,* 28 (2000), 85–119.

Correll, Barbara, 'Scene Stealers: Autolycus, *The Winter's Tale* and Economic Criticism', in Woodbridge, 53–66.

Correll, Barbara, 'Terms of "Indearment": Lyric and General Economy in Shakespeare and Donne', *ELH,* 75 (2008), 242–62.

Critchley, Simon, and Tom McCarthy, 'Universal Shylockery: Money and Morality in *The Merchant of Venice*', *Diacritics,* 34 (2004), 3–17.

Davis, David Brion, *Slavery and Human Progress* (Oxford, 1984).

Delany, Paul, '*King Lear* and the Decline of Feudalism', in Kamps (1995), 20–38.

Deng, Stephen, *Coinage and State Formations in Early Modern English Literature* (New York, 2011).

Derrida, Jacques, *Counterfeit Money*, in *Given Time*, trans. Peggy Kamuf (Chicago, 1992), vol. 1.

Derrida, Jacques, 'From Restricted to General Economy: A Hegelianism without Reserve', in his *Writing and Difference*, trans. Alan Bass (Chicago, 1978), 251–77.

Dobb, Maurice, *Studies in the Development of Capitalism* (London, 1946).

Dolan, Neal, 'Shylock in Love: Economic Metaphors in Shakespeare's Sonnets', *Raritan: A Quarterly Review*, 22 (2002), 26–51.

Dollimore, Jonathan, 'Introduction: Shakespeare, Cultural Materialism and the New Historicism', in Dollimore & Sinfield, 2–17.

Dollimore, Jonathan, and Alan Sinfield, eds., *Political Shakespeare: Essays in Cultural Materialism* (Manchester, 1985).

Donne, John, *The Complete English Poems* (London, 1976).

Dowd, Michelle, *Women's Work in Early Modern English Literature and Culture* (New York, 2014).

Eagleton, Terry, *Criticism and Ideology: A Study in Marxist Literary Theory* (London, 1978).

Eagleton, Terry, *Marxism and Literary Criticism* (Berkeley, 1976).

Engels, Friedrich, Letter to Ferdinand Lasalle, 18 May 1859. http://www.marxists.org/archive/marx/410.htm (accessed 31 August 2014).

Engels, Friedrich, Letter to Franz Mehring, 14 July 1893. http://www.marxists.org/archive/marx/works/1893/letters/93_07_14.htm (accessed 31 August 2014).

Engle, Lars, *Shakespearean Pragmatism: Market of His Time* (Chicago, 1993).

Federici, Silvia, *Capitalism and the Witch: The Body and Primitive Accumulation* (New York, 2004).

Finley, Moses, *The Ancient Economy* (Berkeley, 1973).

Fischer, Sandra, *Econolingua: A Glossary of Coins and Economic Language in Renaissance Drama* (Newark, DE, 1985).

Fischer, Will, 'Queer Money', *ELH*, 66 (1999), 1–23.

Forman, Valerie, *Tragicomic Redemptions: Global Economics and the Early Modern Stage* (Philadelphia, 2008).

Foucault, Michel, *The Order of Things: An Archaeology of the Human Sciences* (New York, 1970).

Foucault, Michel, 'The Use of Pleasure', in *The History of Sexuality*, trans. Robert Hurley (New York, 1985), vol. 2.

Frank, André Gunder, 'The Myth of Feudalism', in *Capitalism and Under – Development in Latin America* (New York, 1967), 221–42.

Freer, Coburn, 'John Donne and Elizabethan Economic Theory', *Criticism: A Quarterly for Literature and the Arts*, 38 (1996), 497–520.

Fulcher, James, *Capitalism: A Very Short Introduction* (Oxford, 2004).

Geschiere, Peter, *The Modernity of Witchcraft: Politics and the Occult in Postcolonial Africa*, trans. Peter Geschiere and Janet Roitman (Charlottesville, 1997).

Glancy, Jennifer, *Slavery in Early Christianity* (Oxford, 2002).

Gosson, Stephen, *Plays Confuted in Five Actions* (London, 1582).

Goux, Jean-Joseph, *The Coiners of Language*, trans. Jennifer Curtiss Gage (Norman, OK, 1994).

Goux, Jean-Joseph, *Symbolic Economies: After Freud and Marx*, trans. Jennifer Gage (Ithaca, NY, 1990).

Grady, Hugh, *Shakespeare and Impure Aesthetics* (Cambridge, 2009).

Grady, Hugh, *Shakespeare's Universal Wolf: Studies in Early Modern Reification* (Oxford, 1996).

Graeber, David. *Debt: The First 5,000 Years* (New York, 2011).

Graeber, David. *Lost People: Magic and the Legacy of Slavery in Madagascar* (Bloomington, 2007).

Graeber, David. *Possibilities: Essays on Hierarchy, Rebellion and Desire* (AK Press, 2007).

Graeber, David. *Towards an Anthropological Theory of Value* (New York, 2001).

Graeber, David. 'Turning Modes of Production Inside Out: Or, Why Capitalism is a Transformation of Slavery"', *Critique of Anthropology*, 26 (2006), 61–85 (accessed 15 February 2012).

Grav, Peter, *Shakespeare and the Economic Imperative* (London, 2008).

Grav, Peter, 'Taking Stock of Shakespeare and the New Economic Criticism', *Shakespeare*, 8 (2012), 111–36.

Greenblatt, Stephen, 'Marlowe, Marx, and Anti-Semitism', *Critical Inquiry*, 5 (1978), 291–307.

Greenblatt, Stephen, 'Murdering Peasants: Status, Genre and

the Representation of Rebellion', in *Representing the English Renaissance*, ed. Stephen Greenblatt (Berkeley, 1988), 1–29.

Gumpert, Matthew, *Grafting Helen: The Abduction of the Classical Past* (Madison, WI, 2001).

Halpern, Richard, *The Poetics of Primitive Accumulation: English Renaissance Culture and the Geneology of Capital* (Ithaca, NY, 1991).

Harris, Jonathan Gil, *Sick Economies: Drama, Mercantilism and Disease in Shakespeare's England* (Philadelphia, 2004).

Hart, James, *Klinik, or the Diet of the Diseased* (London, 1633).

Hawkes, David, 'Against Materialism in Literary Theory', in *The Return of Theory in Early Modern English Studies: Tarrying with the Subjunctive,* eds Paul Cefalu and Bryan Reynolds (New York, 2011), 237–57.

Hawkes, David, 'The Concept of the "Hireling" in Milton's Theology', *Milton Studies* (2004).

Hawkes, David, 'Exchange-value and Empiricism in the Poetry of George Herbert', in Woodbridge, 79–96.

Hawkes, David, *Ideology* (London, 2003).

Hawkes, David, *Idols of the Market-place: Idolatry and Commodity Fetishism in English Literature, 1580–1680* (New York, 2001).

Hawkes, David, 'Sodomy and Usury in Shakespeare's *Sonnets*', *Renaissance Studies,* 14 (2000), 344–61.

Hawkes, David, 'Thomas Traherne: A Critique of Political Economy', *Huntington Library Quarterly*, 62 (2000), 369–88.

Hawkins, Henry, *Partheneia Sacra* (London, 1633).

Heinemann, Margot, 'How Brecht Read Shakespeare', in Dollimore and Sinfield, 202–30.

Heinzelman, Kurt, *The Economics of the Imagination* (Amherst, 1980).

Henderson, Willie, *Economics as Literature* (London, 1995).

Herbert, George, 'The Elixir', in *The Complete English Poems,* ed. John Tobin (London, 1991).

Herman, Peter C., 'What's the Use? Or, The Problematic of Economy in Shakespeare's Procreation Sonnets', in *Shakespeare's Sonnets: New Essays*, ed. James Schiffer (New York, 1999), 263–83.

Higgins, John, *Huloet's Dictionarie* (London, 1572).

Hill, Christopher, *Change and Continuity in Seventeenth-century England* (Cambridge, MA, 1975).

Hobbes, Thomas, *Leviathan*, ed. C. B. MacPherson (London, 1985).

Howard, Jean, *The Stage and Social Struggle in Early Modern England* (London, 1994).

Hoxby, Blair, Letter to *TLS*, 30 Apr. 2004.

Ibarra-Colado, Eduardo, Stewart R. Clegg, Carl Rhodes and Martin Kornberger, 'The Ethics of Managerial Subjectivity', *Journal of Business Ethics*, 64 (2006), 45–55.

Ingram, Jill Phillips, *Idioms of Self-interest: Credit, Identity, and Property in English Renaissance Literature* (New York, 2006).

Ingram, William, *The Business of Playing: The Beginnings of the Adult Professional Theatre in Elizabethan London* (Ithaca, NY, 1992).

Kamps, Ivo, 'Materialist Shakespeare: An Introduction', in Kamps (1995), 1–19.

Kamps, Ivo, ed., *Materialist Shakespeare: A History* (London and New York, 1995).

Kearney, James, 'The Book and the Fetish: The Materiality of Prospero's Text', *Journal of Medieval and Early Modern Studies*, 32 (2002), 433–68.

Kearney, James, *The Incarnate Text: Imagining the Book in Reformation England* (Philadelphia, 2009).

Kellison, Matthew, *The Right and Jurisdiction of the Prelate and the Prince* (London, 1621).

Kettle, Arnold, Introduction to *Shakespeare in a Changing World*, ed. Arnold Kettle (London, 1964), 9–16.

Kiernan, Victor, *Eight Tragedies of Shakespeare: A Marxist Interpretation* (London, 1996).

King, Ros, *Cymbeline: Constructions of Britain* (London, 2005).

Kitch, Aaron, *Political Economy and the States of Literature in Early Modern England* (Burlington, VT, 2009).

Kitch, Aaron, 'Shylock's Sacred Nation', *SQ*, 59 (2008), 131–55.

Knights, L. C., *Drama and Society in the Age of Jonson* (New York, 1937).

Knights, L. C., 'Shakespeare', in *Public Voices: Literature and Politics with Special Reference to the Seventeenth Century* (London, 1971), 30–51.

Korda, Natasha, 'Dame Usury: Gender, Credit and (Ac)counting in the Sonnets and *The Merchant of Venice*', *SQ*, 60 (2009), 129–53.

Krieger, Elliot, *A Marxist Study of Shakespeare's Comedies* (London, 1979).

Laclau, Ernesto, 'Feudalism and Capitalism in Latin America', *New Left Review,* 67 (1971).

Lafargue, Paul, *Reminiscences of Marx* (1890) https:/ /www. marxists.org /archive /lafargue /1890 /xx /marx.htm (accessed 31 August 2014).

Landreth, David, *The Face of Mammon: The Matter of Money in English Renaissance Literature* (Oxford, 2012).

Langholm, Odd, *Economics in the Medieval Schools: Wealth, Exchange, Value, Money and Usury according to the Paris Theological Tradition, 1200–1350* (Leiden, 1992).

Langholm, Odd, *The Legacy of Scholasticism in Economic Thought* (Cambridge, 1998).

Lee, Joseph, *A Vindication of a Regulated Inclosure* (London, 1653).

Leinwand, Theodore, *Theatre, Finance and Society in Early Modern England* (Cambridge, 1999).

LeRoy, Loys, *Aristotles politiques* (London, 1598).

Levinas, Emmanuel, 'The Ego and Totality', in *Collected Philosophical Papers,* trans. Alphonso Lingis (Dordrecht, 1987).

Locke, John, *Of Civil Government* (Toronto, 1924).

Lukács, Georg, *History and Class-consciousness*, trans. Rodney Livingstone (London, 1971).

Lukács, Georg, 'Realism in the Balance', in *Aesthetics and Politics* (London, 1977), 28–59.

Lukács, Georg, 'Shakespeare and Modern Drama', in *Philosophers on Shakespeare,* ed. Paul A. Kottman (Stanford, 2009), 132–42.

Lukács, Georg, *Studies in European Realism* (New York, 2002).

McCloskey, Deirdre, *The Rhetoric of Economics* (Madison, 1985).

McKendrick, N., 'Josiah Wedgwood's Factory Discipline', *Historical Journal,* 4 (1961).

McKeon, Michael, 'The Origins of Aesthetic Value', *Telos* (1982), 62–83.

McNally, David, *Against the Market: Political Economy, Market Socialism and the Marxist Critique* (New York and London: 1993).

McNally, David, *Global Slump: The Economics and Politics of Crisis and Resistance* (Oakland, 2011).

McNally, David, *Political Economy and the Rise of Capitalism: A Reinterpretation* (Berkeley, 1988).

Macpherson, C. B., *The Political Theory of Possessive Individualism: Hobbes to Locke* (Oxford, 1970).

Makaryk, Irena R., and Joseph G. Price, (eds) *Shakespeare in the Worlds of Communism and Socialism* (London, 2006).

Mandeville, Bernard, 'The Grumbling Hive' in *The Fable of the Bees and Other Writings*, ed. E. J. Hundert (Indianapolis, 1997).

Mann, Jenny C., *Outlaw Rhetoric: Figuring Vernacular Eloquence in Shakespeare's England* (Ithaca, NY, 2012).

Marvell, Andrew, *The Poems of Andrew Marvell*, ed. Nigel Smith (London, 2006).

Marx, Karl, *Capital,* trans. Ben Fowkes (London, 1976), vol. 1.

Marx, Karl, 'Debating the Freedom of the Press' (1842), in *Marx and Engels on Literature and Art: A Selection of Writings,* ed. Lee Baxandall and Stefan Morawski (St Louis, 1973).

Marx, Karl, *Economic and Philosophic Manuscripts of 1844,* trans. Martin Milligan (New York, 1993).

Marx, Karl, *Introduction to the Critique of Political Economy* (1857).

Marx, Karl, Preface to *A Contribution to the Critique of Political Economy* (1859), in *The Marx-Engels Reader,* ed. Robert Tucker (New York, 1978).

Mischo, John B., '"That Use is not Forbidden Usury": Shakespeare's Procreation Sonnets and the Problem of Usury', in *Subjects on the World's Stage: Essays on British Literature of the Middle Ages and the Renaissance*, eds David G. Allen and Robert A. White (Newark, DE, 1995), 262–79.

Mitchell, Stanley, 'Lukács's Concept of "The Beautiful"', in Parkinson, 219–35.

Mitchell, Timothy, 'Dreamland', in *Evil Paradises: Dreamworlds of Neoliberalism,* ed. Mike Davis and Daniel Bertrand Monk (New York, 2007), 1–33.

Moore, John, *A Scripture-word against Inclosure* (1656).

Morton, A. L., 'Shakespeare's Idea of History', *Our History,* 33 (1964), 1–18.

Muldrew, Craig, *The Economy of Obligation: The Culture of Credit in Early Modern England* (New York, 1998).

Mullaney, Stephen, *The Place of the Stage* (Chicago, 1988).

Munday, Anthony, *A Second and Third Blast of Retrait from Plaies and Theaters* (London, 1580).

O'Dair, Sharon, *Class, Critics and Shakespeare: Bottom Lines on the Culture Wars* (Ann Arbor, 2000).

Parel, Anthony, Review of *The Aristotelian Analysis of Usury* by Odd Langholm, *Journal of the History of Philosophy,* 26 (1988), 139–40.

Parkinson, G. H. R., ed., *Georg Lukács: The Man, His Work and His Ideas* (New York, 1970).

Partee, Charles, *The Theology of John Calvin* (London, 2008).

Pascal, Roy, 'Georg Lukács: The Concept of Totality', in Parkinson, 147–71.

Patterson, Orlando, *Slavery and Social Death* (Cambridge MA, 1982).

Paulson, Roland, *Empty Labor: Idleness and Workplace Resistance* (Cambridge, 2014).

Perelman, Michael, *The Invention of Capitalism: Classical Political Economy and the Secret History of Primitive Accumulation* (Durham, NC, 2000).

Plato, *The Republic,* trans. B. Jowett (New York, 1892).

Polanyi, Karl, *The Great Transformation: The Political and Economic Origins of Our Time* (New York, 1944).

Prawer, S.S., *Karl Marx and World Literature* (Oxford, 1978).

Rastell, John, 'Of Gentylnes and Nobylyte' (London, 1525).

Rockett, William, 'Labor and Virtue in *The Tempest*', *SQ,* 24 (1973), 77–84.

Rutter, Tom, *Work and Play on the Shakespearean Stage* (Cambridge, 2008).

Ryner, Bradley, *Performing Economic Thought: English Drama and Mercantile Writing, 1600–1640* (Edinburgh, 2014).

Salgado, Gamini, *The Elizabethan Underworld* (New York, 1992).

Sander, Nicholas, *The Ruinate Fall of the Pope Usurie, Derived from the Pope Idolatrie* (London, 1580).

Schalkwyk, David, *Speech and Performance in Shakespeare's Sonnets and Plays* (Cambridge, 2002).

Sebek, Barbara, and Stephen Deng, eds. *Global Traffic: Discourses and Practices of Trade in English Literature and Culture from 1550 to 1700* (New York, 2008).

Shaw, Brent, Introduction to Moses Finley, *Ancient Slavery and Modern Ideology* (Princeton, 1998).

Shell, Marc, *The Economy of Literature* (Baltimore, 1978).

Shell, Marc, 'The Wether and the Ewe: Verbal Usury in *The Merchant of Venice*', in *Money, Language and Thought* (Berkeley, 1982), 47–83.

Smirnov, A. A., *Shakespeare: A Marxist Interpretation* (New York, 1936) https://www.marxists.org /subject /art /lit_crit /works / shakes.htm#a18 (accessed 31 August 2014).

Smith, H. Rick, '*Henry VI Part 2:* Commodifying and Recommodifying the Past in Late-Medieval and Early-Modern England', in *Henry VI: Critical Essays*, ed. Thomas A. Pendleton (New York, 2001), 177–204.

Sorenson, Asger, 'On a Universal Scale: Economy in Bataille's General Economy', *Philosophy and Social Criticism,* 38 (2012), 169–97.

Spengler, Oswald, *The Decline of the West,* trans. Charles Francis Atkinson (Oxford).

Stallybrass, Peter, '"Well grubbed, old mole": Marx, *Hamlet* and the (Un)fixing of Representation', in *Marxist Shakespeares,* ed. Jean Howard and Scott Cutler Shershaw (London, 2001), 16–30.

Stevens, Paul, 'Heterogenizing Imagination: Globalization, *The Merchant of Venice,* and the Work of Literary Criticism', *NLH,* 36 (2005), 425–37.

Sullivan, Jeremiah J., *The Future of Corporate Globalization: From the Extended Order to the Global Village* (Santa Barbara, CA, 2002).

Sweezy, Paul, 'The Transition from Feudalism to Capitalism', *Science and Society,* 14 (1950), 134–57.

Tawney, R. H., *Religion and the Rise of Capitalism* (New York, 1954).

Thirsk, Joan, 'Engrossing and Enclosing 1500–1640', in *Chapters from the Agrarian History of England and Wales,* ed. Joan Thirsk (Cambridge, 1967), vol. 3, 54–124.

Thomas, Keith, 'Work and Leisure in Pre-industrial Society', *Past and Present,* 29 (1964).

Thompson, E. P., 'Time, Work-Discipline and Industrial Capitalism', *Past and Present,* 38 (1967).

Torshell, Samuel, *The Three Questions of Justification* (London, 1632).

Traherne, Thomas, *Centuries, Poems and Thanksgivings*, 2 vols., ed. H. M. Margoliouth (Oxford, 1966).

Turner, Frederick, *Shakespeare's Twenty-first Century Economics: The Morality of Love and Money* (Oxford, 1999).

Vermigli, Pietro Martire, *Common Places of ... Doctor Peter Martyr* trans. Anthonie Marten (London, 1572).

Vitkus, Daniel, '"The Common Market of All the World": English Theater, the Global System, and the Ottoman Empire in the Early Modern Period', in Sebek and Deng, 19–38.

Wallerstein, Immanuel, *The Capitalist World-economy* (Cambridge, 1979).

Wang, Shuhua, 'From Maoism to (Post) Modernism: *Hamlet* in Communist China', in Makaryk and Price, 283–302.

Warren, Roger, et al., (eds) *The Oxford Shakespeare* (Oxford, 2008).

Weber, Max, *The Protestant Ethic and the Spirit of Capitalism* (London, 2001, orig. 1904).

Wennerlind, Carl, *Casualties of Credit: The English Financial Revolution, 1620–1720* (2011).

Westerman, William L., *The Slave Systems of Greek and Roman Antiquity* (Philadelphia, 1955).

Whitney, Charles, 'Green Economics and the English Renaissance: From Capital to the Commons', in *Shakespeare and the Urgency of the Now: Criticism and Theory in the 21st Century,* eds Cary DiPietro and Hugh Grady (New York, 2013), 103–25.

Wood, Diana, *Medieval Economic Thought* (Cambridge, 2002).

Wood, Neal, *Foundations of Political Economy: Some Early Tudor Views on State and Society* (Berkeley, 1994).

Woodbridge, Linda, Introduction, in Woodbridge, 1–18.

Woodbridge, Linda, ed., *Money and the Age of Shakespeare: Essays in New Economic Criticism* (New York, 2003).

Xenophon, *The Economist* in *The Socratic Writings,* trans. H. G. Dakyns (Digireads, 2009).

Zhouhan, Yang, 'Shakespeare's Life and His Major Works', in Makaryk and Price.

INDEX

This index covers the study of economics, chrematistics, wealth, commodity, markets and ethics in Shakespeare's work, in all chapters; these principal topics are further categorized by other headings.

1 Henry IV 134–5, 175
2 Henry IV 154–5
2 Henry VI 95–6, 120
    magic 171
    proletariat 94–6
    self-mastery 12

abstract factors 37
aesthetics 9, 10, 63, 72–4, 85
    class 48–9
    commercialization 9–10, 74, 75–6
    determinism and 45–7, 62–3
    dialectics 47–8, 63–4
    exchange-based economies 69
    free play and 84
    production-based economies 68
affect *see* emotional factors
Agnew, Jean-Christophe 74–5, 76
alienation 38–40, 44, 96–7, 133, 140–1, 168, 181–2
    fragmentation 53, 64, 65
    rootlessness 137
All's Well That Ends Well 149
Althusser, Louis 49

Antony and Cleopatra 124, 176
Appleby, Joyce Oldham 14, 146
Aquinas, Thomas 144–5
aristocracy 47, 65, 119, 121–2, 166
    identity and 175–6
    natural 139
    wages and 127, 134–5
Aristotle 11, 18
    aesthetics 9
    capitalism and 38
    households 7–8
    labour 182
    money 40, 135–6
    possession 161–2
    slavery and 11, 129–30, 132, 136–7, 138
    wages and 136
art *see* aesthetics

Bacon, Francis 171–2
Baker, David 84
banausic factors 5, 129–30
barrenness 148, 150
Bataille, Georges 26–7
bawdry 104–5

beauty 149–50
beggary 92–4
bellum omnia contra omnes
    (war of all against all) 22
bias 101–2
Bloch, Ernst 44
blood 119, 121–2, 134
bodies 138, 155–6, 169
bonds 174
borrowing and lending *see*
    usury
bourgeoisie 36, 43–4
Braudel, Fernand 23
Brecht, Bertolt 43–4
brokers 101
brothels 105
Brown, Doug 53
Bruster, Douglas 29–30, 76–7
bullionists 86, 147
business studies 42–3

Cade's Revolt 94, 95–6
Calvin/Calvinism 21–2, 24,
    155–6
capital 61–2 *see also* money
capitalism 35–6, 38, 67, 81–4,
    177–8
    aesthetics 64, 84–5
    alienation 44
    class 36, 65
    commercialization 61
    determinism and 41, 42–3,
        48, 49–50
    dialectics 53, 65
    equality and 13
    evolutionary history and 31
    labour and 180–1
    land 127–8
    personification 85, 86
    proletariat 128–9

self-interest 22–4
    see also money
Centuries of Meditation
    (Traherne) 113
chrematistics 4, 118
    exchange-value 8–9, 12–13,
        16, 18, 25, 73–4
class 44–5, 46–8, 49–50, 57
    aristocracy 47, 65, 119,
        121–2, 127, 134–5, 139,
        166, 175–6
    bourgeoisie 36, 43–4
    cultural hegemony 48–9, 54
    equality and 38
    labour and 61–2
    land 128
    wages and 133–4
    see also proletariat
coins 86, 153, 177
    counterfeit and 176–7
    semiotics 86–7, 145
    stamps and 153–4, 172, 173
Comedy of Errors, The 100,
    170
commercialization 9–10, 74,
    75–6
    proletariat 61
commodity 99–102
common humanity 59
commonplace book (Jonson)
    140
commons 91–3, 95–6
communism *see* Marx/Marxism
Conservatism 98
consumerism 93
Coriolanus 45
    class 121–2, 134, 139,
        175–6
    equality and 97–8, 135
    proletariat 60, 96–7

slavery 129, 137
  wages 135
counterfeit 173–7
credit 75, 144, 146–7
Critchley, Simon 159
Critobulus 5–6
cultural hegemony 48–9, 54
cultural materialism 54, 56

Davis, David Brion 137–8
dearness 107–8
Debord, Guy 77
Dekker, Thomas 75–6, 169
Delany, Paul 44–5
demonic possession 167
Deng, Stephen 80, 86
Derrida, Jacques 11, 27–9
Description of England
  (Harrison) 92
determinism
  economic 41, 43–4, 45–8,
    49–50, 51, 52, 54, 62–3
  historicism 56–60, 63–5
  materialist 42–3, 45, 48, 50,
    51, 54, 55–6, 57–8
dialectics 51–2, 53–5
  class 61–2
  determinism and 47–8, 51,
    52, 58–60, 63–5
  humanity and 59
  self-interest 53
'Dialogue Between the
  Resolved Soul and
  Created Pleasure, A'
  (Marvell) 113–14
disease 80–1
dissociation of sensibility 53,
  65
Dollimore, Jonathan 56
Donne, John 114

Eagleton, Terry 54–5
econolingua 74
Economic and Philosophic
  Manuscripts of 1844
  (Marx) 40, 133
economic determinism 41, 45–6,
  48, 50, 51, 52, 54, 62–3
  class 46–8, 49–50
  feudalism and 43–4
  self-interest 41, 43
economics 3, 19–20, 21
  exchange-value 11, 111–12,
    113–14, 117–18
  general sense 4, 8, 18–19,
    26–30, 68, 71, 80, 81,
    85, 87–8
  lacking 4
  loss 87
  politics and 123
  property 131, 161, 163–4,
    165–7, 168
  restricted sense 4–5, 19, 28,
    29, 73
  use-value 11, 16, 18,
    111–12, 113–14
  value/worth 111, 113,
    115–17, 118–20
Economics (Aristotle) 7–8
Elegy 19 (Donne) 114
Eliot, T. S. 65
emotional factors 78, 107
  power 167
  sexual factors and 106, 124,
    148, 151, 177, 182–3
  superficiality and 124–5
  unquantifiable 106, 108,
    123, 124
enclosure 94, 128
enemies 7
Engels, Friedrich 35, 52

Engle, Lars 77–8
Epistle to the Galatians 157
equality 38, 97–8, 134, 135–6
    fairness and 13, 79–80
    self-interest and 13
    weight and 135
ethics 17, 20, 42, 123
Eucharist 155–6
evolutionary history 30–1, 62
exchange-based economies 69
extortion 164

family households 3–4, 7–8,
    17–18, 163
Federici, Silvia 31
fetishism 76–7, 93, 116–17,
    122–3, 145, 154–5, 156
    magic 100, 154
feudalism 123–4
    capitalism and 31, 36
    class 43–4, 133–4
    emotional factors and 123
Finley, Moses 4
Fischer, Sandra 73–4
Ford, John 169
forgery 173, 175–6
Forman, Valerie 87
Foucault, Michel 42–3, 87
free play 84
'From a Restricted to a General
    Economy' (Derrida) 27–9

Galatians, Epistle 157
German Ideology, The (Marx)
    57
Glancy, Jennifer 138
gold see money
Gosson, Stephen 75–6
Goux, Jean-Joseph 70
Grady, Hugh 67

Graeber, David 130–1
Gramsci, Antonio 49, 54
Grav, Peter 81–2
groundlings 61
'Grumbling Hive, The' (de
    Mandeville) 24
Gumpert, Matthew 117–18

Halpern, Richard 123–4
Hamlet 124
Harris, Jonathan Gil 80–1
Harrison, William 92
Hazlitt, William 60
health factors 80–1
Hegel/Hegelianism 51–2, 53–4,
    58–60, 65
Heinzelman, Kurt 71, 106
Henry IV, Part 1 134–5, 175
Henry IV, Part 2 154–5
Henry V 116–17, 153
Henry VI, Part 2 95–6, 120
    magic 171
    proletariat 94–6
    self-mastery 12
Herbert, George 158
historicism 56–7, 58–60, 63–4
    materialist determinism and
        56, 57–8
    proletariat 60
    self-interest 64, 65
Hobbes, Thomas 22–3, 163
house ownership 36
households 3–4, 7–8, 17–18,
    163
humanity 59
husbands 8
hypocrisy 173–4

identity 176
    counterfeit and 175–6

households 163
money 176–7
slavery and 98–9, 163–4,
166
idolatry 171–2
fetishism and 116–17,
122–3, 145, 156
magic 156–7
illicitness 100
individualism 5, 22–4, 41, 43
alienation and 38–40, 53,
64, 65, 137
fragmentation and 13
possessive 163
totality and 24–5
*Institutes of the Christian
Religion* (Calvin) 22,
155–6
interpenetration of opposites
see dialectics

James I of England 154, 171
'Jews, The' (Herbert) 158
Johnson, Dr Samuel 59
Jonson, Ben 140
Julius Caesar 37, 166
just price 17

Kamps, Ivo 56–7
King John 101–2, 166
King Lear 106, 123–4
Kitch, Aaron 85
Knights, L. C. 45, 57–8, 60
Krieger, Elliot 47–8

labour 14, 15–16, 141, 180,
181, 182
alienation and 181–2
capital and 61–2
magic and 180–1

time and 181
see also slavery; wage labour
land 14, 15–16, 141, 127–8
enclosure 94, 128
money 164
tenancy and 164–5
landownership 36, 164–5
Landreth, David 85–6
Langholm, Odd 114–15
Lasalle, Ferdinand 34–5
Leinwand, Theodore 78
lending and borrowing *see*
usury
Leviathan (Hobbes) 22, 163
Levin, Richard 36, 49–50
loyalty 133–4
Lukács, Georg 37–8
abstract factors 37
aesthetics 63–4
dialectics 53–4

McCarthy, Tom 159
McCloskey, Deirdre 71–2
Macherey, Pierre 55
Macpherson, C. B. 22–3
magic 100–1, 154, 156–7,
168–70, 171, 180–1,
183–4
demonic 167
personification 154
revenge and 170
semiotics 171
sexual factors 169
Malynes, Gerard de 19
Mammon 85–6
management studies 42–3
Mandeville, Bernard de 24
manufacturing industries 68
Mao Zedong 46
market economy *see* capitalism

markets 17, 74–5
Marvell, Andrew 113–14
Marx/Marxism 33–4, 35,
    36–8, 41, 67–8, 111–12
  aesthetics 9, 45–9, 62–4
  capitalism and 31, 35–6, 38,
    42–3, 44, 48, 49–50, 65,
    67, 83–4
  class 38, 44–5, 57
  determinism 41, 43–4, 45,
    51, 54, 57–8, 60
  dialectics 51–5, 58–60,
    61–2, 65
  evolutionary history and
    30–1, 62
  money and 40–1, 133
  proletariat 61
  usury and 144
  Zeitgeist 34–5
materialist determinism 42, 43,
    45, 48, 50, 51, 54, 55–6
  class 54
  historicism and 56, 57–8
  management studies and
    42–3
Measure for Measure 104,
    150–1, 173
medicine 80–1
mercantilists 86–7, 147
Merchant of Venice, The 34,
    144, 158–9
Midland Revolt 94
'Misapprehension' (Traherne)
    112–13
Misselden, Thomas 19
Mitchell, Stanley 64
Mitchell, Timothy 26
money 8, 11–12, 14–16, 25,
    40–1, 83, 114, 133, 139,
    141, 179–80

bonds 174
coins 86–7, 145, 153–4,
    172, 173, 176–7
  counterfeit 173–4
  equality and 135–6
  fetishism 154–5
  magic and 168–9
  paradox of value 112–13
  personification 85–6
  possession 133, 164
  price and 113
  self-interest 38–40
  semiotics 27, 69–70, 147,
    155
  weight and 120
  see also usury; wage labour
Morton, A. L. 62
Much Ado About Nothing
    111–12
Muldrew, Craig 147
Mun, Thomas 19
Munday, Anthony 76

national economy 20–1
natural aristocrats 139
natural slaves 132, 162, 166
natural wealth 144–5
new economic criticism 65–6,
    68, 69, 70–1, 73, 77–9,
    80, 81, 85, 87–8
  aesthetics and 68–9, 72–4
  capitalism 81–4, 85, 86
  econolingua 74
  emotional factors 78
  health factors 80–1
  money 69–70, 85–7
  redemption 87
  revenge 79–80
  rhetoric 71–2
  semiotics 71

sexual factors 76–7
nomos (custom/law) 114,
157–8

O'Dair, Sharon 38, 84
Oeconomicus (Xenophon) 5–7
'Of Gentylnes and Nobylyte'
(Rastell) 164
oikos (household) 3–4, 7–8,
17–18, 163
Osteen, Mark 72–3
ownership *see* possession

paid work *see* wage labour
paradox of value 112–13
Paul 157
peasantry *see* proletariat
Perelman, Michael 92–3
Pericles 104
Phenomenology of Mind
(Hegel) 53
Plato 11–12
Polanyi, Karl 9, 15, 23
Politics (Aristotle) 18, 138,
161–2
Poor Laws 92–3, 94–5
possession 5–7, 11, 131–2,
165–6, 167–8
alienation and 133, 168
households 7–8
identity and 98–9, 163–4,
166
land 36, 164–5
magic and 167
oppression and 164
slavery and 129, 158–9,
161–2, 166, 179
wages and 162–3
possessive individualism 163
poverty 60, 92–5

praise 107
Prawer, S. S. 33–4
price 17, 106–7, 113
primitive accumulation 92–3,
128
prize 106–7
production-based economies 68
proletariat 60–1
alienation 96–7
beggary and 92–4
equality and 97
land and 94, 128
oppression 60, 94–5
uprising 94, 95–6
wages and 92, 93, 99,
128–9, 134, 136–8,
139–41
prostitution 102–3, 104–6
punishment 60, 92–3, 94–5

Rastell, John 164
reason 11, 42, 102
redemption 87
reification
money 179–80
possession and 98–9, 131–2,
162–3
slavery 132, 138–9
usury 143–4
Republic, The (Plato) 11–12
revenge 79–80, 170
revolt and revolution 94, 95–6,
98
rhetoric 71–2
rootlessness 137
Rowley, William 169
*Ruinate Fall of the Pope
Usurie, Derived from
the Pope Idolatrie, The*
(Sander) 145

saleability 6–7
Sander, Nicholas 145
Sebek, Barbara 80
self-interest 5, 22–4, 41, 43
    alienation and 38–40, 53,
        64, 65
    fragmentation and 13
    totality and 24–5
self-mastery 12
semiotics 27, 29, 69–70, 71,
        86–7, 143–4, 146, 147,
        155, 157–8, 169, 171,
        172–3
    idolatry 145, 156–7, 171–2
    transubstantiation 155–6
service industries 69
servitude see slavery
sexual factors 103, 148–9, 150
    barrenness and 148, 150
    beauty and 149–50
    bodies 169
    emotional factors and 106,
        124, 148, 151, 177,
        182–3
    fetishism 76–7, 122–3
    prostitution 102–3, 104–6
    reproduction and 176–7
    virginity 149
Shakespeare, William 21, 25–6,
        108–9
Shell, Marc 69–70
sight 122–3
sin 21–2, 24
Sinfield, Alan 56
slavery 11, 98–9
    alienation 137
    banausic factors 5
    bodies 138
    masters and 161–2, 163–4
    money and 11–12

natural 132, 162, 166
proletariat and 136–8
semiotics 156–7
time and 181
usury and 158–60
wages and 91, 99, 129–31,
        138–9, 179
Socrates 5–7
sodomy 150
Sonnets 124–5, 149, 150, 151
sorcery see magic
speaking bodies 169
Spengler, Oswald 20–1
stamps 153–4, 172, 173

Talks at the Yenan Forum on
        Literature (Mao) 46
Taming of the Shrew, The 103,
        155
Tempest, The
    capitalism and 180–1
    equality and 98
    magic 183–4
    reification 98–9
    uprising 98
    wages 182–3
tenancy 164–5
Timon of Athens
    capitalism and 82
    money 38–40
    possession 165
    usury 102–3, 151–2
Titus Andronicus 97
total depravity 21–2, 24
totality 24–5 see also dialectics
tragicomedy 87
Traherne, Thomas 112–13
transubstantiation 155–6
Troilus and Cressida 106–7,
        115–16, 117–20

class 127
  equality and 13
  sight 122
  wages 140
Turner, Frederick 82–3
Twelfth Night 140, 174

underdogs 60
usury 101, 141, 144–5, 146,
    150–3, 158–60
  brokers 101
  credit 75, 144, 146–7
  personification 159
  semiotics 143–4, 145–6,
    157–8
  sexual factors and 102–3,
    104–5, 148–50, 151

vagrancy 92–4
'Venus and Adonis' 148
virginity 149

wage labour 91–2, 93, 99,
    127, 128–9, 130–1,
    134–5, 136–40, 162–3,
    164, 179
  alienation 140–1
  banausic factors 129–30
  equality and 134, 135
    loyalty and 133–4
    magic and 183
    sexual factors 182–3
    time and 129
Wallerstein, Immanuel 23
war of all against all (*bellum
    omnia contra omnes*) 22
wealth
  exchange-value and 6–7,
    114–15
  use-value and 5–7, 114–15
  value/worth 120–1
Winter's Tale, The 87, 93, 119
Witch of Edmonton, The
    (Dekker et al.) 169
witchcraft 168–9, 170–1
wives 8
Wood, Diana 131–2, 164–5
Woodbridge, Linda 79
Woodmansee, Martha 72–3
work *see* labour
world economy 23

Xenophon 5–7

Yenan Forum Talks (Mao) 46
youth 148–9, 150, 151

Zeitgeist 34–5